✄ What Everyone is Saying ✎ About *Start Up*

"A comprehensive list of do's and don'ts provides a superb check list for anyone with the guts to start his or her own company. The case histories and anecdotes alone are worth the price of Bill Stolze's book."
—Gary C. Comer, founder, chairman and CEO, Lands' End, Inc.

"Bill Stolze has an outstanding track record as an entrepreneur and as a business school teacher, and *Start Up* combines the best of both worlds. *Start Up* is well researched, clearly written and very logical—a perfect guide for anyone who wants to learn how to start and grow a business."
—Peter S. Prichard, author of *The Making of McPaper*, Sr. V.P. of the Freedom Forum, and former editor of *USA Today*

"In my opinion this book contains important, fundamental reading for any person considering entering the world of entrepreneurism. Bill Stolze has 'been there' and he knows how to help others achieve."
—Tom Golisano, founder and president, Paychex, Inc.

"The health of the American economy—and its competitiveness in world markets—is increasingly dependent upon the work of the American entrepreneur. Bill Stolze's book—*Start Up*—provides an invaluable tool to anyone thinking of starting his or her own business. For those of us in Washington, it provides great insight regarding how public policy can best help the most dynamic sector of American business."
—Congressman John J. LaFalce, New York chairman of House Committee On Small Business (1987-1994), and now Ranking Minority Member

"The merit of this offering is not in its science—it is in Stolze's opinions, points of view, experiences. The man is a sage. Reading and heeding his book will save any first time entrepreneur a lot of heartache. *Start Up* is no Victor Kiam/Donald Trump ego trip. It is an unabashedly humble attempt on the part of a very bright, accomplished man to share his experiences and knowledge with others, to their hopeful benefit."
—Fred Beste, managing partner of NEPA Venture Fund

"*Start Up* is one of the most thorough and powerful presentations I've ever read on the do's and don'ts of starting a business. It's a must read for anyone who has the daring to 'go it alone.' "

—Louise Woerner, founder and CEO, HCR, Rochester, New York

"Anyone who has been involved in forming a new business undertaking will recognize the importance of this book. *Start Up* is a hardheaded and practical guide to starting a new business, whether inside an existing company or as an independent new venture."

—Charles E. Exley, Jr., retired chairman and CEO, NCR Corporation

"I should tell you again what a hit your book has made in my classes. It is brief and easy reading, yet goes straight to the point in a way that more 'academic' textbooks can't seem to match. It has become a mainstay in my teaching 'arsenal,' and I am happy to recommend it to my colleagues."

—Prof. Lanny Herron, Department of Management, University of Baltimore

"Only a founding entrepreneur could possess the wealth of knowledge that Bill Stolze shares with his audience in *Start Up*. It is a 'must read' book for all who are about to embark on an entrepreneurial endeavor. I highly recommend it to all about-to-be entrepreneurs, those entrepreneurs who currently are struggling with day-to-day business decisions, and anybody else who just wants a 'good read.'"

—Mary Woita, assistant director, Nebraska Business Development Center

"I just finished your excellent book, *Start Up*, and wanted to write to congratulate you. Most books on entrepreneurship are too polite and abstract. Yours is down-to-earth and practical and will fill a gap in the literature."

—Peter Faber, partner, the law firm of McDermott, Will & Emory, New York

"In this period when business start ups require unusual devotion and talent, guidance based upon real world experience is invaluable. Bill Stolze provides this kind of guidance, and does so with clarity, verve and style."

—Paul S. Brentlinger, general partner, Morgenthaler Ventures

"A tour de force! Bill Stolze has written the best guide available on how to launch and manage a new venture. He tells it like it is. It is packed with invaluable advice, experience and insights from how to deal with venture investors to how to cash in your chips. If you are involved in a start-up or thinking about a start-up this book is a must read."

—Dr. Warren Keegan, director of the Institute for Global Business Strategy, Pace University, and author of *Global Marketing Management*

"Bill Stolze's approach to venture start-up issues is elegant! It grasps both the problems, and in my opinion, the solutions in a very straightforward way. The section on women entrepreneurs is a real bonus, opening up new dimensions on the traditional view of new business founders."

—Richard G. Schiavo, director of Academy of Learning Centers, U.S., and former dean, College of Business and Technology, Franklin University

"I was given your book *Start Up* for Christmas and read it before returning to work on January 2. It was the most encouraging book I have ever read."

—Jeffrey Medler, founder and president, Exhibit Alternatives

"In your book you convey most of the 'good advice' I try to provide my class; your writing style is direct and to the point, and you speak clearly from an experiential standpoint. I have adopted it for the fall semester, for both the graduate (MBA) and undergraduate versions of my basic entrepreneurship course."

—Prof. Sandy Eustis, director of the Entrepreneurial Center, Xavier University

"*Start Up* is an invaluable guide for the entrepreneur who is starting a business. It doesn't stop there. It also offers excellent guidance for decisions which need to be made when one's business becomes successful. It is full of advice and Bill Stolze's style makes the reader feel he or she can pick up the phone and call a friend."

—Joanne Bauman, regional director of the Small Business Development Center, Binghamton University

"I enjoyed your book immensely. It is full of good common sense that probably cost you a great deal of time, blood and sweat to accumulate."

—Dr. Sylvan Beer, director of the Syracuse University Manufacturers Assistance Center

"Bill Stolze has been able to put into one book all of the essential elements to be a successful entrepreneur and small business owner. I find my students find it a useful reference and a book to use well after graduation. *Start Up* is an essential text for any class that teaches invention, innovation or entrepreneurship"
—Prof. John Kleppe, Electrical Engineering Department, University of Nevada-Reno

"Bill Stolze achieves a goal that is unique—his book *Start Up* contains enough theory about entrepreneurship that should satisfy all those interested in this subject. However, the book's main strength is the practical knowledge it imparts to those who want to start and develop a business. *Start Up* is also a natural for the classroom and I have used it for seven years as the principal textbook in teaching the subject at colleges and universities in the United States and England. I have read all of the well-known books on entrepreneurship and this is the best."
—James N. Doyle, lecturer in entrepreneurship, Simon Graduate School of Business, University of Rochester and former president of Sarah Coventry, Itnl.

"Enclosed is the check I promised to send you for 10 more copies of your great book *Start Up*. Great title; great book; important and useful; straight forward advice and guidance clearly articulated. A winner from a winner."
—Francis X. Driscoll, former venture capital consultant and past president, The New York Venture Capital Forum

"Most valuable book I have had in my college career."
—MBA student, Simon Graduate School of Business, University of Rochester

"We recently read your new book *Start Up*, and we like it. In fact, we like it so much that we now hand a copy to every new client who comes to us for help in launching a new business and we insist that they read it."
—Joseph Hurley, partner, Bonadio & Co., LLP, CPAs

Start Up

An Entrepreneur's Guide to Launching and Managing a New Business

4th Edition

By
William J. Stolze

CAREER PRESS
3 Tice Road
P.O. Box 687
Franklin Lakes, NJ 07417
1-800-CAREER-1
201-848-0310 (NJ and outside U.S.)
FAX: 201-848-1727

START UP (4TH EDITION)

ISBN 1-56414-252-3, $16.99

Printed in the U.S.A. by Book-mart Press

To order this title by mail, please include price as noted above, $2.50 handling per order, and $1.00 for each book ordered. Send to: Career Press, Inc., 3 Tice Road, P.O. Box 687, Franklin Lakes, NJ 07417.

Or call toll-free 1-800-CAREER-1 (NJ and Canada: 201-848-0310) to order using VISA or MasterCard, or for further information on books from Career Press.

Library of Congress Cataloging-in-Publication Data

Stolze, William J.
    Start up : an entrepreneur's guide to launching and managing a new
    business / by William J. Stolze. -- 4th ed.
        p.   cm.
    Includes index.
    ISBN 1-56414-252-3 (pbk.)
    1. New business enterprises--Management. 2. Entrepreneurship.
    I. Title.
    HD62.5.S755   1996
    658.02'2--dc20
                                                                96-23341
                                                                CIP

ᛨ Contents ᛢ

⚔ Introduction ⚖

Entrepreneurship and the Road to Success

This is a book about entrepreneurship and the problems associated with launching and managing a new business. I hope to reach the reader who is either considering embarking on a new venture or who started a business within the past few years and wants to make that business grow.

In writing the first edition several years ago, I thought I could transcribe lecture notes used in an entrepreneurship course I had been teaching. It soon became apparent that to be of any value, a book must include much more than can be packed into an 11-week course. The final product had about three times the number of chapters than was first planned and was a much more difficult project than I ever imagined. Subsequent editions had more chapters still, including a great deal of additional information. It should not have been a surprise, but I learned that writing a book is very hard work.

This fourth edition includes a number of chapters written by others. I did this for two reasons. First, some of this material covers issues on which I do not have much personal experience. The people who contributed are all more expert than I and their comments more valuable. The second reason is to present the other side of certain issues where I have a strong bias that is sometimes

in conflict with conventional wisdom. This, I believe, makes *Start Up* a better book.

Three of the new sections are Chapters 46, 50 and 51, toward the back of the book, which I feel are especially valuable. Chapter 50 is a transcript of my interview with Tom Golisano, founder and president of Paychex, Inc., the fabulously successful payroll service company. This is a good example for the entrepreneur of "How it should be done." Chapter 46 is a transcript of my discussions with Valerie Mannix, founder and owner of Mercury Print Productions, Inc., a very successful woman-owned printing company. Chapter 51, entitled "25 Entrepreneurial Deathtraps," was written by Fred Beste, who has many years experience investing in and working with start-up companies. His comments are extremely perceptive. Do not lay this book down without reading these chapters.

Much of the new material was added at the suggestion of readers who contacted me with their ideas for additions and changes. Without exception, this advice was constructive, of great value and much appreciated.

Even today, when entrepreneurship is in the curriculum at about 500 colleges and universities around the world, there is still disagreement in business and academic circles as to whether this is a subject that can be taught.

I believe it is possible to some extent and use as an analogy the problem of teaching someone to compose music. You can teach a person musical theory, composition, counterpoint and orchestration, but there is only one Mozart. Similarly with entrepreneurship, you can teach a person how to select products, how to identify market opportunities and how to raise capital, but few will be a Bill Gates, Ross Perot, Mary Kay Ash or Steve Jobs.

The approach I follow is to use example after example to illustrate the principles and issues I consider important in starting and growing a business. I draw heavily on my own experience as a founder of a successful high-tech business, as an investor, director and active participant in a number of recent start-up companies, as a teacher of entrepreneurship and as an adviser and consultant to several hundred entrepreneurs in various stages of planning, beginning and running a business.

In teaching this subject, I made extensive use of entrepreneurs as guest lecturers. They told the stories of the founding of their companies with particular emphasis on the unusual problems they encountered. Over the years, nearly 100 have spoken to my classes. Their tales of elation and woe have influenced much of this book.

This is neither a "how to" manual nor an academic treatise. The subjects covered are those I consider essential in determining whether a new company succeeds or fails. My intention is to identify and discuss key issues only.

This means that there are some aspects of starting and running a business that are not covered at all. You should seek guidance on these from others.

Even the subjects I identified as key issues presented a problem, however, in that some are complex and impossible to cover with any degree of thoroughness in a single short chapter. Specialized areas such as selling, franchising, raising venture capital, export marketing and writing a business plan should be and are the subjects of entire books. On these, my goal was to alert the reader to their importance and cover some of the fundamental issues involved.

I spend a lot of time telling about my experience at RF Communications, a company I founded with three associates. My partners were Elmer W. Schwittek, Roger R. Bettin and Herbert W. Vanden Brul. Both Elmer and Roger are extremely creative and very customer-oriented engineers and astute business managers. Herb is also a very able businessman and one of the few entrepreneurial lawyers I ever met. The chemistry between the founders of RF Communications was especially good; we worked closely together through the entire history of the company and share equally in the success we achieved.

I would appreciate suggestions, comments or questions from readers about this book or any aspect of entrepreneurship and starting a business. I can be reached through the publisher.

This book is dedicated to all of you who actually start a business. I hope it helps you along the road to becoming a successful entrepreneur. Good luck.

ᛊ Chapter 1 ᛊ

Decisions,
Decisions!!

One thing that always seems to come as a surprise to a new entrepreneur is the number of decisions that must be made and questions that must be answered before the business even gets underway. Among these are: Should I start the business alone or with partners? What product or service should be the basis of the business? What is my market? Is the potential of the business enough to provide an honest living? How can I raise initial capital? The questions go on and on.

This situation is especially difficult because there is rarely any scientific basis for making these decisions. There are no formulas that will help. There are no equations you can apply.

Eventually you will conclude that there are really no right or wrong answers to these questions. The best you can hope for is an answer that works. You will never know whether a different decision or different answer would have been better or worse. Almost every important decision is subjective. In the final analysis, almost every important decision is based upon the entrepreneur's personal experience and intuitive judgment.

I lecture to groups of entrepreneurs and small business owners at many seminars and meetings. People in the audience ask questions about every possible aspect of starting or managing a business. My response in almost every case begins with, "Well, it depends..." and then I go on to answer as best I can. Comments like "on the other hand," "in another situation," "but then again" and similar qualifying phrases are also generously sprinkled throughout my responses. Sometimes I have the feeling that the answer to every question about starting a business is "It depends."

Long ago I read one author's comment that "Entrepreneurship is a profession for which there is no apprenticeship." No matter how many books you read, no matter how many courses you take or seminars you attend, no matter how much advice you get from "experts," no matter how many small companies you work for, there is no substitute for the actual experience of doing it yourself.

In the words of a great philosopher, "You ain't done it until you've done it." The crucial decisions you make in developing a plan for the business and getting the business underway are yours and yours alone.

Get all the help you can from every source you can identify as having potential value. Much of the advice and many of the suggestions you receive will be contradictory, but doing this still can help in many ways. It will give you more self confidence and help you to avoid some of the mistakes others made.

You hear all sorts of horror stories about the high percentage of new businesses that fail, and these statistics are undoubtedly true. However, there are steps you can take that will greatly improve the odds. I try to describe many of them in this book.

But when the chips are on the table and the go-ahead decisions must be made, you will be on your own. Many entrepreneurs describe this as the loneliest experience of their entire lives and the most difficult decision they ever had to make.

If you do decide to go ahead, pull out all the stops and give it everything you have. Years later many people will ask whether you regret taking this step into the world of entrepreneurism. Almost all entrepreneurs say it was hard. Some regret the move, but many say it was gratifying beyond belief.

In some cases the entrepreneurs become rich, in some they barely eke out a living. Some businesses fail or are abandoned. But in almost every case the process of starting your own business, of being your own boss, of seeing whether you have what it takes, can be the most exciting experience of a lifetime.

⟜ Chapter 2 ⟝

Which Comes First: Whether or How?

Several years ago I led a seminar on "How to Start and Manage a New Business." Five successful entrepreneurs told the stories of the founding and early years of their companies.

During the discussion, a young man in the audience asked a simple question, "Which comes first, the decision to have a company or the idea for the product or service upon which the new company will be based?" My answer was that the idea for the product or service comes first.

After thinking about my own experience for a few moments and asking the other speakers about theirs, it became apparent that in all five cases the opposite was true. I've discussed this issue with many company founders and now I believe that, in the majority of ventures, the founder first starts a company and then struggles, sometimes for years, to find a product or service to use as the basis for the company.

Is this good or bad? On balance I think it is good. There are many reasons people start companies. These include the desire to prove they can do it and the possibility of large financial rewards and dissatisfaction with their present job. One thing seems to be clear: The reasons people start companies are largely unrelated to what the company might do.

I suggest that potential entrepreneurs should first struggle with the question of whether to start a company. Decide if you have the personal qualities needed, the support of your family and friends, the willingness to put in long hours and the ability to make sacrifices and risks.

Only after you have decided to start a company is it possible to address the question of how. This is a complex issue and might include developing or inventing a product yourself, associating with a partner who has an idea for a product or service but no knowledge of how to proceed, buying an existing company, buying a franchise or identifying an unserved market niche that offers an opportunity. This may take a long time and involve one or more false starts.

If you think you want to start a company, don't worry that you have not invented a better mouse trap. First decide that you really have the desire to go ahead and then take on the question of how to do it.

The questions of whether to start a company and how to start a company are, of course, what this book is all about.

Chapter 3

Why People Start Companies

What drives people to become entrepreneurs, to start companies? It's a question with many answers. Often these individuals are not entirely sure themselves, and the answers to the question are apt to change over time as their perceptions change.

I divide the reasons into two broad categories: the reactive reasons and the active reasons. Reactive reasons are those things that are objectionable about working for others. They are the negatives that push you out. Active reasons are those things that are attractive about having your own business. They are the positives that pull you out.

The following list was compiled from many sources over a period of years. I do not necessarily agree with all of them, but they are the reasons most often heard.

Reactive reasons

1. Inequity between contribution and reward

People who are by nature high achievers tend not to get along well in large organizations. They want rewards based on accomplishment, not on seniority, conformity to the culture or political clout. The person who just made a major contribution does not want to be told, "Be patient—your turn will come."

2. Promotion and salary policy

Have you heard the comment "You're too young to make so much money?" When I was 26 years old I had a good engineering management position at RCA Laboratories designing FM and television receivers. I decided to leave New York City, which required changing jobs.

My position at the time involved working with other TV manufacturers, and I had exceptional contacts for someone my age. I interviewed at Stromberg-Carlson, a long-defunct TV manufacturer in Rochester, N.Y., and General Electric in Syracuse. Almost immediately Stromberg-Carlson offered me a job at a 50 percent increase in salary.

During my interview with GE I was asked what kind of salary I expected, so I told the interviewer about my other offer. The man interviewing me was the chief engineer. He gulped, reached into his drawer and pulled out a sheet of paper with a curve on it. He said that if they paid me the money I was asking, I would be the highest-paid person my age at GE. He made me an offer at that salary.

In my evaluation of the two offers I decided that the GE deal was good news and bad news. The good news was that nothing would make me happier than being the highest-paid 26-year-old at General Electric. The bad news was that my new boss would work very hard to get me back on the curve.

I took the offer from Stromberg-Carlson.

3. Adversity

This is one of the most common reasons people start companies. Your position might be in jeopardy or you might be concerned that cutbacks in the organization could limit your future prospects and opportunity. The fear of losing a job, or reduced expectations, causes many people who would not otherwise do so to think about starting a business.

Before I started my company, RF Communications, I was employed in a senior marketing position at General Dynamics-Electronics Division. The company was having some serious business problems and was beginning to make major cutbacks and organizational changes. My boss and I did not work well together and I was convinced I was in danger of being fired. This was an important factor in my decision to start a company.

Since then, I have thought a lot about the subject of job security, and I get very upset when a young college graduate when interviewing for a first job seems unduly concerned about a retirement plan, fringe benefits, etc. Long ago I concluded that there is only one kind of job security that means anything—your ability

to get another job fast. Keep your contacts up, your skills up and your resume current.

During the 1970s, getting a job at IBM was the next best thing to going to heaven. Many new employees began planning their retirement the day they started. Back then IBM employed about 400,000 people. Today, with about half that number, IBM no longer looks like heaven.

Many other major corporations have had large staff reductions and will continue to do so in the future. However, in making such reductions, large companies often provide generous termination pay, sometimes for as long as nine months or a year. Several friends have recently started businesses after receiving these severance packages. This provided them with income for many months while they were getting the new business underway.

4. Red tape and politics

These do not require much discussion. They are shortcomings of all large organizations that drive the entrepreneurial people bananas. Politicians and bureaucrats seldom make entrepreneurs.

5. Champion of orphan products

It's a lonely feeling to try to promote a product that is outside the mainstream business of a large company. In many cases it's more difficult than starting a company from scratch, and even if you do succeed there are probably no significant rewards. Belief in an "orphan product" can strongly encourage the step into entrepreneurship.

Active reasons

1. To be your own boss

Many entrepreneurs possess personality traits that make it difficult, if not impossible, for them to work for others. One sure way to avoid this is to have your own company. Running a company gives you the opportunity to get out of a professional rut, to see a job through from beginning to end and to control your own destiny. These are some big attractions.

Another positive aspect of being your own boss is that you will have much more time flexibility. You can schedule your business activities to be more consistent with the demands of home, children and other commitments and interests.

2. Fame and recognition

It is the opinion of some that this is an important reason people start companies. I do not agree. Most of the entrepreneurs I know are fairly conservative individuals who do not seek the limelight. Ken Olsen, founder of Digital Equipment Corp. (DEC) and a multi-millionaire, for many years lived in the same home he bought shortly after starting DEC. A *Fortune* magazine article said that "Olsen's unostentatious style has kept him from becoming a business celebrity." While there are surely many exceptions, my conclusion is that the extroverted egotist is much more common in the large, well-established company than the start-up. The worst thing that happens to large companies is when their presidents begin to believe what they read about themselves in *BusinessWeek* or *Forbes*.

The struggle to bring a new company into existence is a great lesson in humility.

3. Participation in all aspects of management

Nothing is more exciting than to be broadly involved in the operation of a business. The entrepreneur helps conceive the product or service, helps design it, goes out and gets customers, makes sure that the factory runs well, helps the customer put it in operation and finally sees the effect all of this has on the profits of the firm. What a thrill!

4. Personal financial gain

For some people this is very important, for others it is less so. Gains can come more quickly and can be much greater than when working for someone else; this is not a negligible consideration. This issue is discussed in another chapter.

5. Joy of winning

Entrepreneurs are the ultimate achievers. Starting a company is a good way to satisfy the achievement instinct. Starting a new company, working for a new company, just being involved in any way with a new company is plain fun. It's satisfying and exciting. We spend more hours at our jobs than at anything else we do. Why shouldn't we enjoy it?

I am often asked why I started a company. Here are the reasons that I think were most important:

♦ I wanted very much to stay in Rochester, but for a person with my experience, there was nowhere else to work at the time.

♦ I am an engineer and, in the normal course of my work, I was heavily involved in both the conception and the creation of new products. I met and read about many engineers who had started some very successful companies. Inside of me I had a deep urge and desire to prove whether I had the skills to do it on my own.

♦ The company I worked for was clearly on a downhill slide. I was convinced at the time that my job was in jeopardy. And even if it were not, future opportunity was surely poor.

♦ I had six children, the oldest of whom just entered high school. Providing them a good college education on an engineer's salary would be difficult at best. I thought that if the new company were successful, it might be easier. In a sense it was a "now-or-never" decision.

My reasons, and the others listed, are not the only reasons to start a business. There are many reasons and they are quite powerful reasons. Starting a new company is a great challenge. To those with entrepreneurial instincts, it is very appealing.

◈ Chapter 4 ◈

What Makes an Entrepreneur?

What makes an entrepreneur is a complex question. It includes factors from the environment in which an individual was raised, his or her family situation and his or her personality traits. This question has been the subject of a great deal of both study and research. The following discussion summarizes my own observations, and some of the conclusions of others.

About 20 or 25 years ago if you had asked almost any expert to describe a successful entrepreneur, you would probably have been given a list similar to this:

♦ Male.
♦ Only child.
♦ About 35 to 45 years old.
♦ Bachelors or masters degree in engineering.
♦ Protestant.
♦ Born in the Midwest.
♦ Father owns a hardware store.
♦ As a youth delivered newspapers and sold lemonade.

Should you be concerned if you do not fit this stereotype? Absolutely not. Very few of these are factors that determine whether an entrepreneur succeeds or fails.

However, much recent research and many of my own observations seem to indicate that there are qualities commonly found in successful entrepreneurs, and there are things you can do if you're concerned about any you may lack.

Many writers on the subject seem to be primarily concerned with qualities found in successful entrepreneurs. I look at the question a little differently and believe it is equally important to consider those traits that successful entrepreneurs usually do not have and those traits that, I think, simply do not matter.

Personal qualities common in successful entrepreneurs

Motivation to achieve. In almost every case, successful entrepreneurs are highly motivated to achieve. They are doers, people who make things happen. They are often very competitive. Many researchers have concluded that the most consistent trait found in successful entrepreneurs is the sheer will to win, the need to achieve in everything they do. They do not want to come in third, they do not want to come in second, they want to come in first.

In addition, they are anxious to know how they are doing. They want feedback. Several years ago, after a long business career mostly in marketing, I took a regular faculty position at a graduate business school. One of the things I found most difficult to adjust to was that I never knew how I was doing. Teaching is hard work. Teachers spend 16 weeks preparing, lecturing, grading, counseling, etc., and at the end, the class just disappears. Over the years students will occasionally call or write, commenting about the value of the course, but that is the exception. It is poor feedback at best.

In marketing, on the other hand, you know exactly how you are doing, quickly and with certainty. Either you are getting orders or you are not. It's a clear and simple test of your performance. This may explain why successful entrepreneurs almost always have strong marketing skills. It may also explain why you don't see many business school professors starting companies.

The habit of hard work. Starting a company is hard work. Let no one kid you about that. Some time ago a student reported that one of his other professors said that unless you are prepared to work hard you should not start a company. He asked my opinion. I told him that the statement was nonsense.

I think the correct way to say it is unless you already work hard you should not start a company. There is a big difference. Starting a company is unlikely to turn a lazy oaf into a raging bull.

I worked very hard when starting a company. But I also worked just about as hard for the two companies that employed me before that. Today, when I don't have to work at all, I work almost as hard as ever. I tell my family that I expect to go to the cemetery directly from my office.

An interesting example of a compulsively hardworking entrepreneur is Bill McGowan, the founder of MCI Communications. In 1986, at age 59, he suffered a heart attack that was followed several months later by a heart transplant.

Two weeks after leaving the hospital he visited the office, one month later he began regularly attending board meetings, and within a year of the operation he was back in place as full-time chairman. Some people surely considered Bill McGowan to have been nuts, but I considered him a perfect example of the hardworking entrepreneur.

One motivational speaker said, "It's a dog-eat-dog world out there—for 40 hours a week. But when you get to 50 hours, suddenly there aren't as many dogs. When you get to 60 hours or more, it's downright lonely."

In his excellent book, *Winners*, published by Holt, Rinehart and Winston, Inc., Carter Henderson quotes Nolan Bushnell, the founder of the Atari game company and Pizza Time Theater, as saying it all comes down to one critical ingredient: "Getting off your ass and doing something." In summary, entrepreneurs are almost always very hard workers.

Nonconformity. Entrepreneurs tend to be independent souls, unhappy when forced to conform or toe the line. They are people who find it difficult to work for others, who want to set their own goals. It is hard to imagine anyone more nonconformist than Steve Jobs and Steve Wozniak, the founders of Apple Computer, or Bill Gates, founder of Microsoft.

Strong leadership. Starting a new company can be a harrowing experience, full of uncertainty and risk. Successfully bringing a small organization through these trying periods requires a lot of leadership skills.

Street smarts. I do not know quite how to put this. Shrewd or sharp might be a better word. Paul Hawken describes it as "trade skill" in his book *Growing a Business*, published by Simon and Schuster. We all know owners of some very successful businesses who were lucky to finish high school and never even considered college. Yet they always seem to make the right moves. Call it common sense, instinct, whatever you want. Successful entrepreneurs seem to have intuitive good judgment when making complex business decisions.

Personal qualities not found in successful entrepreneurs

Compulsive gambling. Almost without exception people who start companies are not gamblers. They are attracted to situations where success is determined by personal skill rather than chance. They strongly prefer that their destiny be determined by hard work and conscious decisions rather than by the roll of the dice.

High risk-taking. Contrary to popular opinion, entrepreneurs do not take excessive risks. Through careful product and market selection, creative financing, building a good team and thorough planning, the real risk of starting a new business can be quite low. In the world of small business, optimism is truly cheap and high risk takers die an early death.

Compulsive hip shooting. Snap decision-making is not a common entrepreneurial quality. In fact, excessive caution is more apt to be a problem. Entrepreneurs tend to be careful planners.

Irrelevant factors

Age. This simply does not matter any more. During the 1950s, 60s and 70s the majority of people starting companies were in their 30s and 40s. Not true during the 1980s or today. Several years ago I invested substantial personal funds in a company headed by two 26-year-old entrepreneurs, both younger than my youngest child. Shortly after that, I helped two 19-year-olds plan a business and secure financing.

Steve Jobs and Steve Wozniak were both in their early 20s when they started Apple Computer. At the other extreme, Ray Kroc was 59 when he started the McDonalds restaurant chain.

A recent national survey indicated that a greater percentage of teenagers than adults were interested in someday launching their own businesses. This may be the result of high-visibility role models or the result of hearing their parents discussing whether or not they will be able to survive the next major layoff at their company.

Sex. Here again, it just does not matter. Until recently, entrepreneurship was considered by many to be the last bastion of male dominance in the business world. This is no longer true.

Not long ago I read that more businesses are now being started by women than are being started by men. I know many women who have started successful companies in recent years, and I do not mean only gift shops or snack bars. I mean building contracting, bicycle manufacturing, real estate, printing, newspaper publishing, market research, law firms, accounting firms, and on and on. Later chapters discuss in more detail some of the unique problems faced by women entrepreneurs.

Marital status. This is almost, but not quite, irrelevant. For a woman, being pregnant or having several preschool children may not be the best time to take the step into entrepreneurship. For a man, who is the sole support of the family, having two or three children in college may not be the best time.

But this in no way means they should not start a business. It means that perhaps they should have done it several years earlier or wait a few years longer. The question is when to start a business—not whether.

Educational level. Knowledge and skill are very important. How you acquire them is less important. Too many college degrees may be a handicap rather than an asset. One researcher suggested recently that one of the biggest handicaps you can

have when you start a business is a Ph.D.

Bill Gates, founder of Microsoft, the country's largest software company, quit Harvard after his sophomore year. Interestingly, the information I have shows the educational level among women entrepreneurs to be significantly higher than among men.

Other. After writing this section of the book, something gnawed at me. Somehow I felt that I had overlooked an important personal quality. It occurred to me that intelligence was not on my list. People with below-average intelligence should probably not start businesses, but it is not necessary to be a genius.

Somehow or other, being smart—whatever that means—ought to be better than being dumb, but I do know quite a few very average people who have started some very successful companies.

I watched a television program recently on which the founder of a major company with millions of dollars of sales was interviewed. He said he had graduated last in his high school class of 230 students. Then he added that he did not think he graduated at all, but they just wanted to be rid of him.

As I said at the start, if you do not fit the mold, don't panic. Every entrepreneur is an individual with different skills, different strengths and weaknesses, and different personality traits. Your smartest strategy as you start or develop your business is to be aware of your own special set of skills, strengths and weaknesses, and build on these.

◈ Chapter 5 ◈

Upside/Downside: Reward and Risk

Conventional wisdom is that starting a company is an extremely risky proposition. Data from many sources show that a high percentage of new businesses in the United States fail within the first few years. These statistics put fear in the heart of anyone thinking about launching an enterprise. I urge you not to be too concerned; it's not as bad as many people seem to think. In fact, the odds can really be quite good.

First of all, the above quoted data includes all startups, i.e., corner grocery stores, gasoline stations, trendy restaurants and similar businesses that have a notoriously high attrition rate. Conclusion: Avoid these businesses entirely and your chances of surviving will increase dramatically.

Secondly, many people starting businesses are doomed almost before they begin because of poor initial strategy. The most frequent error, in my view, is to select an offering (either a product or service) that is distinguished from competitors only by price. If you heed the advice later in this book on "Start up Strategies That Work" and find ways to concentrate, differentiate and innovate in every aspect of the business rather than selling price alone, the odds of success will be better.

Finally, I suggest that instead of thinking only about the risks of starting a business, consider the potential rewards at the same time. After all, the relationship between reward and risk is much more important than either alone. If the potential rewards are very great, it may be worth taking a higher level of risk than you would otherwise consider.

Risks and rewards come in many forms. The most obvious are financial, but for many entrepreneurs the financial issues are of less importance than others. The two I want to discuss first are professional and emotional. What different people consider acceptable risk will vary substantially. More things than money must be considered.

The professional rewards of starting a company and succeeding are obviously very great and do not need further discussion.

The most important professional risk of starting a business and failing is the possibility of suddenly becoming unemployed. The question to ask is how two or three years of managing an unsuccessful start-up company would compare to the same two or three years with your former employer when it comes to reentering the job market. My belief is that the broad experience and extensive contacts that come with being the head of a company, even though it fails, would make it easier to find a job. If this is true, or even almost true, it means that the professional risks of starting a company are low.

Emotional risks and rewards are another matter—the rewards can be very great but the risks may also be great for both you and your family. Let us look first at the reward side. I started a company from scratch. We had two employees in addition to the four founders. Eight years later, at the time of our merger with Harris Corp., RF employed about 800 people—today it is closer to 2,000. These were jobs that would not have existed otherwise. Most employees have a spouse and children. There are suppliers and merchants in the community where our employees spend their income. All in all, I estimate that the company I started supports 10,000 to 12,000 people in the Rochester area. Is this an emotional reward? You better believe it is!

Starting RF Communications was financially rewarding to the founders. My living standard and lifestyle moved upward considerably but not nearly as far as my income. Suddenly I had resources available for other purposes. I often tell friends I increased my skill at earning money faster than my wife increased her skill at spending it.

Important to me in my life were the educations my three daughters and three sons received in private Catholic high schools. It was during the 1960s and early 70s, which were very hard times for young people. As a result of the success of RF Communications I was able to donate an athletic field to each of the two high schools my children attended, plus a dozen or so scholarships that will help other young people get a similar education.

On the downside, the emotional risks associated with starting a business can be great whether the business succeeds or fails. Consider how your complete dedication to and immersion in the new venture will affect your marriage and family. When you spend every waking hour dealing with business problems, it may not leave much emotional energy to deal with family problems. Are your spouse and children able to make the emotional investment needed for you to start a business? If your venture goes down, will you be able to prevent your marriage and family from going down as well?

These are scary questions that deserve a lot of attention. While the emotional rewards of entrepreneurship can be great, so can the risks. Each person must assess whether and how they can handle these.

In addition to these two areas, where the risks and rewards must be carefully balanced, there is a long list of others where only reward is possible and the risk is zero. These include things such as being your own boss, being involved in all aspects of the business, getting away from the politics, red tape and bureaucracy of a large company, and many more. If these things are important to you, and they usually are, there is only an upside.

Chapter 6

Five Ways
to Get Rich

It is widely believed that the most important reason to start a business is to make a lot of money. My personal feeling is that the possibility of financial gain is one reason to start a company, but not necessarily the most important.

A survey of about 500 successful male entrepreneurs showed that the prospect of making a lot of money ranked sixth in importance in a list of 10 reasons for starting a business. A similar survey of 113 women entrepreneurs showed the prospects for large financial rewards ranked 11th in a list of 16 reasons.

Each October *Forbes* magazine devotes almost an entire issue to listing the 400 wealthiest people in the United States, along with estimates of each person's net worth at that time. Rush to your nearest library to get a copy—it is fascinating. About half of the top 100 people on the 1995 *Forbes* list made their fortune by starting their own businesses. Here are a few names you may recognize:

Name & Company	Est. Net Worth
Walton Family, Wal-Mart	Too high to count
Bill Gates, Microsoft	$15 billion
David Packard, Hewlett-Packard	$3.7 billion
Gordon Moore, Intel	$2.8 billion
Ross Perot, Electronic Data Systems	$2.6 billion
Philip Knight, Nike	$2.4 billion
Ted Turner, Turner Broadcasting	$1.9 billion
Michael Dell, Dell Computers	$740 million
Henry Singleton, Teledyne	$600 million
Leonard Abramson, U.S. Healthcare	$560 million
Edward DeBartolo, Shopping Centers	$520 million
Thomas Monaghan, Domino's Pizza	$500 million
Frederick Smith, Federal Express	$395 million
Henry Block, H&R Block	$360 million

It is estimated that about 2 million U.S. men and women are millionaires and that nearly 90 percent made their fortunes by starting their own companies. The point here is to emphasize the unarguable fact that by starting a company it is possible to make an amount of money that staggers the imagination. It has been done, it is being done now and it will continue to be done in the future. The potential financial rewards of entrepreneurship are huge.

How about the downside? At RF Communications each of the four founders invested $5,000. That doesn't sound like much now, but in 1961 it was about one-third of a year's salary. And worse yet, none of us had $5,000. We borrowed, put the touch on relatives, cashed insurance policies, etc. As difficult as it was to scrape up the money and as uncomfortable as it felt at the time, the situation was not all bad.

We knew exactly what our downside financial risk was—$5,000. Since this represented about two or three years of savings, we concluded that it was an acceptable risk. Most important, the ratio of potential financial reward to known financial risk was high.

As it turned out, eight years later RF Communications merged with Harris Corp. and the four of us made a great deal of money, far more than we would have dared dream when we started the company. We did not become as rich as Bill Gates, Deon Sanders or Steve Forbes, but we became very comfortable.

I emphasize this point to my entrepreneurship classes by giving a short exam. I ask the class to list the five best ways to get rich. Try it. These are my answers:

◆ The best way to be rich is to be born rich. No close second. On the *Forbes* list most people who did not start companies became rich by inheritance.

◆ The second best way, also by a wide margin, is to marry rich. This is a problem since many people are young when they marry and aren't smart enough to recognize the importance of picking a wealthy mate.

◆ Third place is to win a state lottery. Unfortunately, the probability of winning a state lottery is far lower than the probability of being born rich.

◆ Fourth place, in a close finish, is show business. Be an Elizabeth Taylor, a Johnny Carson, or a Michael Jackson. Show business, unfortunately, requires that you have some talent. Incidentally, both Elizabeth Taylor and Johnny Carson seem determined to do the best they can to help a number of people marry rich.

◆ The fifth way is to start a company. This is the only way available to most of us, and it clearly has the best odds.

Several years ago I decided to do a bit of rigorous scientific research on this subject in an attempt to confirm the above premise. The research was conducted at the Rochester Yacht Club where I am a member and where I docked my 44-foot sailboat. Using the boat population of the club as my sample, I first ascertained that the crossover between a "small" boat and a "big" boat occurred at about 35 feet. Almost without exception the "big" boats were owned by people who had started their own companies. The "small" boats were owned by Ph.D. chemists from Kodak.

There is no doubt in my mind that the only opportunity available to most people to make a lot of money is to start a company. The prospect for large financial reward may not be your primary motivation for starting a company but it certainly has a lot of appeal. Be aware that the potential for huge returns is there and the downside, in comparison, can be acceptably low.

⨍ Chapter 7 ⟣

Entrepreneurship for the Retiree

A strange change has taken place in U.S. industry over the past 10 years or so. Many large and prestigious companies have had major staff reductions, with more still to come. The change that I refer to is that no longer do they give their terminated employees two weeks notice, accrued vacation pay and a pat on the back to send them on their way. Recently it has become far more common to pay them anywhere from three months to a year or more of continuing salary (usually depending on years of service), continuation of health benefits for an extended period and a considerable amount of assistance in retraining and in finding a new job.

A few years ago one of my sons took what I refer to as voluntary/involuntary termination from a major computer company after working there as a salesman for about 11 years. I strongly encouraged him to do this because 11 years of direct selling was enough, even though he had moved up through progressively more responsible positions. It was time for a career change for him, with broader marketing responsibilities.

His termination package included about 50 weeks of pay, along with other benefits. He called me at the end of his last day on the job and said he had not been as happy and excited for as long as he could remember. Immediately he took off for several months to participate in long-distance sailboat races on Lakes Michigan, Huron and Ontario, as well as in Key West, Florida.

After about seven months, he accepted a position as director of marketing for a nonprofit organization at a significant reduction in pay. He is getting much more diverse experience, and my guess is that in several years he will team up with someone and go off on his own.

Obviously my son is not a retiree, but the benefits he received are an example of how generously laid-off professionals may be treated by big companies these days.

In early 1991 the Eastman Kodak Company embarked on a planned cutback of 3,000 people on a voluntary basis. Their eligibility requirement was that age plus years of service had to equal 75. Guess what? By the end of the year more than 8,000 people accepted the offer. Interestingly, I understand that most people who left Kodak were in their early 50s, much younger than I would have expected.

In late 1993, Xerox announced a planned reduction of 10,000 employees over the following two or three years. Recently AT&T announced that it plans to split the company into several semi-independent units, which will include a staff reduction of about 40,000 people. These reductions will undoubtedly include many layoffs, as well as voluntary retirements.

In my opinion many of these people are too young to retire. You may have heard the story about the recent retiree's spouse saying, "I married you for better or for worse, but not for lunch." Sitting in the sun in Florida is not part of my life, nor is a rocking chair on the back porch in Rochester. By and large many of these retirees have immensely valuable business skills and a large number are seriously considering starting a business of their own. This chapter is devoted to some of the issues involved in a decision of this sort.

My first reaction when thinking about a 50-year-old retiree starting a business was that the problems were about the same as for anyone starting a business. But I soon decided they were different in a number of ways.

As I mentioned in the Kodak case, the company was extremely generous in its termination benefits. I was told it included a year's pay and health benefits for life. In addition, a senior manager in his or her early 50s, for example, had the choice between a monthly-payment lifetime annuity and a lump sum payment. The annuity would be in the range of 60 percent of base pay before retirement and the lump sum payment could be well into six figures. Most people starting a business have neither the financial security of an annuity nor access to personal financial resources in the six figure range.

Another difference is that most employees in their 50s or older have reached a stage in their lives where financial demands have decreased. Their children are probably through college, they probably have little or no remaining mortgage on their homes and, since their salary was in many cases substantial, they may also have additional financial resources from savings and investments.

In comparison, when I started a company, I had six children between the ages of 4 and 14, a large mortgage on my home, a car loan, no outside income and a sizable debt as a result of the money I borrowed to get the business going.

It seems to me that the retirees from these big companies have the opportunity to start a business with minimal financial risk. They can take as much time as needed to analyze market opportunities, build prototypes of products, test a new service on an experimental basis and do a top-notch job preparing a business plan. And they probably know dozens of others in the same boat with whom they can form teams that bring together complementary skills. Raising outside capital may be harder because of their age, but borrowing from a bank may be easier.

In talking to a number of friends who took early retirement from Kodak in recent years, I learned two other things that came as a surprise. First, many were unprepared emotionally to retire so suddenly, and quite a few were extremely upset when they learned their former employer, to whom they'd given their entire professional life, suddenly considered them dispensable.

The second thing I learned was that many of them had been "unfulfilled" in their professional careers. Even though they had done well and held responsible positions, they'd always worked under conditions where team performance was emphasized rather than individual performance. Many believe they still have what it takes, and they are highly motivated to reach the top of their profession and succeed on their own.

And they have some very high-visibility role models. Ray Kroc, for example, started the McDonalds restaurant chain at the age of 59. Colonel Sanders started Kentucky Fried Chicken at age 65. All of these things say "go ahead."

But there is a downside too. If these people had the personal qualities needed and the inclination to be entrepreneurs, why didn't it surface 20 or 30 years sooner? Some questions you should consider are whether you are really ready to work the long hours that will probably be required, is your spouse ready to support such a decision and do you really understand the nonfinancial risks of starting a business? Health can also be an issue because it is in the early 50s that the old body begins to show wear and tear.

Finally, many professionals who spent their entire careers in large organizations may have led fairly sheltered business lives. They may never have read a financial statement, surely never had to meet a payroll and may or may not have developed management skills to complement their other professional skills. Is it reasonable to expect to teach such an old dog so many new tricks?

Another point worth mentioning is that it almost always makes sense to start a new business in an area related in some way with your previous job. By doing this it is possible to take maximum advantage of knowledge and experience that took years to acquire. However, care is needed to avoid violating the restrictions in any employment agreements with former employers. One way to minimize this particular risk may be to discuss your plans with your former employer before you actually start the business. Hopefully, you can get their active support and perhaps even an investment.

So the problems of starting a new business and becoming an entrepreneur are not the same for a recent retiree as they are for the younger entrepreneur. I do not suggest that you should not try. But I do suggest that you recognize very clearly what you are getting into before you decide it is a path you really want to travel.

✧ Chapter 8 ✧

When Is the Right Time to Start a Business?

When RF Communications was about three years old, I spoke to a local business group describing our early experiences. By then we had reached several million dollars in sales and had achieved a good level of profits. The start-up days were behind us. It seemed almost certain that we would survive and, in all likelihood, continue to do well.

At the end of the presentation someone in the audience raised his hand. His comment was, "Boy, you guys were really lucky. You started your business at just the right time."

I had never thought about that and had to stop for a moment before responding, "Boy, when we started our business it sure didn't feel like the right time." Three of the founders had quit their jobs, we had not raised any outside capital, we'd invested all of our meager savings and personal borrowings in the company, we were operating out of a vacant beauty parlor, we had a half-finished product and we had no orders.

Were we really lucky? Did we really start the business at the right time? Who knows?

In retrospect I now believe it is either always the right time to start a business or never the right time. If you need an acceptable reason to put the decision off forever, "It's a bad time" is as good a reason as any.

The company that I had considered a model early in my professional career was Hewlett-Packard. That company was started in a garage by two Stanford University graduate students in 1939—the middle of the Great Depression. If there was ever a wrong time in the history of the world to start a company, I would say that David Packard and William Hewlett did very well in finding it.

I do not suggest for a minute that you should rush out and quit your job before you are ready. Carefully evaluate the market opportunity, get as far along as you can in developing your product or service, prepare a good business plan, try to make arrangements for the capital you think you need and then get on with it.

If all the pieces do not fit, perhaps it may be prudent to go back over the planning process. Perhaps you should delay if you decide it is necessary to revise your fundamental strategy to match changes in the economic conditions or the availability of capital. Consider as best you can the circumstances and difficulties you are likely to face.

Remember most of all, though, that it is always difficult to start a company. It is never easy. The issue is not whether it is the right time or the wrong time. The issue is that you must adjust your strategy and your plan for the business so that they match the times. And when you look at others who built successful businesses, do not think that those entrepreneurs were fortunate enough to have found an easy road. In all probability they were just as scared and just as apprehensive as you, regardless of the times.

Chapter 9

To Team or
Not to Team

There are two ways to start a company—alone or as a team. Whether to team with one or more other entrepreneurs, rather than go it alone, is a complex decision that depends mostly upon the personal qualities and skills of the individuals and the nature of the business you are considering. My opinion is that starting a company with a team is usually desirable and greatly improves your chances of success. However, teams are not without problems. Below is a discussion of some of the pros and cons of teaming.

Factors in favor of teaming

Complementary skills

The most important benefit of starting a company with others is that it brings together complementary skills. Most people starting a company have never run a business before, and it would be quite unusual for them to have all of the skills needed. Teaming, for example, can bring an engineering/operating type together with a marketing/promoter type. I describe this as an inside/outside combination.

In a high-tech start up, the inside person would help conceive the product and be responsible for its design and manufacture. The outside person would be responsible for raising money and selling the product. In a service business, such as an investment advisory firm, the inside person would carry out the necessary research and make investment decisions, while the outside person would concentrate on finding clients, managing relations with customers and generally promoting the business. There is obviously much overlap.

Be sure each team member brings a key skill to the situation. More than three or four people are unlikely to be needed, since in most start-up situations there are only a few key skills required. For instance, in my experience, a controller or financial manager need not be part of the founding group. Financial management is a skill that is easy to hire on a part-time basis.

On the other hand, many entrepreneurs, especially those with technical backgrounds, are often unwilling to or do not recognize the importance of having a marketing or sales person as a key member of the team.

Risk reduction

Companies formed by teams of three or four people have lower risk than companies formed by one person. If the founder should be unable to perform his or her duties for any reason, one of the other team members could step in and perhaps save the day. The chances for survival are better with a team.

Emotional support

Starting a new company can be a very lonely job. It seems that every decision you make, if wrong, might mean failure. I describe managing a start up as being equivalent to walking down a road that is covered with banana peels. If you step on one, the game is over. A team of equal or near-equal partners makes it possible to share the emotional burden. For me, this was very important. I don't think I could have started a business alone.

Investors like teams

The importance of this depends on how you go about raising capital and how much capital you need. Investors, either individuals or formal venture capital organizations, seem to be much more comfortable with a team than an individual entrepreneur. This may be a good enough reason to form a team even when it might not otherwise be needed. If your business has to do any bank borrowing you will probably find that bankers are also more likely to lend to companies formed by a team of entrepreneurs.

Improved likelihood of success

In his excellent book entitled *Entrepreneurs in High Technology,* published by Oxford University Press,

Prof. Edward Roberts of MIT suggests that the failure rate of technology companies formed by teams of entrepreneurs is much lower than companies formed by individuals, especially if the team includes a marketing person. A recent study of fast growth companies showed that only six percent were founded by one individual, 54 percent had two founders and 40 percent had three or more.

Hewlett-Packard and Teledyne are classic success stories of companies started by teams. More recently, Apple Computer, Microsoft, Ben & Jerry's Ice Cream and Genentech are a few of the more notable ventures started by teams of entrepreneurs.

Factors against teaming

Dilution of ownership

Many entrepreneurs are unnecessarily generous in sharing ownership in their new venture. Contributing to this is the common belief that the stock in their venture has no value. Gordon Baty in his book *Entrepreneurship for the Nineties,* published by Prentice Hall, suggests that stock in their venture, i.e., a share of the ownership, may be the most valuable thing a new company has. Clearly it is unwise to give away ownership unless the recipient can contribute in a meaningful way.

He also suggests that sharing ownership, either as an outright distribution or as an option, should only be done with key people as a way of providing incentive for future contributions, not as a reward for past contributions. There are other, less expensive ways to give rewards.

Possible serious conflict

I have never seen a start-up business that did not, sooner or later, suffer from conflict among the team members. In my mind, the question is not whether there will be conflict but how bad it will be.

Conflict can be caused by the emotional strain of running the new business, a feeling that one partner is not carrying his or her weight, simple personal incompatibility, a spouse who feels their marital relationship has been hurt by the demands of the business, and on and on. I have seen such conflict range from a disagreement that can be resolved by a candid discussion to one so serious that the only solution was selling the company. Recently I read about two partners in a business who actually resorted to fist fights with each other to resolve disagreements.

Inequalities in responsibility

In most companies formed by a team of entrepreneurs, one is usually selected as president. The others may hold lesser key positions, such as vice president of research or vice president of marketing, but they are almost always directors of the firm, as well. On the board of directors everyone is equal. The problem results from the president being boss part of the time and an equal at other times. This can be a difficult relationship to deal with.

Bad decisions: hard to undo

When you bring in a team member as an officer and director and give that person stock in the firm, it represents a commitment for both the individual and the company. You may hope the commitment is greater for the individual but, in fact, it may be greater for the company. If team members do not meet performance expectations or if their degree of commitment changes, it is difficult to remove them from the job, even harder to remove them as directors, and it may be impossible to get the stock back. So be careful.

Let me describe two rather bizarre teaming arrangements as extreme examples of the situations in which otherwise rational people find themselves. In one company that I had business dealings with there were four founders with essentially equal ownership. They agreed that the presidency would rotate among the group annually, with each taking a turn. As you might imagine this worked great for one year until it was time for the first president to step down. In another situation, a spin off from an aircraft company, there were 17 almost-equal founding partners. It would take another book to describe the problems this caused, but it took years to unravel.

In summary, teaming arrangements in most start-up companies can be a powerful strength that greatly reduces the risk and increases the probability of success. But they almost always generate problems of some sort that may be hard to resolve. To be aware of this is to some extent to be prepared.

᚛ Chapter 10 ᚜

Stolze's Law: The Peter Principle in Reverse

In my reading of books, periodicals and articles relating to entrepreneurship and the management of new ventures, I have never seen any mention of the Peter Principle and its effect on the competitive behavior of a start-up business. The discussion in the following paragraphs is of immense importance and represents one of the most valuable competitive strengths of a new company.

First let's talk about the Peter Principle. This comes from *The Peter Principle,* by Dr. Lawrence J. Peter and Raymond Hull, published by Bantam Books. I recommend this book highly to any student of management. It is a very easy read and quite humorous, but its conclusions are indeed serious.

Dr. Peter suggests that in a large organization, managers tend to be promoted to positions they are no longer qualified to hold, and then they are not promoted again. He says that in a mature organization, most positions are held by those who have reached their "level of incompetence."

You can reasonably ask whether this principle is real or nonsense. You'd better believe that it is real, and the larger and more bureaucratic the organization, the more real it is likely to be.

The second question you might ask is whether the Peter Principle applies to start-up ventures. It absolutely does not and, in fact, the opposite is likely to be true. In most start ups that I know of, the key managers have stepped back from much more responsible positions in larger companies, and this gives the new company an immense competitive advantage. I call this Stolze's Law.

At RF Communications, three of the four founders came from General Dynamics, Electronics Division, in Rochester, N.Y. There, I held the second senior marketing position as general product manager in a business unit with about 6,000 employees. Two of the other founders were chief engineer and assistant chief engineer of the communications laboratory.

What were our jobs at RF Communications? In my case, I had the title of president but my position was salesman—plain and simple. My main responsibility was to get orders. How did I do this? I wrote the sales literature, compiled mailing lists, dug out prospects, visited potential customers, made sales calls, wrote proposals, prepared quotations and, most important, closed orders. At General Dynamics, I supervised a product management department of about 40 people. At RF I was a sales-man and spent most of my time trying to get orders.

How about the two engineers? At General Dynamics, they supervised a group of about 150 people. At RF Communications they worked at the bench designing our products.

Why is all this so important to the start-up company? It means that most of the people in the small firm, at least for a while, have stepped back in position. They are working below their highest skill, not above their highest skill. As a result, they are much better at their jobs. As a practical matter, managers of smaller firms almost always know their markets better, know their customers better, know their products better, make decisions faster and work much more effectively than their counterparts in larger competitors.

Notice that I say "counterpart," not the same position. RCA was one of our competitors, but my counter-part at RCA was not its president, it was the salesman calling on the same customers in the U.S. govern-ment that I called on. And I was bet-ter at that job than he was.

A big company has many com-petitive advantages over the small firm, but this is one instance in which the smaller firm clearly has the edge, and it is a very important edge.

♪ Chapter 11 ♫

The Theory of
Distinctive Competence

It is always valuable to look at companies that you consider to be exceptionally good and analyze the reasons for their success. Ask the questions, "What is this company really good at that distinguishes it from its competitors?" "What represents its most important competitive strength?" Try to identify its distinctive competence. If you do this in a totally objective manner you will be surprised at some of the conclusions you draw.

An example that I especially like to use is the Coca-Cola company. When I ask students to name the distinctive competence of Coca-Cola, they usually suggest:

♦ Secret formula.

♦ Youthful image.

♦ Unique advertising program.

♦ Taste.

♦ Distribution system.

♦ Licensed franchised bottlers.

Which do you think is the best answer? In my mind the distinctive competence of Coca-Cola, by far, is its distribution system. There are more than two million outlets for Coca-Cola soft drinks, more than for any other product in the world. Wherever you may be on the face of this earth, if you decide to have a Coke you can usually find one within a hundred feet or so.

How important is this immensely powerful distribution system? My guess is that Coca-Cola could put anything into a bottle or can, and within months it would be among the top 10 soft drinks.

Now stop and think for a moment of the problem you would face if you decided to start a company with some kind of new soft drink as your product. You would surely have to think of some way to overcome the power of the Coca-Cola distribution system. It would be hopeless to try to compete with them head on. One approach might be to develop a unique soft drink product that served a market niche that did not depend upon such intensive distribution. Gatorade accomplished this successfully.

A few years ago a new company entered the soft-drink market with a product called Jolt. Its distinctive quality was high caffeine content. Their motto was "Twice the caffeine. Twice the sugar." It was an immediate success, attracting national media attention. Obviously they addressed a very specialized market niche with a highly differentiated product. As of this writing, they are working feverishly to establish strong national distribution. An interesting twist on this is that they recently announced a new product—Low-Cal Jolt. With "Twice the Caffeine and Twice the Sugar" as its marketing thrust, Low-Cal Jolt is a little hard for me to understand.

Several years ago Judy Columbus, the founder of one of the most successful real estate firms in Rochester, spoke to my entrepreneurship class. I define her success not in terms of total sales volume or number of employees, but in terms of sales per employee. Her people usually average $3 and $4 million of sales a year, the highest of any realtor in the Rochester area. If her employees don't measure up to this, they do not last very long.

Before starting her own company, Ms. Columbus was one of the top real estate salespeople in the entire United States; however, now she no longer handles clients herself. If she no longer sells, what does she do that makes her company so successful? She hires, she trains and she supports her staff of very competent, highly motivated producers. At one time her distinctive competence was selling, now it is hiring and training. To her firm, this is a much more important skill than selling.

Try listing the distinctive competence of a few other companies. You will find that the larger the company, the more likely that its distinctive competence will be some aspect of marketing. This is important from a small company viewpoint, because marketing is one of the most

difficult and time-consuming competences to develop. Marketing, by and large, depends upon relationships— relationships between a company and its customers, between a company and its distributors, etc. Establishing relationships takes time. They must be earned, they cannot be bought. Time is the one thing a new company has least of.

As an entrepreneur, you can consider the issue of distinctive competence from two directions. First, you can examine your personal skills and the skills of others in your organization to determine how they can be used as the basis for a strategy. Or you can examine the market you wish to address and the competitors you will face, and try to identify the skills and competences that are needed to succeed in that market.

Another quality found among the great companies of the world is that they tend to concentrate their activities in relatively narrow areas— narrow niches. In recent years, there have been as many examples of large companies selling off lines of business to *un*-diversify as there have been of companies diversifying.

Recently I read an article telling how Honeywell made a major comeback after years of poor performance. You may recall that Honeywell tried very hard to diversify into and become a major player in the computer business. They devoted vast resources and spent huge sums of money on computers, only to abandon the program not many years later. The article mentioned that now Honeywell's key products are process, heating and air-conditioning control equipment. Honeywell is a smaller, but very profitable company today. They went back to their basics and it apparently worked.

Not too long ago, Kodak made a major effort to enter the pharmaceutical business by purchasing a number of large drug companies. When it became obvious that this strategy was not working, the board of directors removed the head of the company and hired George Fisher, then president of Motorola. One of his early moves was to sell off most of the pharmaceutical companies it purchased just a few years earlier. Kodak is again concentrating on photography, both chemical and digital, and succeeding—another example of a company returning to its niche.

It is also important to recognize that not only is it possible that the distinctive competence of a firm will change over time, but it is likely. I have often thought about the distinctive competence of Xerox. At the beginning, it was clearly superior technology—the electrostatic imaging process they acquired from the inventor, Chester Carlson. Several years later, when they introduced the fabulously successful Model 914 Copier, they expected considerable sales resistance because of its high cost. Their ingenious solution was not to try to sell copiers, but to sell copies instead. Their sales pitch was, "Let us put a machine in at no cost—just pay us 10 cents a copy." Customers did not have to make a front-end investment to have the use of a Xerox copier.

Today Xerox is still a great company but everyone has access to its basic technology, and selling copies rather than machines is no longer fashionable. So what is Xerox's present distinctive competence? I think it is two things. One is an outstanding line of advanced, high-end copiers with a multitude of sophisticated features, and the other is its marketing force, which is still about the finest in the industry.

So when developing a business strategy for a new company, it is very important to identify or develop some special, unique competence that distinguishes you from those with whom you compete. This can be in the area of marketing, pricing, manufacturing, service, product, etc. In most new companies, the main thrust is a unique product or service, but the other areas may be just as significant.

Of crucial importance here is that it is not necessary for you to be good at everything. But, it is extremely important that you be very good at something.

❦ Chapter 12 ❧

<u>Why Small</u> <u>Companies Are Better</u>

When developing a fundamental strategy for a start up business, give a great deal of serious thought to identifying the intrinsic strengths of small companies compared to the intrinsic strengths of large companies. Where are small companies stronger? Where are big companies stronger?

Then, when you develop a strategy and select products and markets for your new firm, you should try very hard to maximize the advantage you get from your intrinsic strengths and do whatever you can to minimize the effect of the intrinsic strengths of the larger firm. You cannot hope to completely overcome the strengths of the larger company, but you may be able to reduce the advantage it gives them. This process will also make you more aware of obstacles you may face.

Let's talk first about large firms, and try to identify the areas where large companies have an intrinsic advantage over small companies.

Intrinsic strengths of large companies

1. Financial resources

This, without question, represents the most important competitive advantage of larger companies. The lack of financial resources influences every decision in a small business. Some advantages large companies get from their greater financial resources are:

♦ Economies of scale. Large firms can build large plants and manufacture their products in large quantity, thereby benefiting from economies of scale. High production rates usually mean lower cost and, probably, lower prices.

♦ Full product line. The large firm can have an extensive product line, rather than isolated products. In a start up you must first develop, build, sell and generate cash flow from one product before you have the resources to consider a second. Developing a meaningful line may take years.

♦ Investment in product development and marketing. Large companies can undertake product developments that require millions of dollars and years of time. They can establish large sales organizations and undertake huge introductory marketing promotions. These are completely out of the question for a small firm.

2. Momentum/marketing

Big companies have momentum. In business this is the ability to go through down periods or survive bad decisions with a minimum of disruption. It's the ability to weather a recession, a bad product, changes in management, etc. In my view, momentum is achieved by strong marketing, which is one of the most difficult, time consuming and costly skills for a small company to develop.

3. Credibility

If you want to know the importance of this, try selling an expensive product to someone who has never heard of your company. You will soon learn how difficult it is to persuade a tough purchasing agent that your company, operating on a shoestring, will stand behind its product when it is far from certain that you will even be around a year in the future.

4. Structure

Large firms have support organizations carrying out functions that are almost invisible when you work there, but require big investments of time and money to duplicate in a start-up company. Included are quality control, purchasing, incoming inspection, publications and many others. Early in the history of RF Communications, I received a call from a customer asking about the status of a recent order. I said I would find out and call back. To my amazement and embarrassment, I learned the order had somehow been lost between marketing and manufacturing and that work had not even started. Obviously, we did not have, and desperately needed, an order-entry system.

Together these represent a powerful set of advantages that large companies have over small companies. As a practical matter, the small company can do nothing other than become large.

Intrinsic strengths of small companies

At this point you might wonder how the small firm can hope to compete when all these chips are stacked on the other side of the table. Well, all is not lost, because there are some areas in which small companies are stronger than big companies. They are just as important, though harder to identify.

1. Senior people working below their highest skill

This was discussed in an earlier chapter. It may be the most important strength of a small company. You have to replace the Peter Principle with Stolze's Law.

2. Greater flexibility

Small companies are more flexible and have the ability to react much faster on almost any issue than can a large firm. You can respond rapidly to changes in your competitor's product line or marketing strategy, you can customize your product to better meet your customers' unique needs, and you can make decisions in almost every aspect of the business in days rather than weeks, months or years.

After years as president of Abbott Laboratories, Kirk Raab became president of Genentech, the incredibly successful biotechnology company.

According to Raab, it took about 100 meetings to change Abbott's course a noticeable amount. At Genentech, he said, being president was like being at the helm of a PT Boat.

3. Determination to succeed

I was once asked what I considered to be the most important factor in the early success of RF Communications. After a few moments, I answered, "Our compulsive desire to succeed." I cannot be certain that this was the most important factor, but it was significant. My guess is that employees of large companies never hear the words "compulsive desire to succeed" used by a senior manager. Like Avis, small companies try harder.

4. More fun

Finally, there is the intangible factor that working in a small start up can be more fun. People who truly enjoy what they are doing are likely to do it better. An atmosphere of fun and excitement can be a powerful strength. This is one reason so many large companies are desperately trying to introduce "entrepreneurial spirit" into their operations.

These factors should influence the basic strategy of a start up company. Clearly, you should avoid those areas where the large company has an intrinsic advantage and emphasize those areas where the small company has an advantage. The small firm holds more chips than most people realize. As a practical matter, there is nothing a large company can do about these except become small, which is the least likely response.

☞ Chapter 13 ☜

Start-Up Strategies That Work: Picking Your Product and Market

All new companies must make two very important initial decisions: 1) selection of the product or service that the new company will offer; and 2) selection of the particular market to which it will be offered. These are by far the most important decisions in a new venture.

In deciding on your product or service and selecting the market you intend to address, you should strive to develop a strategy that is different from the strategy of your potential competitors, concentrate in fairly narrow niches, and be innovative in significant ways. Remember these words. Write them on your sleeve. Engrave them on your consciousness.

- Differentiate.
- Concentrate.
- Innovate.

If you can figure out how to include these three ingredients in your new venture, the probability of succeeding will be greatly enhanced.

Differentiate your offering, be it product or service. Rarely is it possible to achieve conspicuous success by following others. Offer your customers benefits that are significantly different than other solutions to their problems. *This is very important.*

Concentrate your efforts on a fairly narrow offering in a fairly narrow market niche. It's not possible to be good at everything. By concentrating in a narrow or specialized market niche, you may be able to avoid head-on competition with larger, well-established firms. Attack your competitor in his toe, not in his heart. *This is very important.*

Innovate your offering in meaningful ways. Innovation of product or service is obvious. However, it is possible to innovate in anything—pricing, promotion, customer service, distribution, etc. *This is very important.*

All exceptionally successful companies do these things well—the more you can do, the better. You might ask "How can a small start-up company with almost no resources achieve these qualities in actual practice? How should it approach the problem?"

We have already discussed the issue of distinctive competence. Identify what you and your associates are really good at, and select a market in which these competences will be valued.

Next, I suggest you think again about the intrinsic strengths of a small company compared to those of a large company. This will help you develop a business strategy that avoids the areas in which large firms have a natural advantage and concentrate on the areas where small firms have a natural advantage.

From here on, this chapter will try to identify a number of specific issues related to product/service selection and market selection that are of paramount importance to the small firm. It includes a lot of do's and don'ts and a number of examples that should help you address the very important questions of what product or service should be offered and what market should be served.

You may have noticed by now that I am a product person. My experience is largely with companies that sell physical products rather than services. However, the things that I say apply to service businesses equally as well as to product businesses. The ideas that I am trying to develop and the principles I describe are the same for both.

Product/service selection

First, we will list several things that a new company should avoid when selecting its initial product.

Advanced technology

It is my belief that new companies should not try to pioneer advanced, new technologies. Pioneering a dramatically new technology usually takes a long time, requires substantial capital and involves great risk. This seems to be the natural turf of large firms, even though there are some notable exceptions—Polaroid, which pioneered both polarized optics and instant photography, is one, and Xerox, which pioneered electrostatic imaging, is another. Many people will probably disagree with this position, but I still think the risk and cost are usually not right for a start up.

New concepts

Pioneering a new concept is different from pioneering a new technology, even though the impact is similar. For example, the new cellular telephone system was a dramatically new concept that utilized existing technology. Only a very large company like AT&T could have successfully introduced such a concept.

Volume production

A very large investment in plant, equipment and working capital is needed to build most things in large volume. Where scale is important, only large companies can succeed.

What then should a new company do if it cannot offer new technology, promote new concepts or manufacture in large quantity? There are a few things.

Operational innovation

This is not obvious. What I mean by this is to offer products that, even though functionally similar to competitors, have unique operational features. Make your product smaller, lighter in weight, easier to use, easier to install, easier to service, etc. Emphasizing operational innovation can provide powerful benefits to your customers and is perhaps the most effective product/service strategy for a start up.

The following are a number of examples of companies that used the concept of operational innovation as the main thrust in starting a business. If you were to ask the managers of any of these companies whether operational innovation was their main start up strategy, they would probably not know what you were talking about even though they seem to be doing exactly as I suggest. I've never seen this approach to an initial strategy mentioned in other books about entrepreneurship, yet it represents one of the best ways for an entrepreneur, with limited financial resources, to get a business off the ground.

In the product area, the early Apple II personal computer is a classic example of operational innovation. It was built with parts readily available from an electronics parts distributor, and it employed computer architecture and programming techniques well-known for years. I read recently that the Apple II was discontinued in late 1993, after 16 years and production of over five million units.

Digital Equipment Corp. (DEC) is a company that now has sales exceeding $8 billion. It was started in the 1950s by Ken Olsen, an MIT engineer, and two partners. Olsen's concept was to build minicomputers— small dedicated machines intended for specialized applications, such as monitoring engineering experiments and controlling factory processes. These computers were fairly inexpensive and located right in the work place. Before DEC pioneered this idea, most computers were large mainframes, installed in environmentally controlled computer rooms and run by trained computer staff. DEC revolutionized an industry. It was years before IBM responded to Olsen's operationally innovative strategy.

Compaq Computer is a company that began in 1982 with a personal computer product competing with three well-established companies— Apple, IBM, and Radio Shack. Compaq had sales of more than $100 million in its first full year in business and became one of the fastest-growing companies in U.S. industrial history. Compaq's first product was a portable computer. All the pieces were packaged into a single unit with a handle so the computer could be lugged around without too much difficulty. Even though it weighed about 30 pounds, the product was an instant success. By today's standards a 30-pound PC is the equivalent of an elephant, but back then the concept was unique.

Until recently, Compaq was able to stay ahead of competition with a series of new products that were a little more operationally innovative. They were faster, smaller and more versatile—no big technical breakthrough—just more ingenious and imaginative. A few years ago, Compaq went through some hard times, but after a number of major management changes, they are again one of the leaders in their industry.

A small company, Terry Precision Bicycles For Women, came into existence in 1985. Georgina Terry, the founder, is an avid bicyclist and a mechanic... ...engineer w...th an MBA degree. W...... she star...ed her company, s... routinely ...cycled 5,000 miles or ... ...re a year.

At ...that tim...... bicycles were design... for me... ...d gave little or no c...siderat... ...o the different phys... characteri...stics of women. Gen...... ...a wom...an has longer legs and ... sho...er to...so, narrower shoulders...... ...er ar...ms and wider hips tha... a man. T...is means that to fit properly, a bi...cle intended for a serious woman cyclist should be longer from the saddle to the pedals, shorter from the saddle to the handle bar, and have a narrower handle bar and wider saddle. Even though a bicycle such as this is straightforward to produce, none was available on the market. Georgina Terry formed her company to custom manufacture bicycles, priced in the $1,200 to $1,500 range, for serious women cyclists.

After several years she decided that to increase sales, her company must have a lower priced line than was possible with a small, custom manufacturing operation. She entered into an agreement with a Japanese manufacturer of quality bicycles to supply her with a line of products, built to her specifications, that could be sold for about half of her previous price. Over time she shifted entirely from manufacturing to distributing and her business has grown to almost $1 million in annual sales. Interestingly, the Japanese partner was so impressed with Terry's conceptual knowledge of cycle design and ability to distribute such a product, that it arranged a loan for her through a Japanese bank to finance inventory.

Several U.S. manufacturers offered similar products for a few years but have since dropped out. For all practical purposes, Terry now has this specialized niche market to herself.

More recently Terry has developed another new and unique product that is very successful. It is a bicycle saddle designed specifically for women. I won't try to describe its features but it seems incredible to me that a product so obviously desirable should have taken so long to reach the market. Georgina Terry clearly understands the needs of serious women cyclists and it took someone with her skills and knowledge to design and introduce this new saddle.

In the service area, H&R Block provides an excellent example of operational innovation. Its business is the preparation of income tax returns for tax payers with uncomplicated returns. H&R Block has more than 9,000 offices, about 40,000 seasonal employees and is the most successful firm in this business on a national basis. It offers the same generic service as tens of thousands of public accountants, but it better meets the needs of its target market. Service is fast, inexpensive and provided by trained specialists. As a result, H&R Block has an incredibly high percentage of loyal customers who come back year after year. My daughter, who has her own accounting firm specializing in taxes, has nothing but good things to say about H&R Block.

Domino's Pizza, headquartered in Ann Arbor, Mich., rocked the pizza industry when it introduced fast home delivery as a key part of its operating strategy. Today almost every neighborhood pizza shop provides the same service. The popularity of home-delivered pizza was at least partly a result of the popularity of microwave ovens. Some people think the most important reason to buy a microwave oven is to reheat home-delivered and leftover pizza.

A friend of mine, the former owner of a video rental store, introduced a new twist to this business. He made a deal with a local pizza shop in which they would deliver both a pizza and a video rental at the same time. People staying home on Saturday night to watch a rented movie with the family may very well be interested in both. Why this idea did not succeed, I do not know, but it strikes me as being very innovative and sensitive to the needs of a focused market segment.

Perhaps the best example I know of a service business that used operational innovation as their initial business strategy is Paychex, Inc. The company provides payroll preparation services to companies with between one and 200 employees. Tom Golisano, the founder of Paychex, previously worked as sales manager for a large, well-established firm that provided similar services, but mostly to large clients.

For a small business with only a handful of employees, the weekly or semimonthly paychecks can certainly be done by the boss's secretary in just a few hours. Several simple PC software programs are now available that help with the task. But the problem that Paychex identified was the preparation of the many complex reports required by federal and state governments. Companies have to report income tax withholdings, Social Security, disability, unemployment, etc. In New York State, every corporation must file about 42 reports a year. Some states require a larger number. Now this is something a secretary cannot do in a few hours.

You could make the point that while these reports are admittedly difficult for the small business, why don't they just have their accountant do them? But even for the accountant, it is both time-consuming and expensive. In fact, a high percentage of Paychex's clients are referrals from accountants who realize this is an area best done by a specialist. Paychex now has offices all over the country and prints more than two million paychecks a week for its 225,000-plus clients.

Did Paychex have a revolutionary idea or great invention? Absolutely not. What Tom Golisano did was identify a need in a very focused market that was not being served by companies already in the business. Through his very astute planning and brilliant management, he built one of the most successful start up companies this country has seen in recent years.

A later chapter of this book includes the transcript of a lengthy interview I had with Tom Golisano. He tells about the decisions he made and the programs he followed building Paychex. It provides a superb example for any entrepreneur who wants to learn the right way to start and build a company.

The ability of small companies to conceive and develop operationally innovative offerings is largely a result of the entrepreneur's better understanding of potential users and their problems.

Customer accommodation

When a large company sets up an elaborate manufacturing facility and produces a product in large quantity, it completely surrenders the ability to modify or adapt that product to meet the specialized needs of a small market segment or individual user. You cannot have economies of scale and flexibility in the same package. Because the small company cannot have economies of scale, it should adopt a strategy that emphasizes flexibility.

Early in the life of RF Communications, I traveled to Washington to demonstrate one of our products to the chief engineer of a large government agency. When the demo was over, I asked him how he liked our radio. He said, "It looks great, but it does not meet our requirements." When asked what he meant, the answer was that they wanted the cabinets of all the communications equipment in their radio room to be the same color—green. Our radio was gray. What do you think I said? Obviously, my answer was, "We'll make it green."

There were a few other more technical changes he wanted, which we agreed to for a small additional charge. The sales people of our larger competitors would not even know who in their organization to ask for such modifications.

Through the years, RF secured many very large orders because of its willingness and ability to adapt its very complex products to the unique requirements of individuals or small groups of customers.

Many new ventures have been built on a willingness and ability to accommodate small market segments and even individual customers. This can indeed be a powerful strength of the small company to which the large firm simply cannot respond.

Market selection

Here are a number of factors in the area of market selection that can be of value to a new firm.

Identifying market opportunities

Many new entrepreneurs spend a great deal of time and effort designing the product or service they intend to offer, and almost no time confirming that a market exists or can be created for that product or service. This is frequently true of engineers. The best way to identify market opportunities, in my opinion, is preliminary research. The entrepreneur should spend whatever time necessary visiting potential customers, talking to people already in the business and generally becoming as knowledgeable as possible in the market in which they have an interest. This is true even if it is a business in which they are already working.

Several small companies that I counseled recently used formal market research studies to determine the existence of a market by having the work done by an outside consultant *after* the company was under way. This was clearly wrong. First, it is a waste of financial resources to be investigating market opportunities after the company is under way. This should have been done during the early planning stage of the business. Second, formal market research usually provides a lot of data, but little knowledge. Unless the entrepreneur already knows about the industry and market, he or she will be unable to interpret the data intelligently.

In the software area, a company whose strategy I find very impressive is Intuit, a Menlo Park, California firm, whose product is a simple check writing program called Quicken. In its original form, Quicken did one simple job and did it extremely well, and that was to manage a personal checking account. It set up a file of the names and addresses of the payees to whom checks are regularly sent, printed the check, maintained a check register, assigned each transaction to a category and included a simple procedure for printing reports. It did not attempt to be a double-entry accounting system, an inventory management system or an investment advisory system. All it did was manage a checkbook. Intuit successfully avoided head-to-head competition with much larger software firms by identifying a very focused market opportunity.

Intuit's marketing strategy was also quite ingenious in that it sold the program at a very low price, somewhere in the $30 to $40 range. In general, I do not like the idea of emphasizing low price as a key selling strategy, but Intuit had something else going for it. Many of its customers wanted preprinted checks to use with the program, and these Intuit sold at industry-competitive prices. In effect, it became the Gillette of the software industry. Give away the razor but sell plenty of blades.

Over the years, Intuit added many other features that made the product easier to use, more versatile and that helped sell a lot of upgrades. I use Quicken to manage both my personal and business checking accounts, and I recommend it to all of my family and friends. Even my tax accountant uses Quicken. It drastically reduces the time I need to do my income tax summaries and it's fun to use.

My guess is that there are thousands of computer programmers with the skills to write a program like Quicken. But there are very, very few computer programmers with the skills to identify the need for, and so successfully sell, a program like Quicken.

An interesting problem recently faced by Intuit is that with more and more computers being used by small businesses and in the home, check book management software has become a very attractive market opportunity for some of the giants in the industry. For example, Microsoft, the world's largest software company, recently introduced a product directly in competition with Quicken, and they put a large effort into promoting the product. To date, Intuit seems to be one of the few companies in the software industry able to successfully survive a direct assault by Microsoft.

A year or so ago, Microsoft tried to acquire Intuit to strengthen its position in this market. But the deal was never consummated because of regulatory concerns.

Nothing can replace the intuitive knowledge and experience of the entrepreneur when it comes to recognizing a market opportunity, but it is necessary to spend the time and effort to be sure the information is properly used.

Niche markets

By concentrating in a small, highly specialized niche market, a start-up company can eliminate the need for an extensive distribution or sales organization. Niche markets can be efficiently served by a new company with limited resources.

Several years ago I spent time with two very creative scientists who were considering starting a company. They described four products they thought could serve as the basis of their new business. The products were a camera that could photograph the inside of an eyeball, a fiber optics skylight for department stores to bring natural daylight into a clothing department, an infrared system for locating tanks on a smoke-covered battlefield and an aerial mapping system. All of these seemed like very unique and innovative ideas.

When they asked my opinion, I suggested that trying to introduce all of these products into four totally different, completely unrelated markets at the same time was a sure way to guarantee failure. Any one of the ideas alone could serve as the basis of a successful venture. Attempting all four would be their downfall.

As an alternative, I suggested that a possible way to capitalize on their obvious creative streak was to start an "inventing business." Their products would be ideas, carried to prototype stage and then sold or licensed to others who had the marketing skills and resources to develop them into a business. As it turned out, they did not take any of my advice. When the Star Wars program took off, they were awarded several major government research studies, which was perhaps the best niche of all for their inventive skills.

In addition to simplifying the marketing process, by concentrating on niche markets it is possible for the new company to minimize the advantages that large firms get through volume manufacturing.

A great example of a company that identified and found success in a niche market is Southwest Airlines, which began operations in 1971. It was founded by an attorney named Herb Kelleher. He had an extremely difficult time getting Southwest "off the ground" because of legal challenges from other airlines that were finally resolved in the Supreme Court.

Most airlines use the hub-and-spoke concept and try to serve their large markets with flights going into and out of a few hub cities. To travel on American Airlines from any northeastern city to the southern states you will almost surely go through Raleigh-Durham. To travel across the country on United Airlines you will almost surely go through Chicago.

Southwest's strategy is different— it serves many mid-sized and smaller, regional markets and operates city to city directly. It started out by using only a single type of aircraft (the fuel-thrifty Boeing 737's) and had found ways to reduce time on the ground way below its competitors. Other cost saving strategies? It offers no connections, no luggage transfers, no meals and most of its planes make 11 trips a day. Because of these and many other efficiencies, its fare structure is below competitors, yet in 1990 it was one of the few profitable airlines in the country. I read recently that Southwest could set prices 25 percent below its larger competitors and still operate at a profit. Dallas-based Southwest Airlines has made money for over 20 straight years. Wow!

Agency Rent-A-Car Company addresses a niche market generally ignored by the giants such as Hertz and Avis. If your car is damaged in an accident and your insurance coverage provides for a rental car, chances are your agent will refer you to one of several rental cars companies you never heard of. One of these is Agency. They are the nation's largest renter of insurance replacement rental cars. They have no rental booths at airports, they are usually not near hotels or in downtown locations, but because of the unique insurance situation they operate under, their rates are likely to be very low.

In general, offering a narrow line of products or services that by their nature are directed at fairly narrow niche markets is a better strategy for the new firm than trying to get too big too fast. Start by being very good at what you do and growth will come.

A friend of mine, who is both a very successful entrepreneur and a venture investor, says that every business, not only start up businesses, must adopt a niche strategy to have any hope of achieving exceptional success. Trying to be "everything" to "everybody" just does not work.

Several years back, Eastman Kodak learned this lesson when they tried to become a major factor in pharmaceuticals, and Xerox learned it when they acquired a major insurance company. Both of these "diversification" strategies failed.

One word of caution: The ultimate niche market is one that has only a single user. Designing a product or offering a service where there is only one potential customer clearly has a lot of risk and in most cases should not be done.

What I suggest is that you should seek niche markets that are the "right size" for your specific situation. They must be large enough to be meaningful to your company, yet small enough so as not to attract too many larger competitors.

Use of external selling channels

Since a small company cannot reasonably expect to have a large direct sales force, it should not try. It must either select markets and/or products that do not need extensive selling organizations or use channels external to the firm. In almost every industry, there exist representatives, distributors, agents, dealers, wholesalers, etc., that are geographically diverse and well-established with their target customer base. These individuals or organizations are often willing to represent small firms. I encourage new companies to locate and use external selling channels to rapidly increase marketing strength at a minimum cost. This is discussed in more detail in another chapter.

The following story is an indication of what an innovative mind can do to overcome the powerful distribution system of a huge competitor. Some years ago I read that Dr. Pepper and Coca-Cola were battling in court over whether Dr. Pepper, the soft drink, was legally defined as a cola. I remember thinking that while the world has many overwhelming problems, the question of whether Dr. Pepper was a cola did not seem to be one of them. As I recall, Dr. Pepper, which was a small company at the time, won the case and their soft drink was officially not a cola.

Shortly after that, I attended a management seminar and sat next to the president of Dr. Pepper at dinner one evening. I asked him what the big deal was in the dispute with Coca-Cola. He said it was extremely important to his company, since he had managed to persuade a number of franchised Coca-Cola bottlers to distribute Dr. Pepper. The problem was that these bottlers would not be permitted to handle the product if it were a cola. Gaining access to Coca-Cola's distribution system was clearly a major achievement for Dr. Pepper.

Let's review the principles that a new company might follow in selecting products/services and markets.

♦ Start with a well-defined, distinctive competence that can be used as the basis of the business. You should identify what you and your associates are good at that distinguishes you from competitors.

♦ Think about the special strengths of small, new companies compared to those of big companies. Try to take maximum advantage of the intrinsic strengths of small companies and avoid those where large companies have an advantage.

♦ Differentiate your offering in meaningful ways, concentrate in a fairly narrow product area and fairly narrow market niche so that your limited resources can be used as efficiently as possible. In this way, you will be avoiding head-to-head confrontation with larger, well-entrenched competitors.

♦ Be innovative. It is possible to be innovative in almost every aspect of a business, including pricing, personnel policy, distribution, sales promotion, etc.

♦ Emphasize the benefits your product or service provide your customers, and avoid a strategy that emphasizes low price as your most important competitive thrust. This particular issue is discussed in more detail in another chapter.

Although large companies have competitive advantages that seem impossible to combat, small companies have many strengths that the larger firms cannot duplicate. The challenge faced by the start up is to select an offering and identify a market that takes advantage of these strengths.

⨍ Chapter 14 ⨎

Product/Market Matrix

A helpful tool in selecting the product offering and target market for a new company is a Product/Market Matrix. An example is shown below:

Along the horizontal axis, I show product categories, i.e., Existing Products, Modified Products and New Product. Along the vertical axis, I define market conditions, i.e., Existing Markets, Identifiable Markets and Unknown Markets. Written in each cell is a specific product offering. I chose examples based upon the conditions that existed when the product was first introduced, not the situation that exists today. Think about the specific products as we go through the discussion of the comparative attractiveness of each cell for a new company.

Existing product/existing market

Start-up companies should avoid this cell at the top left of the chart at all costs. Why should you knock yourself out trying to do better what is already being done well enough? Entry costs into such a market are likely to be extremely high and the profit potential questionable.

An example I use here is women's shampoo. I was staggered when I learned that a number of years ago Gillette, a major consumer products firm, sent out 20 million free samples to introduce a new shampoo product named Silkience.

	Existing Product	Modified Product	New Product
Existing Market	Women's Shampoo	Alternative Greeting Cards	Solid State Still Camera
Identifiable Market	Clothes For Professional Women	Overnight Package Delivery	Specialty Sports Car
Unknown Market	Mobile Pet Grooming Service	Personal Computers	Video Disks

When entering an existing market with an existing product, about the only competitive moves available to build sales is to lower price. As I discuss later, this is almost never an acceptable strategy. For a start up to compete in this cell is hopeless.

New product/unknown market

Shown at the bottom right of the chart, this is very dangerous territory for a new firm because of the large uncertainly in both the product area and the market area. The example I use, the video disk, has been a disaster business for a number of companies. Both RCA and N.V. Philips invested huge amounts of money trying to introduce competitive technologies. Both failed. The market just did not want a product that could play videos but not record. On the other hand, the video cassette recorder (VCR), with which you can both record or playback, was a huge success.

Modified product/ existing market or existing product/ identifiable market

For a new business these two cells, top middle and left middle, probably represent the lowest risk. The examples I use are alternative greeting cards and clothes for professional women.

The greeting card industry is dominated by three giants, Hallmark Cards, American Greetings and Gibson Greetings. Over the past 15 years, dozens of small entrepreneurial card companies have come into existence featuring niche themes not addressed

by the big three. These include such things as love themes, humor, inspirational messages and sex. Many of these start ups survive and thrive with sales levels in the $1 million to $10 million range. At that point they encounter a common problem: gaining sufficient distribution in the face of the large marketing organizations of the entrenched giants.

Liz Claiborne launched her clothing business in 1976, selling fashions for professional women. The business has been extremely successful. Ms. Claiborne identified this probable market opportunity long before others and tried unsuccessfully to persuade her employer to switch from junior dresses to clothes directed to fashion conscious, highly paid, working women. They refused and Liz Claiborne, Inc., was born shortly thereafter.

Existing product/unknown market, modified product/ identifiable market, new product/existing market

In these cells, from bottom left to top right, we take a step up in risk— and a step up in opportunity. All things considered, these may be good cells for a start up. They give ample room to differentiate, concentrate and innovate. The opportunity for reward is high and the risk is reasonable.

The three examples used here are a mobile pet grooming service, overnight package delivery and solid state still cameras. The first is an easy-entry service business. The other two would require large amounts of capital, but all might be good opportunities under the right circumstances.

Modified product/unknown market or new product/identifiable market

Many dramatically successful new ventures are in either of these two cells, bottom middle and right middle, as are some notable failures. High potential rewards are combined with high risk. Generally speaking, these two cells take considerably more vision and guts than you are apt to find in a large firm, yet the risk level may be acceptable for the more venturesome entrepreneur.

The examples I use are the personal computer, which was a huge success for Apple Computer and many companies since, and the specialty sports car, which was a disastrous failure for John DeLorean.

This type of analysis is far from fail-safe. It is often difficult to decide in which cell a product fits best, the cells can be moving targets and the process might be criticized for being too simplistic. Yet, I still believe that thinking through your fundamental strategy in this way can only be beneficial.

Notice that I have not included price as part of the product/market matrix decision process. Nor should I.

Chapter 15

Supply-Side Strategy

When developing a strategy for a business, most entrepreneurs look out at the market they intend to serve and try to identify characteristics and needs of existing or potential customers to which competitors have not responded. This is, of course, a good way to develop a strategy, but it is not the only way.

Another approach is to put yourself in the position of the customer and to look back at the suppliers from the user's perspective. Try to identify ways suppliers can serve their customers better. Doing this can help you identify opportunities your competitors are not aware of. I call this supply-side strategy.

The following are some situations that might indicate an opportunity for a new business.

◆ No recent entries in the market.

◆ A reasonably large market being served by a small number of suppliers.

◆ The only suppliers are large firms.

◆ Little or no recent change or innovation in the products or services being offered.

◆ An existing network of distributors or dealers who do not have access to a product.

◆ Complacency among suppliers, possibly a result of some kind of government regulation.

◆ Suppliers that treat customers poorly.

Here are several examples of what I mean:

During the late 1970s, three U.S. companies dominated the market for office copiers—Xerox, IBM and Kodak. All three sold their products using large, direct-sales organizations. At the same time there existed in the U.S. an extensive network of independent office equipment distributors. These organizations sold to the same people in the same companies as the Xerox, IBM and Kodak salespeople. Yet these office equipment distributors did not have access to a line of copiers with which to compete with the big three.

When Japanese copier companies came into the U.S. market, they discovered that they could get access to an existing network of quality distributors who were anxious to add a line of copiers to their offering. This gave the Japanese firms an instant sales capability that in many ways may have been better than those of the big three, especially for smaller copiers. Today, 15 years later, some of these Japanese copier companies have switched to direct selling, but others stayed with the distributors.

Another example is Federal Express Company, which provides overnight parcel delivery anywhere in the United States and several other countries as well. It accomplishes this by having its own fleet of cargo planes pick up parcels at the end of the day at airports all over the country. These planes then fly to Memphis, Tenn., where the parcels are sorted. Within a few hours, the planes take off again heading for outlying cities. The parcels are delivered by local truck early the next business day.

This concept was revolutionary. During its early history, Federal Express had a lot of difficulty raising sufficient capital. It took a series of large outside financings, mostly from venture capital firms, and two or three close escapes from the edge of doom before its unusual service produced a satisfactory revenue stream. Today, Federal Express is an important part of the business communications system. It is hard to imagine the business world functioning without Federal Express and its clones.

What had Federal Express done? It certainly identified a market opportunity that it addressed in an aggressive and extremely innovative manner. But it entered an industry with at least three of the supply-side characteristics listed earlier:

♦ No recent entries in the market.

♦ Little innovation in the services being offered.

♦ Customers being treated poorly.

A few years ago, I sent an Express Mail Letter from Rochester, N.Y., to a destination in Indiana. Express Mail is the U.S. Postal Service's competitive response to Federal Express. Delivery is guaranteed the following day or you get your money back. The fee was something like $11. The letter was not delivered the next day as promised. As a matter of curiosity, I decided to see how hard it would be to get a refund. It was harder than I expected. This is what happened:

1. I telephoned the person to whom the letter was sent to get a copy of the receipt showing the time of mailing and the time of delivery.

2. I mailed this to the post office branch from which the letter was sent, requesting a refund.

3. The response I got was a special form that had to be filled out and mailed to a central refund processing location. I did this.

4. Next, I received a call from a person, who did not identify himself, telling me to come in for my money. Unfortunately, I was not in the office and took the call from my answering machine.

5. I confused the name of the branch where I was to pick up the refund. When I got there, I was directed to the correct branch.

6. I went to the correct branch and asked the clerk for my money. I was told in no uncertain terms that I could not get a refund until I had filled out a special form and sent it to the central processing point along with evidence of late delivery.

7. I tried, to no avail, to explain that I had already done that.

8. By coincidence the postmaster walked by and heard an argument developing. He interceded and said he remembered the call and that I could have my money.

That's service?

Several weeks later I decided at about 3:30 in the afternoon to send a package that day to Florida by Federal Express. The package had to be there the following morning. This is what happened:

1. I called the local Federal Express office and was told I would have to call an 800 number.

2. When I did this, a woman on the other end asked if I could get the package to one of their local deposit boxes before 6 p.m.

3. I said I could not and she said they would handle it. An hour or so later, a Federal Express truck arrived at my office and picked up the package.

4. When I tried to pay in advance, the driver said they would bill me. I said I had no account with them. He said it was fine, they knew my name and address.

5. The package was delivered the next morning, on time.

That's service! I do not recall what Federal Express charged for pickup and delivery. I don't care. I don't know how hard it is to get a refund from Federal Express. I never had to try.

I could give many examples of companies who discovered an unexpected opportunity by putting themselves in the customers' position and looking back at the suppliers who serve the customers. This can be an offbeat but very effective way to develop a strategy for a business.

Chapter 16

Fads vs. Trends

Defined, a fad is a short-lived but widespread phenomenon. A trend, on the other hand, reflects a relatively long-term direction.

It is extremely important for entrepreneurs to decide whether the business they are considering is a fad or a trend. In either case it may be a good opportunity, but your operating strategy must be different if you hope to succeed. The basic distinction between the two is short term versus long term. If you guess wrong you could be in for big trouble.

Relatively early in the life of RF Communications, we had to decide whether to enter the citizens band (CB) radio business. For the reader unfamiliar with CB radio is it is a group of channels that can be used by ordinary citizens without the complexity of securing license assignments from the Federal Communications Commission. It was used for gab-fests and was especially popular among truckers. One common use was for the truckers to warn their buddies of the location of police radar traps.

The cost of a CB radio was only a few hundred dollars and many private citizens used CB for emergency communications while on the road. To a certain extent CB has been replaced by the now popular cellular telephone.

At the time, our products were single sideband, long-range radio communications equipment for military, commercial and industrial customers. When we faced this decision, the CB market was experiencing explosive growth and U.S. companies serving the market were expanding by leaps and bounds. They were all very profitable.

I personally felt nervous about entering the CB business. We had the technical skills and financial resources, but I was unsure that the market would last. Was citizens band radio a fad or a trend? If it was a fad, we had no interest, if it was a trend, we had no alternative.

Since we did not have good market research skills in our company, we sought counsel from a large management consulting firm that had just completed a major, multi-client, international communications market study. Their conclusion was that CB was here to stay and that within a few years, most new cars would include a CB radio as original equipment. They predicted that the market would continue to grow for the foreseeable future. In effect, they suggested that CB was a trend and that we had better move fast.

I still felt uncertain. Because we had several other opportunities at the time that were more attractive than the CB radio business, we decided not to enter that market. Within a year or so, the CB market collapsed and many companies in the business went down the tubes. I don't know whether we were lucky or smart, but I guess it doesn't matter.

Approximately 20 years ago, Apple Computer pioneered the personal computer—a dramatically new and innovative product sold into a market that did not exist a short time earlier. Predictions were rampant that within several years we would find a PC on every office desk, in every classroom, in every home. Was the personal computer a fad or a trend?

Even though I was not in the business at the time, I concluded that it was probably a trend. Shortly after that, IBM apparently made the same decision, and the rest is history. It is hard to think of a new product that so quickly became a necessity in almost aspect of our lives than the personal computer.

Another interesting product that looked like a fad when it was first put on the market was the Walkman personal cassette player, introduced a number of years ago by Sony. I remember reading that all of the market research that Sony did indicated that the world did not want this product. However, the personal judgment of Sony's chairman was that the world did want this product. Obviously, he was dead right and today, years later, the Walkman and countless variations are still extremely popular.

I learned a few years back about a company named Safety First Inc.

that sold over four million of the yellow and black diamond shaped signs that say "Baby on Board!" These were usually put in car windows. This sign was a fad if there ever was one. When sales of the sign tapered off, however, Safety First began selling other safety products for babies that they marketed through several large national retail chains, supermarkets and drug stores. Safety First apparently thrived with a fad-type product that gave it the resources and impetus to expand into a more attractive, long-term type of business.

On the other side of the coin, is Pizza Time Theater, a California-based company founded by Nolan Bushnell, who previously started the Atari game company. Chuck E. Cheese/Pizza Time Theater was a chain of company-owned and franchised pizza restaurants that, in addition to food, featured animated cartoon characters, including Chuck E. Cheese, and a large room full of video games. The quality of the pizza was excellent, the characters unique and the video games interesting.

Business boomed for several years and then the parent company failed, as did many of the franchised, privately owned Pizza Time restaurants. I am not certain of all the reasons, but two things seem clear. One was that the concept was too dependent on the popularity of video games, which itself was a fad, and the other was that the world can only support so many specialty restaurants of this type. What Bushnell and his investors apparently thought was a trend seemed to have been a fad.

A few years ago, another company took over Pizza Time Theater, modified the concept somewhat and cut back drastically on the number of restaurants. I spoke with the owner of five franchises and was told that business was good and the organization was growing again.

It is easy to suggest, with 20/20 hindsight, that the answers in these situations should have been obvious. But believe me, when RF Communications decided not to enter the citizens band radio market, it didn't feel obvious.

Several issues are important here. One is whether a fad-type of business is ever right for a start up company. You can make a very strong point that a start-up firm has a number of qualities that make fad businesses attractive. For instance, they are willing to take risks, they are responsive, they can move fast, etc. Surely, to succeed in a fad business, these qualities are essential. Yet my personal belief is that it is usually best for a new company to avoid fad-type businesses. To succeed, management has to have the foresight to get out at the right time and the skill to get out fast and decisively. These are rare qualities.

In thinking about the fad vs. trend question, I tried to list a number of notable fad-type products. They include hula hoops, Nehru jackets, quadraphonic sound, crock pots and electric carving knives. You can surely think of others. All were booming businesses at one time, but try to buy any of them today. For some companies, these may have been profitable businesses for a short time, but my guess is that they had to be pretty fast on their feet to come out whole. A year or so ago, I spoke at a meeting of a local business group. They gave me an electric carving knife as a gift. I could hardly believe my eyes.

Trend businesses clearly are attractive. They permit sensible planning, have desirable long-term benefits, greatly reward the creative and responsive entrepreneur, and do not require skills unlikely to be found in a start-up company. The big problem in deciding between a fad business and a trend business is telling them apart early enough. In another chapter I tell how being street smart or having instinctively good moves is an important personality trait of successful entrepreneurs. This is a business area where being street smart can really save the day.

Chapter 17

Product/Market Zig-Zag

Entering a new market with a new product or service is very difficult for any business. The risks are always high and it is an excellent example of "leading from weakness." When you introduce a new product or service you can never be sure that it will perform satisfactorily or have the right features. When you enter a new market in which you do not have experience or knowledge, you can never be certain that your product or service will meet the customer's needs.

Every company starting in business is faced with the challenge of entering a new market with a new product or service. Almost without exception, the company is trying to sell something that it has never sold and it is trying to sell to users who have never before bought anything from that new company. This is a tough situation and is one of the reasons starting a business is so difficult.

As you overcome this difficulty and your business grows, before long you will seek opportunities for expansion. You'll try to develop new products and services and identify new market opportunities. My very strong advice is that it is almost always wrong to try to do them at the same time. A better strategy is what I call "Product/Market Zig-Zag."

Let us assume that after a year in business, your firm has successfully introduced its initial product, Product A. It's been accepted by your customers, it can be produced efficiently and all the bugs are out. This product is being sold into what we'll call Market A. You have a small sales force that calls on the customers in this market, you have established a series of strong distributors and you are competing effectively. Everything is great. Product A is selling well in Market A. However, you have some extra financial resources that you want to invest in growth.

My advice is to either take your existing product and try to sell it to a new group of customers or develop a new product and sell it to your existing group of customers.

♦ New product to an old market.

♦ Or old product to a new market.

♦ But never, ever, a new product to a new market.

This is shown in the chart on the following page.

Later, after you've established the new product or penetrated the new market, you can consider doing the same thing again. This time, you will be doing it from a stronger base. *Zig-zag between product and market.*

Paychex, Inc., is a company that provides payroll preparation service to small businesses. Its strategy is described in detail in other sections of this book. The market it targets includes companies with between two and 100 employees. Paychex is a fast growing, very profitable and very successful company by any standard.

A number of years ago, Paychex decided to diversify by introducing a service called Jobline. Jobline tried to match individuals interested in changing jobs with companies interested in hiring. This was done on an experimental basis in the Boston area.

Paychex collected and published long lists of condensed resumes. When a firm had a need, it could contact Jobline and, for a fee, get a list of candidates who might be qualified for the position. This business did not succeed, and after a few years, the project was abandoned. This is a good example of the difficulty of trying to

penetrate a brand-new market with a brand-new offering.

More recently, Paychex began packaging fringe benefit programs, such as health, disability and workman's compensation insurance, that could be offered to the same client base that buys its payroll service—small companies who do not have benefit specialists on their staffs. It also began selling employee handbooks customized for individual users. Here Paychex has put together several innovative offerings that are sold to its existing customers. These programs are a success.

Another example is Xerox. At one point, Xerox made a major effort to enter the computer business. As I recall, it paid something like $1 billion to purchase Scientific Data Systems, a fast-growing, independent West Coast computer company. Over the years, Xerox made other major moves to enter into this market. For example, its Palo Alto research center is credited with pioneering the use of graphical user interfaces in personal computers, a technique that is so successful in Apple's Macintosh line and in Microsoft's Windows

Software. And Xerox was one of the earliest companies on the market with a personal computer product.

Now you should ask, "How important is the computer business to Xerox today?" As best I know, the answer is, "Not very." It is still the world leader in electrostatic copiers, introducing new and almost revolutionary products on a regular basis, but its computer-related business is small. My belief is that the reason for Xerox's failure with computers is that it was trying to enter a market it did not understand with products it did not understand. Computers are completely different, both in technology and in marketing, than copiers.

Introducing a new product or entering a new market is always a formidable challenge for a business. If you try to do only one at a time, you have the benefit of at least some strength and experience helping the process.

Chapter 18

Buying a Franchise: Another Way to Own a Business

Buying a franchise in an established business is another way to become an entrepreneur. This approach has its own pros and cons, some of which will be discussed here. However, buying a franchise is a very specialized undertaking. There are numerous books and magazines devoted to franchising, and you should read some of these. There are also lawyers, accountants and franchise consultants who are experts in the field who you should consider using before you sign on the dotted line.

In 1990 there were more than 500,000 franchised outlets in operation in the United States, with annual sales exceeding $700 billion, about one-third of all retail sales. The franchise industry employed more than 7 million full-time or part-time people. There are about 3,000 U.S. companies from which franchises can be bought, representing about 60 different industries. From this data, you can see that franchising is big, big business.

The larger franchise companies, such as McDonalds, Holiday Inn and Wendy's, frequently require investments in excess of $1 million, and as a practical matter, simply are not an alternative for the average person interested in owning a business. On the other hand, there are many other franchises available, some very small and serving focused markets, where the required investment is modest.

Lists of franchise opportunities are included in franchise guides and handbooks that can be obtained from most libraries and many book stores. If you are seriously thinking of buying a franchise, be sure to read some of these at the very beginning of your search, so you get a feel for the scope and diversity of franchise businesses.

There are two different types of franchises: One is called a product franchise where the franchisee obtains the rights to purchase and sell the product of the franchiser, perhaps operating the business under his or her own name rather than the franchiser's name. The most common of this type is an automobile dealership.

If you want to buy a new Chevrolet, you don't go to a Chrysler dealer. However, in recent years, it has become more common for a single dealer to offer more than one brand of automobile, such as a U.S. brand plus a Japanese brand. In these cases, they must obtain separate franchises for each brand, each with its own individual restrictions.

The other type of franchise is called a business format franchise. Here it is usual to operate the business under the franchiser's name. Typical of these is a McDonalds or Holiday Inn franchise. In these cases, it is often difficult for customers to know whether they are in a franchised unit or a company-owned unit.

The main advantage of buying a franchise rather than starting a business from scratch is that the failure rate among franchised businesses is lower than among independently created businesses. You are buying a proven business idea, and you get a lot of help running it.

For example, you begin with a known product or service, you usually receive training and expert guidance in the operation of the business, you benefit from the advertising and promotional efforts of the parent company, you may receive volume buying economies, you follow standardized procedures and operating methods that have proven successful for others, and you may get the benefit of new products or services developed by the franchiser. All of these can give you a valuable headstart compared to developing a business strategy of your own. In effect, you are in business for yourself—not in business by yourself.

Some of the disadvantages are that the up-front costs may be considerable, there are probably continuing carrying costs in the form of royalties and advertising sharing fees, and you will probably have to accept many restraints and limitations on your freedom to zig and zag in directions you evolve on your own. These restraints may reduce the upside potential and long-term financial rewards. And if the franchiser goes bust or gets into financial difficulties, your life can become very complicated.

All sellers of franchises are required by the Federal Trade Commission to give the potential buyer a document called a Franchise Offering Circular. This provides detailed information about the franchiser's business and is intended to protect the buyer. Be sure to read it carefully. Many states also have laws that regulate the operation of franchises. Learn about these.

If you are serious about buying a franchise, you should consider attending one of seven or eight expositions or trade shows held each year that will have as many as 400 franchise companies exhibiting. For information about these, contact International Franchise Expos, Inc., at 407-647-8521.

Buying a franchise is far from a fail-safe way to have a business. You should go about the selection of a franchise in a thorough and rigorous way. Evaluate the product or service, analyze the market, study your competitors and learn all you can about the business from others. Write a business plan of your own. The contents of the plan may be different than for other types of businesses, but the importance is equally as great.

When buying a franchise, unlike many business situations, you are free to talk to other franchisees who have gone down the same path you are considering, and the likelihood is that they will be willing to share their experiences. One important thing to know is how many units of that franchise were abandoned or sold by the owners within a short period of time. Also, you should be sure that you have reasonable geographic protection and that the franchiser cannot open other units so close as to negatively affect your sales. I read an article recently where a disenchanted franchisee of a major fast food chain was quoted as saying, "It's just buying a hard, low-paying job with long hours."

In summary, I view buying a franchise as one of a number of acceptable ways of being an entrepreneur. But you should be just as careful and just as diligent as you would in starting a business of any kind.

Chapter 19

Why People Buy: Value, Benefits and Price

This section is about pricing. You are not likely to hear the things that I say about the subject in pricing courses in a business school, even though everything I say is consistent with sound economic principles.

Before we get to the details, I suggest you make a list of what you consider to be the five or six best companies in the United States. Define "best" in any way that you like. List any type of companies from any industries. Write down your choices before reading further. My list includes the following companies:

- Microsoft.
- Bristol-Myers.
- Hewlett-Packard.
- Bloomingdale's. **(Now Macy's?)**
- Coca-Cola.

Your list is probably entirely different. One quality common to all of the companies on my list is that rarely do their customers make their purchase decision because of price. In no case are these companies the low price player in their industry and in many cases they are the high price player. Yet, they are almost always the most profitable. How do you explain this?

I explain it by using the following very simple formula:

$$Value = \frac{Benefits}{Price}$$

This formula suggests that buyers, when making a purchase decision, select what they consider to be the best value—all things considered. And it suggests that value is equal to the benefits they perceive, divided by the price. Price is only one part of the purchase decision process.

If you want to increase your customers' perceived value of your product, you can do so by either increasing the benefits or decreasing the price. It is almost always preferable to work on the benefits, which should make it possible to sell at a higher price. Unless you do this, the likelihood of your company being reasonably profitable is small.

Surely, at this point, some readers will suggest that these companies are either lucky or that they can demand high prices only because they dominate their markets. First, I reject the idea that luck has anything to do with it. Consistent winners are always lucky. As Malcolm

Forbes, Sr., once said, "The harder you work the luckier you get."

Second, I reject market dominance as the key issue. Instead, I suggest that all the companies on my list, and probably your list as well, follow the pricing approach described above as a deliberate strategy. They consciously surround their offering with so many benefits of such great value to their customers that they can invariably command a higher price.

It is because of this that they are able to dominate their market. Anyone who suggests that good companies can justify higher prices because of market dominance has the cart before the horse. It may be possible in the short term but in the long term, it is just not true. A large, dominant company that is going bad may be able to demand higher prices for a while based upon its reputation; however, unless it keeps its offering sharp, this dominance will not last.

For a new company, the only way to get high prices is to have an offering that provides benefits for which users are willing to pay a premium. Doing this is the best way to gain market share and be profitable at the same time.

Another way of looking at this is to consider what happens if your offering (product or service) is identical to your competitor's. In this case, the only thing you can do to increase sales is to cut your price. Your competitor's reaction is predictable, i.e., drop price further than yours. And you have only one move. In the long term, selling price seldom works.

If you permit your company to develop the mind-set that emphasizing price is an acceptable strategy, sooner or later your business will be in trouble. The alternative to price cutting is to increase the benefits of your offering.

How can you do this? You can include innovative features in your product that your competitor does not have (as does Microsoft). You can offer a continuous stream of new products (as does Bristol-Myers). You can build an extremely effective marketing organization with a great product offering and concentrate on being a safe, dependable buy (as does Hewlett-Packard). You can offer a combination of unique products and an exciting buying environment (as does Bloomingdale's). Or you can concentrate on extensive distribution and availability (as does Coca-Cola).

You can reasonably stop me here to point out that the benefits I list are things that are often not available to a small start-up firm. Extensive distribution systems and the perception of dependability take years to develop. True. But earlier, we identified a number of strengths of small companies. The ability to customize products for small market segments or individual customers, fast response to changes in the market and better understanding of customers' needs are just a few of the ways that small companies are better than big companies. Convert these strengths into benefits.

In summary, I suggest that the only pricing strategy that makes sense is to work very, very hard to surround your product or service with benefits, both tangible and intangible, both rational and emotional, both large and small, that will cause your customers to perceive a value that is greater than their alternative. Then you will have justified a higher price. Companies, large or small, that continually emphasize low price as a competitive strategy are almost always lousy companies that sooner or later either reverse the strategy or find themselves in very serious trouble.

In discussing the above approach to pricing to business groups or classes in entrepreneurship, I am always challenged by someone who names companies that seem to be exceptions. Usually they are retail chains that, through volume buying and a willingness to operate at lower margins, are able to sell at lower prices. My response is to accept the fact that there may be exceptions, but I also name a long list of similar companies that also emphasized low price as their main strategy that are no longer in existence.

My point is that by emphasizing benefits rather than price you are more likely to have a profitable, successful business.

✧ Chapter 20 ✧

Marketing Means Selling

It is an absolute truth that unless a start up company can sell its offering, and sell it fast, it will not survive. Getting orders, selling your product or service to paying customers, is of crucial importance to a new firm. I cannot emphasize this enough.

This may sound obvious and trite, but you would be amazed at the number of entrepreneurs who simply do not understand both the importance and urgency of getting orders. For a company to survive, it must have positive cash flow. Sooner rather than later, its cash receipts from orders must be greater than its cash expenditures. Early on, cash is generated by the personal investment of the entrepreneur, by borrowing and/or by raising outside equity capital. But these sources only last a short time. It is imperative that the new firm generate positive cash flow, through the sale of its offering to paying customers, before its start-up capital is depleted.

The only way to do this is to get orders. Getting orders is the main game in a new business.

Many people in both the business world and in academia go to a lot of trouble to differentiate between marketing and selling. They consider marketing to be more dignified than selling and in fact, many marketing programs do not even include selling as part of the agenda. My solution to this is that you can call the process anything you want, but the basic problem remains the same, especially for a small or new company, and that is getting orders. Exactly what you do, which element of the marketing process your choose to follow, will vary depending on the exact nature of your business. But whatever you call the process, the goal remains the same: to get orders.

How does a new start-up company go about getting orders? First, you do not do the thing you're likely to learn in a business school marketing course. You don't do market research, quantitative competitive analysis or consumer surveys. These should have been done before you started the company. You do not develop long-term marketing strategies and you do not do computer modeling.

You do communicate information about your products and services to as many potential users as possible, and most importantly, you sell. Finally, you do all this in the most efficient and effective way possible within the financial constraints of the small firm.

The reality is that selling, influencing the decisions of others, is something we spend more time doing in both our business and personal lives than almost any other activity. Let me give a few examples:

♦ You get up in the morning and ask your 2-year-old what she wants for breakfast. She says, "ice cream" and you say, "cereal." You have to sell!

♦ You ask your boss for a raise. The response is, "Why do you think you deserve a raise." You have to sell!

♦ Before you leave the office in the evening, you call your spouse and say, "I've had a hard day, let's go out to dinner." He or she says, "Great, where will we go?" You say, "How's McDonald's?" Your spouse says, "I had Chez Paree in mind." You both have to sell!

♦ Hopefully, as an entrepreneur you are also spending a lot of time selling customers.

If you think about it, you can only conclude that our entire lives are devoted to "sell, sell, sell!!!" Having emphasized how important selling is, I will now tell you what a difficult job it is for the small firm and suggest some things that might be done.

Selling direct

Many large companies sell with a direct sales force of company-employed sales people. This is very expensive and takes years to implement. The only way a small firm can hope to sell direct is to focus on a very narrow niche market that can be addressed by a small number of people. I have already stressed this point.

High-level selling

In a start up, the head of the company is almost always an effective sales person. He or she knows the customer better, knows the product better, works harder and can make decisions on the spot. Every buyer likes to deal with the head of the firm. When making a call or setting up an appointment, few people will refuse to see "the president." Clearly, this is one of the most effective uses of the time for the head of a start-up company. Getting orders is crucial and the best person for getting orders is the boss.

Ross Perot was a star IBM field salesman before he started Electronic Data Systems. Later he continued as a star salesman for EDS while being an effective chief executive, as well.

Another good example is Bill Gates, the founder and head of Microsoft, the world's largest software company. Yes, Bill Gates has a great knowledge of computers and computer software, but what he really does well, and does constantly, is to promote Microsoft products using every form of marketing and selling ever invented. In my opinion, the main factor in the amazing success of Microsoft is Bill Gates's selling skills and understanding of the market for its products.

In many big companies, the president rarely sees a customer.

Using external channels

The next alternative, and most small companies follow this course, is to use some type of marketing channel external to the firm. Use marketing intermediaries such as agents, representatives, distributors, jobbers, wholesalers, retailers, dealers, etc., whichever are appropriate in your business. The number of marketing intermediaries available in the U.S. is great, and they are available to sell almost every imaginable product or service. Shown below are some of the pros and cons of a small firm selling through independent marketing intermediaries.

Pros

- No fixed cost, they are only paid when they get orders.
- They can be put into place fast.
- If they have complementary lines, the strength of their offering may be greater than yours alone.
- They often handle installation, training, warranty and service.
- You, as a new and unknown firm, can benefit from their reputation with their customers.
- They know the territory.

Cons

- It is difficult to train and monitor external marketing organizations.
- They tend to emphasize the things that are easy to sell, which may not be yours.
- If they are very successful, they become hard to control.

- Your customers may have more loyalty to your representative than to you.
- They require a lot of support.

In most situations, the pros far outweigh the cons. However, managing an external marketing force is complex. Here are a few key issues:

- A large part of your selling effort must be devoted to finding, managing and keeping top-quality members of your distribution channel.
- Philosophically, you should operate as if the selling intermediary is part of your organization, not an outsider.
- You must compete constantly for their attention and effort.
- You must treat them fairly by such actions as paying generous commissions, paying promptly, backing up your product, being responsive to their inquiries and keeping your promises.

Managing external channel members is a specialized skill that requires maximum attention.

Licensing and private-label resale

Other alternatives that I have used successfully on a number of occasions are private-label resale and license arrangements. If you have a very strong product offering and limited marketing and selling skills, you may be able to find an established company that will purchase or license your product to resell it under either its name or yours.

In recent years a number of small software companies with products such as spelling checkers, data compression techniques, virus detectors, etc., have licensed the use of their very specialized products to larger, better known software companies with better marketing skills, either for incorporation as a feature in their products or to sell as part of their product line.

The advantages and disadvantages of these arrangements are:

Pros

♦ Access to skills that might take years to build in your own company.

♦ Single large order, with delivery scheduled over an extended period.

♦ No credit risk or collection problem.

♦ You may be able to negotiate advance payment.

♦ Quick access to the market.

♦ The larger firm's reputation carries over to your company's product.

Cons

♦ You don't develop marketing strength in your company.

♦ You may be subject to price pressure.

♦ You build no reputation for your firm with the end user.

Franchising and multilevel marketing

These are two somewhat different ways of selling, which have become very popular in recent years. Another chapter gives a description of each, along with its pros and cons.

Advertising/sales promotion

Promoting your offering and communicating information about it to potential customers is another complexity. The traditional way to do this is through media advertising—trade journals, magazines, newspapers, television and radio. This is expensive. As an alternative, small companies should make extensive use of new product releases—which trade magazines usually publish at no cost—papers in professional journals and presentation of papers at seminars and meetings.

If you decide to use paid space advertising, choose your media with care and imagination. I had a very interesting experience that really opened my eyes on how innovative you can be in the area of product promotion at very low cost.

RF Communications' products, as I mentioned earlier, were two-way radios sold to military and government customers all over the world—a very hard market to target. Even though we made no products used by amateur radio operators, our most effective advertising medium turned out to be a magazine called *QST*, the official monthly publication of the amateur radio fraternity. Why would we advertise in this magazine when we made no products bought by amateurs? Because most communications engineers in countries all over the world are amateur radio operators, and you see *QST* lying around radio rooms everywhere. Only a tiny fraction of the readers of *QST* were potential customers, but almost all of our potential customers were readers of *QST*. And because it was the publication of a club, a private society, space costs were fairly low. Through the years, RF Communications received a number of very large orders that could be directly traced to these ads.

Direct mail selling

For a small company, direct mail is another selling alternative that should be considered. It can be efficient and cost effective in focused markets. I read recently that in 1990, more than 50 percent of American adults purchased products through mail order—more than twice as many as in 1983. In any one year, there are more than 8,000 different catalogs mailed out in the United States, and consumers and businesses spend more than $175 billion on mail order products.

If you have trouble finding a mailing list, incidentally, contact your advertising agency. There are lists available for every specialized market segment imaginable.

Here are some examples of lists that you can purchase at very modest cost:

Mailing Lists

Category	Number
Sperm banks	20
Rubber band manufacturers	30
Windmill wholesalers	80
Air ambulance services	80
Dude ranches	240
Spiritualists	430
Tattoo shops	500
Banks with assets between $5 and $9.9 million	950
College bookstore managers	3,545
Baptist churches	55,520
Medical specialists	614,146
Small businesses	2,300,000

And of course, another source of lists is other users of lists. Almost every magazine is willing to sell you its list of subscribers, and almost every company in the mail order business is willing to sell you its list of customers. I have heard that for some companies in the mail order business, selling its list of customers is a more profitable business than selling its products.

Mail order selling requires you to have a good catalog or brochure describing your offering and probably an 800 number over which you can take orders. In addition, you must be able to accept payment with credit cards and have the facilities to store, pack and ship your products. During the starting phase, these services can all be purchased from specialized outside organizations at fairly reasonable prices. These are called "Fulfillment Companies." As your business grows, you will undoubtedly decide to do some of them yourself.

Incidentally, when you do this kind of mailing, be sure that the letters are signed in blue ink and that they always include a P.S. Experience has shown that people usually read postscripts, often before they read the body of the letter. Also, some mailing experts recommend that stamps be used for postage, rather than bulk rate preprinted mailing envelopes. Envelopes with stamps are more likely to be opened rather than thrown in the trash barrel, even when bulk rate stamps are used. My personal preference is to send everything first class. However, my mailings are usually fairly small.

Selling by mail, or mail order marketing as it is now called, has been the strategy of many very successful companies in recent years. One that I find especially intriguing is Lands' End. It was founded in 1962 by Gary Comer, a copywriter at Young & Rubicam and an avid sailor. Initially, Lands' End sold specialty yacht hardware, but it soon found that men's and women's clothing and high quality canvas luggage were more profitable. Today, it mails out millions of its monthly catalog, employs more than 6,000 people and is one of the premier firms in this highly competitive industry. It emphasizes quality products, outstanding service, competitive prices and a return policy with no questions asked. I have never purchased anything from Lands' End without being completely satisfied with the experience.

Another interesting example is Calyx & Corolla, based in San Francisco. This company, founded by Ruth Owades in 1988, sells fresh flowers and plants with a mail order catalog. She sends out six seasonal catalogs a year. Sales in 1995 were about $20 million. Calyx & Corolla has about 50 full-time employees and several times that many part-time people during the heavy selling seasons—Easter, Valentines Day, Mothers Day, etc. When an order is received, it is forwarded to one of 25 growers in Florida and California with whom Calyx & Corolla has a strategic relationship. The flowers are shipped in insulated boxes by Federal Express. Owades has been quoted as saying that flowers are the ideal gift. They are "nonfattening, low cholesterol, moderately priced and even politically correct."

Lillian Vernon is another big-time mail order player. It mails out more than 137 million catalogs annually to more than 12.5 million people.

The Direct Marketing Association is a source of information and material about this form of marketing. Its publication entitled "The DMA Catalog Start Up Resource Guide" is a collection of tips and guidelines for starting a mail order business. It is available from the association at 212-768-7277.

Infomercials

Over the past few years another selling method has emerged that made it possible for several new companies to achieve amazing success over a very short period of time. An "infomercial" is a 15-minute or longer television program produced by the selling company and put on the air or on cable as a paid advertisement.

These are often aired during late-night hours when rates are lower. Those that are most successful seem to use well-known personalities as part of the program. Even though the viewers may never have heard of the company or its product, they will have heard of the individual promoting the product.

Two examples are Victoria Jackson Cosmetics, which sells a line of facial foundations and other makeup products, and Anthony Robbins who sells a program for increasing one's confidence and self-esteem. Victoria Jackson uses movie personalities, such as Ali McGraw, and Anthony Robbins uses football star Fran Tarkenton.

I read recently that Victoria Jackson had a great deal of difficulty raising initial capital for her venture. She was quoted as saying, "Anyone who takes no for an answer isn't an entrepreneur."

Recently I have noticed that many more infomercials on TV and cable are for some type of exercise or body-building equipment. They all seem to include a musclebound man and a very shapely young woman explaining how you can improve your physique and general health by purchasing one of their odd-looking machines.

Whether infomercials are appropriate for your business depends on the nature of the business. But many companies now using this innovative approach to selling have achieved outstanding results.

Publicity

Most entrepreneurs begin marketing their companies through advertising, telemarketing, direct mail or trade shows, but one of the best and least expensive ways to generate interest in a company's product or service is through publicity. You know, getting your name in a newspaper, being interviewed for a TV newscast or perhaps participating in a radio program. Anything you do that gets a mention of your company, your product or service, or your employees in the media is considered publicity.

It may surprise you that a large percentage of stories appearing in your local newspaper come directly from press releases and information provided by publicity-seeking organizations. Be sure to take advantage of every opportunity to communicate with the media, alerting them to interesting happenings at your company. Publicity is often called "free advertising," because you are featured in a published article or broadcast, but you don't pay for it. The advantages of publicity are:

♦ It's free. Your only costs are for sending information to the media in the form of press releases, announcements or letters.

♦ Articles and editorials are considered much more credible than advertising. You receive an implied endorsement from the publication or station just by being mentioned.

♦ You often have more space in an article (vs. an ad) to explain exactly what your company does or what your specialty is.

♦ The more publicity you get, the more successful you are perceived to be.

Some of the disadvantages are:

♦ You have no control over the content of a news story or article. Editors will use the information if they have space, and it may or may not say what you want it to.

♦ There is no guarantee that if you are interviewed for a story, you'll actually be mentioned. Editors sometimes cut part of an article because of space constraints or discard it altogether.

Like other marketing methods, publicity can help generate sales leads, educate potential customers regarding what you are selling and project a company image of professionalism and success.

My most convincing example of the power of getting your name out happened when I was trying to sell the first edition of this book, which I self-published. I was a guest on a Saturday morning program called "Sound Money" on National Public Radio, which was carried by about 95 stations. When I got back to my office from New York City on Saturday afternoon, I had about 40 calls on my answering machine from people who wanted to purchase copies. I sat taking calls the rest of Saturday and all day Sunday and Monday, and sold several hundred books all at the cover price. And this was without an 800 number. So you can see the power of publicity.

Make it easier for the customers to buy

Finally, an approach to selling I never read about in the marketing literature is, simply, to make it easier for your customer to buy. Analyze the buying practices and habits in the markets that you selected. Try to identify the things that make life difficult for the person making the buying decision, and then do everything possible to remove those obstacles. Make his or her job easier.

Selling to communications customers in places such as Tanzania, Nigeria, Saudi Arabia and Indonesia was difficult for RF Communications. We analyzed the problem and discovered that the buying process was unbelievably complex. Consider the problem of the director of communications for the army in any one of these countries. First of all, he is not sure what he needs to buy. Then, when he figures that out, he has difficulty finding out where such equipment might be available. After that, he must design the system—select operating frequencies, antenna locations, etc. Then comes the preparation of a purchase specification and competitive bidding. He must get the purchase approved at a very high government level, perhaps even by the president of the country. Funds must be put into the national budget and foreign exchange established (extremely difficult for some countries). After a supplier is selected, the order must be placed, confirmed letters of credit set up (the normal payment process) through at least two international banks. Then the equipment must be inspected before shipment and cleared through the buying country's customs.

Finally, all that remains to be done is unpacking, installing and

putting into operation in some remote area of the world an elaborate
configuration of high-tech electronics, some of which might have been
damaged or lost in shipment.

How do you like that for a buying process? What an opportunity for
a creative, innovative seller! Some of
the things we did were to prepare
instructional material that helped
the customers' engineers design the
system, and we wrote a detailed specification in our brochure that was
good enough for procurement purposes. We included in our standard
catalog and price list every accessory
and piece of installation material that
they could possibly need, we offered
a variety of spare parts kits so that
the entire package could be bought
from one source and we offered training in either our plant or the user's
facility. In short, we tried very hard
to simplify the buying process for the
user and make RF Communications
a more attractive supplier.

Why companies fail

In closing this chapter, I would
like to say a few words about why
companies fail. Early in my career I
worked for a man who told me about
a company he and his brother started.
He said that the business was a
great success, but it failed because
they ran out of money. I had little
management experience at the time,
but what he said bothered me. Something about it seemed wrong.

Years later, after I started my own
business, I think I figured out why
his statement bothered me. First of
all, being a success includes not running out of money. Second, I do not
believe that companies fail because
they run out of money. They fail because they run out of orders. Sure his
company ran out of money, but that
was not the cause of the problem—it
was the result of the problem. I don't
know what their business was but it
seems to me, if they were halfway-
decent managers and had been more
successful selling whatever it was they
were making, they would not have
run out of money and the business
might not have failed.

In summary, the problem of getting orders, selling, is crucial to any
new business. It must be done well
and done fast if the firm is to have
hope for survival.

✿ Chapter 21 ✿

Other Ways to Market: Franchising and Multilevel Marketing

Two other ways for a small company to sell its products or services are franchising and multilevel or network marketing (sometimes called direct selling). Both of these are fairly complex. They are often under attack by regulatory agencies and require considerable care in setting up in order to avoid problems at a later date. I strongly advise anyone considering either approach to consult an attorney, expert in these areas, at an early stage. A neophyte or amateur proceeding on his or her own is almost certain to encounter some difficulty that could have been avoided by seeking advice and counsel from a specialist. Caution is strongly suggested.

The subject of franchising in general terms and from the viewpoint of the franchisee are discussed in an earlier chapter. We are now talking about the other side of franchising, but the fundamentals are similar. They will not be repeated here.

Multilevel marketing is a selling approach where the company sells its product to others, frequently called independent distributors or independent consultants. Typically, they buy products from the company and resell to the ultimate user. This is often done through house parties, group sessions, door-to-door selling and selling to friends, relatives, neighbors and acquaintances. The product, when purchased by independent distributors, is discounted from the retail price so they can realize a profit on the transaction. Normally the distributors operate as independent contractors rather than employees of the company. They take title to and pay for the product in advance of making a sale.

There's even more appeal to this selling approach. The independent distributors are then encouraged by the company to recruit other distributors, and in return, receive a percentage commission on the sales of their recruits. They cannot be paid a fee for finding a recruit. Their payment must be in the form of a commission on the sales of the recruit.

This arrangement may extend through several levels. If you're good at recruiting others to sell the product, you don't have to sell as much yourself to have a good income.

Amway, Mary Kay Cosmetics and Tupperware are some better-known companies using multilevel marketing as their main distribution method. I have heard that there are about 2,000 companies that use this approach, most of their independent distributors work part-time and about 80 percent are women. Information and very good publications about multilevel selling can be obtained from the Direct Selling Association at 202-293-5760.

From the company's viewpoint, there are several key benefits from franchising and multilevel marketing:

♦ The company can recruit a large sales force without the expense of adding full-time employees.

♦ You can view either of these approaches as an inexpensive way of securing capital for your business. Both the franchisee and the multilevel marketing distributors are independent contractors, owners of their own businesses. Little investment is required from the company. In fact, the franchisee usually pays a fee in advance and then raises capital to build the facility to carry out the franchiser's business. In the case of a Holiday Inn, for example, the building costs may be in excess of $50,000 per room. Holiday Inn has about 1,400 franchises. I have no idea how many rooms are in the average Holiday Inn, but you can see the immense capital investment that would have been required to accomplish this through normal financing channels.

♦ Franchisees and distributors tend to be entrepreneurs or individuals working part-time to augment their income. They will often have more drive, spirit and enthusiasm than will regular, full-time employees.

Both of these methods of selling have come under recent criticism for various reasons.

In the case of franchising, this happens when the franchiser establishes a company-owned operation in the same area after the buyer of the franchise invested a lot of money and years of effort establishing the market, or when the franchiser holds back on the training and management assistance that was promised. Also, if the franchiser goes out of business, this could leave the franchisee without the support it already paid for and expected to receive.

This means that if you are selling franchises to others, you must take it as serious business not as a windfall source of capital. The franchiser has an obligation to fulfill its commitment and to do everything possible to help the franchisees succeed. One thing not too many people selling franchises do is qualify the buyers. This means you should be sure the franchisee has the necessary knowledge, experience and capital and is committed to being successful. One seller of franchises that I read about receives more than 5,000 requests a year for information. After initial discussions, it invites about 200 to informational meetings and ends up selling franchises to only about 50.

In the case of multilevel marketing, the company must have a valid product or service. However, a frequent criticism here is that some of these situations may resemble a pyramid scheme where the people who get in early can get rich, but the latecomers are taken for suckers.

Another criticism of multilevel marketing is the great emphasis on recruiting new distributors. This implies that, because of the override commissions across several levels, the distribution costs become excessive. In most cases, I do not believe this is a valid criticism. For example, it is not unusual in the normal distribution of consumer products to have a company salesperson selling to a commission representative selling to a distributor selling to a retailer selling to a consumer. Add all the markups in this "conventional" distribution process and you may find the costs are similar to or even higher than those in the multilevel process. And the multilevel marketer will usually deliver the product to the user's home at no cost, which in some cases may be an important benefit.

In both cases, these objections can be overcome by the franchiser and multilevel marketer by their doing business in an open and ethical manner and making sure that the buyer knows and understands the risks involved. Obviously, not every kind of business is suitable for franchising or multilevel marketing. For those where it is suitable, it may provide an opportunity to greatly leverage your marketing and selling capability in a way that would not be possible to do on the company's own resources.

✄ Chapter 22 ✃

Forms of Business

"What form should my business take? Should it be a sole proprietorship? A partnership? A corporation?"

This is one of the first questions the start up entrepreneurs should ask. This question has many legal and tax implications, varies greatly from state to state and from time to time, and has been the subject of numerous books, pamphlets and articles. My intention here is to review briefly these various forms in general terms and then suggest that probably the best answer is to incorporate.

Sole proprietorship

In a sole proprietorship, the individual entrepreneur owns the business. In the state of New York, all that seems to be necessary is to go to a county clerk's office, pay a small fee and register the business as a DBA. This means "Doing business as...," which permits you to operate a business under a name different than your own.

This is simple, fast and inexpensive. The main drawback is that all assets owned by the entrepreneur may be at risk if the business runs into trouble. This could include house, car, savings account, etc.

In a service business, you may be able to secure business liability insurance to protect you from this risk. In a product-related business, insurance of this sort can be prohibitively expensive, if available at all. In a sole proprietorship, the profit and loss of the business flows through to the owner each year for tax purposes.

Partnership

This is similar to a sole proprietorship but has more than one owner. Typically, a partnership agreement is desirable to define the relationship. Normally, a partnership ends at the death of any partner, but this problem and other situations can usually be provided for in the partnership agreement.

All partners are liable for the acts of all other partners, which can be a serious drawback considering the insurance situation. Should you decide on this business form, one piece of advice I can give that may save you a lot of grief later is to discuss and put in writing at the beginning exactly how the partnership will be dissolved, considering as many different circumstances as you can think of. You will find that it is much easier to reach agreement when the business is worth nothing than later on when real money may be involved.

Some legal experts suggest that the spouse of each partner also be asked to participate in and sign any agreement, since they may suddenly become involved in the event of a divorce or estate situation.

This form is not quite as simple as a sole proprietorship, because tax returns must be filed for the partnership even though the partnership pays no taxes. Profit and loss from the business flow through to the partners in proportion to their ownership.

Limited partnership

This is a special form of partnership in which the general partner has liability, but the limited partners do not. Each year profits flow through to all partners in proportion to their ownership. Again, the partnership must file a tax return even though it pays no taxes. Not too long ago, this was a popular business form, but recent tax law changes have reduced its attractiveness except in special situations.

C-Corporation

This is a business form that has a life of its own. It is usually chartered by and subject to the laws of the state in which you choose to incorporate. Many companies incorporate in Delaware, because its business law is considered more "friendly" to corporations. A corporation is owned by shareholders whose liability, with several exceptions, is limited to the assets of the corporation.

Some of the advantages of a corporation, in addition to limited liability, are that its shares can be sold to others as a way of raising capital, and the company survives the death of individual shareholders (owners). Its

shares can be traded, with various restrictions, thereby providing some degree of liquidity to investors. Profits and losses stay inside the corporation, unless paid out in the form of dividends and/or capital distributions.

The downside of incorporating for a small business is that there are significant overhead costs. Everything you do seems to become more complex. I once had a small software business that I formed as a hobby and made the mistake of incorporating too soon. It cost me $500 to form the corporation, about $1,000 a year in franchise tax and legal and accounting fees, and it cost about $1,000 to terminate the corporation.

Sub-Chapter S Corporation

This is similar to a conventional corporation, except that profit and loss flow through to the shareholders each year for tax purposes in proportion to their ownership. The corporation files a tax return, but pays no taxes. Sometimes companies start as Sub-Chapter S Corporations when they expect to lose money and then convert to a standard C-Corporation when they get into the black. This transition can be done only once. Like the limited partnership, the popularity of Sub-Chapter S Corporations is influenced by prevailing tax laws.

Limited Liability Company

Recently, the government has authorized states to permit businesses to use a new business form known as a Limited Liability Company (LLC). It has some of the advantages of a corporation, is less complex than a Sub-Chapter S Corporation and has many of the advantages of a partnership without the liability. It is much less costly to set up and avoids some of the complications of corporate reporting.

Since an LLC is neither a partnership nor a corporation, how it is taxed depends upon how the LLC operates and how it is organized.

New York State recently made the LLC a legal business form and it is also a legal business form in many other states. Some legal experts believe the LLC will be the predominant business form in the not-too-distant future. Since the details of what a business must do to qualify as an LLC are somewhat complex and vary from state to state, it is recommended that the entrepreneur consult a lawyer familiar with LLC's before making a decision.

Joint venture

This is a special business form where two or more individuals or corporations associate with each other for the purpose of performing a single specific task or business activity. The joint venture usually ends when the task or activity is completed. A joint venture agreement defines the tasks each party will perform, their responsibilities to each other, how the profits will be divided and under what circumstances the venture will terminate.

There may be other alternatives of which I am not aware. My advice to an entrepreneur is to consult both an attorney and a tax adviser to be sure that all the implications of this decision are fully understood. The legal and tax aspects are complex and vary considerably from state to state and from time to time.

⚜ Chapter 23 ⚜

Setting Goals

There are two approaches to setting goals for a business. The first is to set goals that are difficult to achieve and represent a very tough challenge for your entire organization. The second is to set goals that are realistic, or even on the conservative side, that you have a good chance of both meeting and exceeding. I like the second approach.

Most entrepreneurs, when making sales and profit projections and setting goals for their company, lose all sense of reality. They seem determined to set goals they have almost no possibility of achieving. This is bad for a number of reasons. If you consistently fail to meet your goals, you will quickly lose credibility—with your employees, with your investors, with your bank, etc. It is demoralizing for an organization to work hard and always fail to meet its goals. Nobody likes to be a loser.

On the more practical side, consistently missing goals has a devastating effect on profits. High expense budgets tend to go hand-in-hand with high sales projections. You can be assured that most people are very good at meeting expense budgets. However, if your sales fall short of projections and expenses are not cut back quickly and decisively, you are certain to have large losses. Cutting back is a very disagreeable task, because

it usually means laying people off. Because of this, the temptation is to hold off on expense reduction until it is so late that such cuts no longer produce the results you need.

As an alternative, suppose you set your sales goals on the conservative side—goals that you are almost certain to meet or exceed. Then you should budget expenses consistent with these conservative goals so that if this is your actual level of operations, you will have a modest profit.

Now let's assume you exceed your sales goals by a significant amount. Expenses are not likely to expand as fast as sales and the result will be an exceptionally profitable company. This is called, "planning for the worst and hoping for the best."

There is always the possibility of having more orders than you can handle and thus facing cancellations or loss of business to a competitor. This doesn't happen very often. Most organizations have a way of rising to the challenge of coping with excessive orders. Somehow or other, they fumble their way through.

When I talk to entrepreneurs planning to start a business, I ask what they consider the most serious problem they are likely to face. You would not believe how often they answer, "Expanding production fast enough to handle a sudden inflow of orders!" Of all the problems that I enjoy having, it is trying to keep up with unexpectedly high orders. What fun!

If you routinely set conservative sales goals, goals that you have a good chance of exceeding, and set expenses accordingly, you will have discovered one of the best ways to have a very profitable company. Another way of saying this is that expenses almost always lag revenues. If expenses lag revenues when revenues are increasing, you will have a very profitable company. If expenses lag revenues when revenues are declining, you may lose your shirt.

This approach is frequently criticized as being too short-term oriented. I am often asked how I balance short-term performance against long-term performance. Many managers pressured by their company for short-term profits become confused when trying to plan for the long term. I have no problem with this. It all depends on how you define good long-term performance. I define good long-term performance as good short-term performance five years in a row.

I once fired a division manager for unsatisfactory performance. His explanation was that he would never sacrifice long-term goals for short-term profits. I did not debate the question, but that was exactly the reason I fired him.

Long ago, I concluded that there are three kinds of people in the world. They are winners, losers and non-winners. Winners and losers are easy to identify. They are obvious. It's the nonwinners, the people who always fall just short of success, who are the real menaces in the business world. If you are successful in weeding out the nonwinners from your organization, you'll have a far better company.

I suggest you run your company so that it achieves profitability early and so that it stays profitable. The way to have a profitable big company is to grow it from a profitable small company.

At RF Communications, we decided early that operating the company at a profit was a very high priority goal. I'd like to take credit for this approach, but it was really the contribution of one of the other founders, who was a very profit-conscious manager. As a result, we reached profitability in our second quarter of existence and stayed there for the eight years we were an independent company. We ran RF Communications to make a profit. Before long, every employee understood that no other way was acceptable.

The philosophy of goal setting that I describe here will help you put your business in the black and keep it there.

✧ Chapter 24 ✧

What? Me Write a Business Plan?

More has been written on the subject of planning in general and the preparation of business plans in particular than almost any other business discipline. An immense amount of material is available telling you how to write a business plan. I urge you to read as much as you can. Some of it will be great, much contradictory and some wrong. That does not matter. The more you read, the better understanding you will have of the process. Then, follow the suggestions contained here. It is good advice that will put you well on the road to having a good business plan.

How important is the business plan? It is crucial! I urge everyone even thinking about starting a business to write a business plan before you go very far down the road. Modify and change it when necessary, but do not try to run your business without one. It has been said, "If you don't know where you're going, any road will get you there."

Appendix 1 and 2 are samples of two very good business plans. These will give you a good idea of what several entrepreneurs used to guide them in planning, and/or starting and/or managing their businesses.

Recently I have thought a lot about this subject and came to the conclusion that I should differentiate between a "business plan" and a "plan for the business." Many would say that these are the same, but I suggest that they are different. A business plan implies a written document, while a plan for the business implies a strategy, which may or may not be in writing.

You can reasonably ask which is most important, the plan for the business or a written business plan. Is not the process of thinking it through and making the fundamental strategic decisions more important than putting it in writing? The answer is yes, the thinking process is more important than the document, much more important. But the discipline of putting the plan on paper will make the thinking process more effective, and you will end up with a better plan for the business. Also, a written plan can be shared with others.

Before you prepare a business plan for your company, you must decide on the main purpose of the plan. In general, you prepare a business plan for one of two reasons: 1) as a road map for managing your business, or 2) as a sales document for raising capital or securing a loan. The information in either of these plans should be substantially the same, but the emphasis will be different. For example, a plan intended to be used as a road map does not need to include detailed biographies of the key management. In a plan intended as a sales document for raising capital or obtaining a loan, the background and experience of management may be the most important part. I suggest that you first prepare a business plan to be used as a road map, an operating plan for running the business. This can then be modified for use as a sales document.

How long should a business plan be? How many pages should it have? Many entrepreneurs rebel at the prospect of writing a business plan, but when they finally decide to do so, they write one about 200 pages long. Most business plans are far too long and detailed. As a result, they are less effective than they might be. I believe 40 or 50 pages is long enough, perhaps even too long. Longer plans are much less likely to be read.

Consider the problem of presenting a 200-page plan to the venture capital firm from which you are seeking an investment. Even a medium-sized venture fund is likely to receive several dozen business plans each week. With this number to review, and investment decisions to be made, the following is apt to be the sequence of events:

◆ Four out of five plans will be reviewed and discarded in 10 to 15 minutes or less after a very cursory scan.

◆ Of the remainder, four out of five will be read thoroughly, an hour or more, and then discarded.

◆ The rest may be of sufficient interest for the venture investor to either visit the company or invite the management to their office for further discussion. Then four out of five of these will be turned down.

◆ The remainder, or about one out of 100 of the business plans originally submitted, may survive to the point of serious discussion and perhaps negotiation of detailed terms. More of these will fall short than will pass.

◆ In most cases, only one out of several hundred plans submitted will result in an investment.

The general partner of a medium-sized venture fund told me recently that he sees about 1,200 investment opportunities a year and invests in four or six. This means that your business plan better be a pretty darned good selling document to have a prayer of surviving to the end.

Then there is the question of who should write the business plan. Many entrepreneurs are uncomfortable writing such a formal document. Scientists and engineers in particular are often intimidated by the process. They frequently assign the task of writing the business plan to others, such as a business plan consultant, their lawyer or their accountant. I do not advise using a lawyer or accountant, but under certain circumstances, using the services of a professional business plan writer may be the right thing to do. But please remember that the planning decisions for an enterprise must be the effort of the key person or small key group if it is to make any sense at all. Get help with editing, get someone to correct your spelling and grammar, even get someone to write the plan for you. But be sure that the key strategic decisions about the business are yours. Any knowledgeable reader will know in an instant when a business plan was prepared entirely by a surrogate.

Following, there's a brief section prepared by the owner of a business-plan-writing company about some of the benefits of using her services.

As far as the format of the plan is concerned, again I suggest caution. Today we are in the age of desktop publishing and multimedia. Computer magazines are full of articles about how to include graphics, color, different typefaces, many types of charts, etc., in your written documents. Physical appearance is fast becoming more important than content. I suggest you forget all of this and keep your plan simple. Use only one or two different typefaces. In the text, use a typeface with serifs, such as Times Roman, with proportional spacing to make it easier to read. And use graphics only where they add meaning to the plan—not for the purpose of adding flash.

Another thing to consider in writing a business plan is whether or not to use a PC software program, which guides you through the process. There a number available with prices in the $100 range. I have some experience with one of them and it did a pretty decent job. In essence, what these programs usually consist of is a simple word processor, an outline for a plan and one or more sample plans.

Now let's get to the details.

Shown below is an outline of a business plan that I like. This is an outline of a plan intended to be a selling document. There is nothing magical or unique about it—it just covers all of the bases and puts the contents in logical sequence.

Business plan outline

- ◆ Title page.
- ◆ Table of contents.
- ◆ Executive summary.
- ◆ General description of business.
- ◆ Goals and strategy.
- ◆ Brief background.
- ◆ Product/service description.
- ◆ Market description.
- ◆ Competition.
- ◆ Marketing and selling.
- ◆ Manufacturing/quality.
- ◆ Organization and management.
- ◆ Board of directors.
- ◆ Financial plan.
- ◆ Present stock ownership.
- ◆ Capitalization plan.
- ◆ Return to investors.
- ◆ Assumptions and risks.
- ◆ Supporting material.

The rest of this section will include brief comments on each individual part of the plan and a description of its purpose.

1. Title page

Obviously, the title page should include the name of the company and the words "Business Plan." Not so obvious, it seems, is that it should also include an address, telephone number and FAX number. On a number of occasions I have had to call the information operator in order to learn the telephone number of the company whose plan I was reading.

2. Table of contents

This should be a page or so long and is more important than you might think. Many readers have hot buttons. They like to read about marketing strategy, cash flow or some other narrow interest before reading the entire plan. The table of contents directs them to the right place. Obviously, the pages must be numbered.

3. Executive summary

Here you must capture the entire essence of your business in one, two or three pages. Some people write this first—others write it last. I think last is better. It is a critical part of the plan and the only part some audiences may read. Many will read no further if the executive summary does not whet their curiosity. You cannot spend too much time working on this section.

4. General description of business

Here's where you present the "Big Idea." What is your offering (product and/or service) and what market will you address? Why did you choose this offering and market and why are they attractive? Be sure to comment on your distinctive competence and how it supports your selections.

5. Goals and strategy

State briefly the goals you have for the business and the general strategy you intend to follow to achieve these goals.

6. Brief background (optional)

This is to set the stage for the remainder of the plan, if appropriate. It could include a description of other ventures in which individuals on your team have been involved, and anything else you want to highlight by way of introduction.

7. Product/service description

This and the next section are the heart of the business—and the heart of the business plan. Identify the important attributes of your product/service and the benefits that it provides to your customers. Be certain your proposal differentiates, concentrates and innovates in meaningful ways, as we have already emphasized so strongly.

8. Market description

Include comments about the resources you need and what you consider to be major success factors. Forecast how you expect your market will grow or change over the next few years. Brief descriptions of market research studies and projections by industry experts might be included to substantiate your projections.

9. Competition

List your competitors and identify their strengths and weaknesses. Include estimates of their market shares and profit levels, if possible. This section will give the reader an idea of how tough it will be to get your business going. One venture investor I know says that when he sees the words, "We have no competition," in a business plan, it is almost a sure predictor of failure.

10. Marketing and selling strategy

This should be an action plan on how you expect to get customers to buy your product or service. Selling strategy is a serious weakness in many plans. Do a good job here. Make it a strength. Describe available distribution channels and how you intend to use them.

11. Manufacturing and quality control

Include some comments on how you will produce your product or deliver your service and how you will assure continued good quality. While this will, you hope, become an important operating problem in the future, it is not often a key part of the business plan.

12. Organization and management

This is considered an extremely important section by many investors. Include a description of your organization and how you expect it to develop over the next few years. Your management team is of critical importance. Be sure you've identified the key skills that are needed, and that you have first-rate players covering these key skills. I am a strong believer in including references in a resume or biography, especially if you can use people who are known to the intended reader. Include addresses and phone numbers because you want it to be easy for the reader to contact your references if they choose to do so.

Do not make individual resumes too long. Academics are the worst offenders. They often equate quality with length.

13. Board of directors/advisors

List the people you have or expect to have on your board of directors or board of advisers. Do not load your board with either relatives or employees. Investors like to see a fairly small board, which includes successful business people with strong skills in functional areas key to your business. Tell how often the board meets and whether the directors or advisers have a financial commitment to the company.

14. Financial plan

Financial projections are a key part of a business plan. They provide the reader with an idea of where you think the business is going. Perhaps more importantly, they tell a lot about your intrinsic good sense and understanding of the difficulties the company faces.

Often, financial projections are optimistic to an outlandish extent. And they are always prefaced with the words, "Our conservative forecast is..." Do not use the word "conservative" when describing your forecast. Be careful not to use the "hockey stick" approach to forecasting, that is, little growth in sales and earnings for the first few years, followed by a sudden rapid upward surge in sales and totally unrealistic profit margins. Many are the business plans I've read where after tax margins of 40 percent and higher are projected in an industry where 10 or 15 percent is considered good performance.

Excessively optimistic projections can ruin your credibility as a responsible businessperson.

Include monthly cash flow projections (remember, this is different than profit), quarterly or annual order projections, profit and loss projections, and capital expenditure projections. In making financial projections, it may be a good idea to include "best guess," "high side" and/or "low side" numbers.

15. Present stock ownership and investment

Include a list of all present shareholders with a comment about what they contributed to get their stock—money or otherwise. If the list of shareholders is too long, use a summary, but be sure to include the large shareholders. Investors like to see the founders of a company have a cash investment in the business, in addition to "sweat equity." The level of this investment should have a reasonable relationship to their personal resources. But remember, your chances of raising capital from others will be much easier if you have invested some of your own money.

16. Capitalization plan

This is the financial deal that you are trying to sell. Tell the potential investor how much money you're trying to raise, which should be consistent with your cash flow projections, and what percentage of the company they will own in return for their investment. This can be done in terms of number of shares, percentages or both. Be specific in describing the type of security you're trying to sell (common stock, preferred stock, warrants,

etc.) and other alternatives you will consider.

17. Use of funds

Include a description of how you expect to use the money and of any major capital items you need to get the business going. On large items, it may be appropriate to reference actual quotations from credible sources.

18. Return to investors

Sensible investors want to know what returns they can expect and especially how they will achieve liquidity. Tell them, again perhaps with some alternatives.

19. Assumptions and risks

This is another very important part of the plan, even though I suggest it be placed toward the end. It could be a good idea to suggest other strategies you might consider, to reduce risk in the event your original assumptions do not materialize.

20. Supporting material

Brochures, short magazine articles, technical papers, summaries of market research studies, references from people acquainted with the company or the founders can be included. Be careful not to go into too much detail.

You may ask how you can possibly pack all of the above in 30 to 50 pages. The answer is, "With great difficulty." But remember, people who read business plans appreciate brevity and view it as an indication of your ability to identify and describe, in an organized manner, the important factors that will determine the success of your business. If the plan is so long that it intimidates the reader, you are the one who suffers.

Using professional business plan writers

This section was written by Marcia Layton, the president of Layton & Co. (716-256-6224), a Rochester-based business and marketing consulting firm. Layton & Co. provides small and mid-sized companies with guidance in growing their businesses through improved marketing, increased sales and/or additional capital. Marcia is a graduate of Wellesley College and the University of Michigan MBA Program. She is the author of Successful Fine Art Marketing *and co-author of* The Complete Idiot's Guide to Starting Your Own Business.

While I agree with Bill Stolze that you should never have a "surrogate" develop your company's business plan, I do not believe that all business plan writers are surrogate planners. The majority of business plan writers that I am aware of would never attempt to prepare a business plan without significant input from the entrepreneur or business owner. And when I say significant input, I mean participation in the form of face-to-face or phone interviews, providing important business documentation and going through several iterations of editing and revising a plan.

Extensive interviewing is necessary, because you, the business owner or entrepreneur, need to have your own words in the plan. Your business plan should reflect your goals and personality.

The business plan writer does *not* make business decisions for you, nor should they. It is foolish and even potentially dangerous to hire a firm or consultant to write a business plan and turn over all the goal-setting and decision-making activities to that person. Only *you* know what you want to achieve with your business and how you want to go about it.

A plan writer can tell you what your plan is missing, asking questions that can help you make decisions about your business. Through these questions and queries, the plan writer can lead you to a more complete plan that addresses all the important issues you will probably have to deal with.

For those of you who are unfamiliar or uncomfortable with financial statements, a business plan writer can help you prepare reasonable projections for your business, based on your knowledge of what revenue and expenses are typical for your type of business. With your input and guidance, the business plan writer can create the financial statements your banker, venture capital group or investors will want to see.

Working with someone who can speed the process of organizing and writing a plan can be beneficial.

Benefits

Some of the major benefits of working with a professional business plan writer may include:

1. Saving time—If you're a slow writer, you can have someone who writes business plans for a living work with you and speed the process. If

you've never written a plan before, you can potentially spend hundreds of hours researching and studying the process of creating a business plan, or you can choose to hire a professional who does this on a daily basis to help you. Finally, even if you've written a plan before, you may simply not have the time to devote to running your business and writing a plan. By working with a business plan writer, you can make progress in getting it done without investing countless hours yourself.

2. Better quality—While a business plan that you write on your own may be successful in helping you to secure financing and manage your business, it can also hurt your chances for funding if you haven't done a thorough job.

I've heard from numerous bankers and financiers that the quality of a business plan can play a major role in their decision to provide financing. If the plan is well-written and easy to understand, and it demonstrates that the entrepreneur has carefully thought through the potential opportunities and problems the business will face, the banker or investor comes away with the sense that the entrepreneur is capable. But often business plans that bankers and financiers review are not thorough or easy-to-read, and so they may end up sitting on someone's desk for days or weeks.

By working with a knowledgeable consultant who specializes in preparing business plans, you can be con-fident that the information your banker or investors need to see is going to be in the plan. In many cases, this significantly improves the readability of the plan and success in financing.

3. Direct access to financiers— Most business plan writers I know maintain close contact with financing consultants, brokers, venture capitalists, investors and bankers as a normal part of doing business. Business plan writers need to be aware of what the financing community wants to see in a business plan, so that they can prepare a plan that exactly meets the standards and needs of the bankers and investors who will ultimately be reviewing the plan.

Selecting a business plan writer

By working with a business plan writer, you typically get advice and introductions to financing sources you would otherwise not have met. For many entrepreneurs, this network can save time and money. If you are considering working with a business plan writer to complete your plan, make sure that he or she is qualified to assist you. Just because someone can write or create financial statements does *not* qualify that person to advertise as a business plan writer.

Ask to see work samples, which should demonstrate an understanding of the format and presentation of a business plan, and discuss educational background and training. Does this person have the financial knowledge, marketing training, writing experience, etc. that is necessary to understand and create a comprehensive plan? Or does he or she have work experience directly related to business planning?

The answers to at least some of these questions should be yes.

Being a business plan writer, one should be qualified to provide suggestions regarding issues you have not yet encountered or considered; so make sure you'd feel comfortable taking advice from this person. Working with a business plan writer who takes your vision and communicates it clearly on paper for you can save you time and money and improve your chances of securing financing, if that is your goal.

ᓚ Chapter 25 ᓗ

Homemaker's Theory of Cash Flow: Forecasting Capital Needs

About 17 years ago, I began teaching a course entitled "Entrepreneurship and New Venture Management" to second-year MBA students at a prominent graduate business school. To my amazement, I discovered that the students had virtually no understanding of cash flow, particularly as it applies to a start-up venture. Since then, I have read informational booklets written for entrepreneurs by several national public accounting firms. To my further amazement, I found that the discussion of cash flow in some of these booklets was almost useless to an entrepreneur.

Cash flow is by far the most important financial control in a start-up venture and almost every small business, and every entrepreneur must understand its significance.

The accounting definition of cash flow is "net profit plus depreciation," both being noncash items in the operating statement. A better way to define cash flow, at least for a start up, is that it is the difference between cash receipts and cash expenditures—between the money you take in and the money you spend.

It is imperative in planning a new business, or in managing a growing business, to do a cash flow projection on a regular basis. A cash flow projection must be a key part of your business plan. It is the only way for you to have any assurance you will be able to meet the financial obligations of your business. It is the only way to be sure that you will not come to the office some day and suddenly discover that the business is insolvent. You cannot meet a payroll with depreciation. Some people describe managing a start-up venture as "a race against insolvency," and they are right.

The most useful way to forecast cash flow in a meaningful way is to first project cash receipts from all sources. Subtract from these the projected cash expenditures. This is a very simple concept. Keep track of the cash input to the firm and subtract the money you spend. I call this the Homemaker's Theory of Cash Flow.

The average homemaker is a master at managing money. This includes the housewife, professional woman or man—whoever is managing the finances. This person doesn't worry about profit and may not even know what depreciation means. What he or she does know is that if more is spent than is taken in there will soon be big trouble. So it is with a new company. Almost every new company begins its life with limited capital and it is necessary to project and manage cash flow carefully to manage the business intelligently.

When I say cash receipts, I mean cash in the bank. Orders are not cash receipts and invoices you send out are not cash receipts. A deposited check is close. Cash receipts are cleared checks. Even here you run some risk that you will have returns.

On the other side, a purchase order placed with a supplier, a bill or even a mailed check is not a cash expenditure. A check that clears your bank account is a cash expenditure. By keeping all of the above in mind, you can forecast cash flow in a reasonably intelligent manner.

As an example, the illustration is this chapter shows a cash flow projection for a typical start up.

When projecting cash flow, you must consider when orders will be received, shipping schedules and collection delays. In this example, I assume the company has three products that go into production within a few months of each other. I also assume a collection cycle of two months. Expenses, of course, start almost immediately. A personal computer and a spreadsheet program will be of immense help in projecting cash flow.

This example is somewhat over simplified and may be unrealistic in a real-life situation.

These projections are very difficult to make with any degree of confidence. About the only thing you can be sure of in a forecast of cash receipts is that it will be wrong. Should that stop you from making the forecast? Absolutely not. What it does tell you is that projections of cash receipts must be constantly reviewed and updated.

Projecting cash expenditures, on the other hand, is easy. Most expenditures are both known and controllable and can be projected with a fair degree of accuracy. However, here again, they should be constantly reviewed—not so much for accuracy, but to be certain that your spending rate is consistent with the most current projection of cash receipts.

Any dunderhead can forecast expenses, but it takes real business sense to project orders, shipments and cash receipts. Students doing a business plan for the first time invariably get bogged down when they try to project cash receipts. They simply cannot deal with the uncertainty.

I suggest doing these projections on at least a monthly basis; they might even be done weekly. For a new company, a quarterly or annual cash flow projection is of no use. The bottom line in the projection is cash flow on a cumulative basis.

I find cash flow most understandable when plotted as a graph. A critical point for all small businesses is when cumulative cash flow reverses direction from negative to positive and starts to head north. This is a milestone that every company must reach sooner or later, the sooner the better.

Sample Cash Flow Projection

	Jan	Feb	Mar	Apr	May	June	July	Aug	Sept	Oct	Nov	Dec
Receipts												
Product A												
Units Ordered	5	5	7	7	9	9	9	9	9	9	9	9
Units Shipped	0	3	6	7	8	10	10	9	9	9	9	9
Cash Receipts	0	0	0	24	48	56	64	80	80	72	72	72
Product B												
Units Ordered	0	0	2	5	5	5	3	3	4	4	4	4
Units Shipped	0	0	2	3	4	4	4	4	4	4	4	4
Cash Receipts	0	0	0	0	10	15	20	20	20	20	20	20
Product C												
Units Ordered	1	1	3	3	3	3	3	3	5	5	10	10
Units Shipped	0	0	0	1	2	2	2	4	6	8	8	8
Cash Receipts	0	0	0	0	0	10	20	20	20	40	60	80
Total Cash Receipts	0	0	0	24	58	81	104	120	120	132	152	172
Expenditures (All cash)												
Rent	5	5	5	5	5	5	5	5	5	5	5	5
Salaries	10	15	20	30	40	40	40	40	45	45	45	45
Benefits	2	3	4	6	8	8	8	8	8	8	8	8
Telephone	2	2	3	3	3	3	3	3	3	3	3	3
Materials	2	2	8	10	12	20	50	50	50	50	50	50
Capital Equip		15				8					10	
Misc.	1	2	2	4	1	1	2	2	2	2	2	2
Total Cash Expenditures	22	44	42	58	69	85	108	108	113	113	123	113
Net Cash Flow	-22	-44	-42	-34	-11	-4	-4	12	7	19	29	59
Cumulative Cash Flow	-22	-66	-108	-142	-153	-157	-161	-149	-142	-123	-94	-35

The cash flow projection is also important for forecasting the capital needs of the company. The lowest negative point in the graph indicates in simplest form how much capital the company will need.

In planning the financing of the firm, you should obviously include a safety factor to allow for contingencies. I already suggested that the only thing you can be sure of is that these projections will be wrong. This means that when you begin raising capital, you should aim at raising 25 or 50 percent more than your projections indicate will be needed. In this example, where the projection shows that about $160,000 will be needed, you should probably try to raise between $200,000 and $250,000.

This approach to forecasting is a simple yet effective way to project the capital needs of a business and will be of great value to the entrepreneur.

Finally, you might ask, who in the new company should make these projections? The only one qualified is the head of the company. Do not let your accountant do the job. He or she may be able to handle the expense projections but is sure to panic when trying to project orders, shipping schedules, revenues and cash receipts.

That is all there is to cash flow. Do not let anyone tell you that it is complex. It is not. It is extremely simple in concept, yet crucial to the new firm.

Sample Cumulative Cash Flow

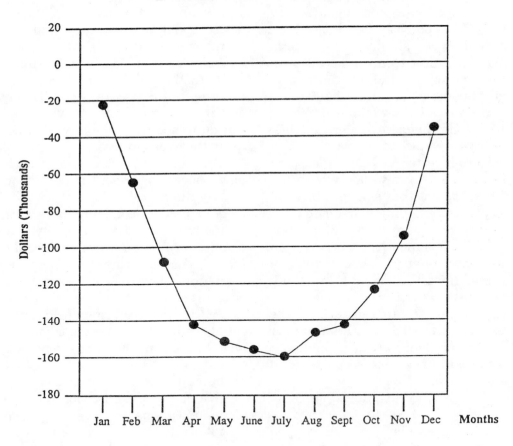

Chapter 26

How Much Money Is Enough?

The previous section suggested a way of estimating the capital requirements of a new business by using detailed cash flow projections. This gives you an idea of the capital you can expect to need, based upon the scale of operations suggested in your business plan. It is the amount of capital that you would like to have to get the business underway. Ideally, you would like to approach a venture investor and say, "Please let me have $...," and walk away with a check. It's not that simple. The capital projection is only a first step.

The next step is to try to determine how much capital you can raise, and what you should do if you cannot raise the amount you think you need. Further questions are: Should you try to raise all of the capital you need at one time, or should you do it in stages? And, is it desirable to raise more capital than you require?

Suppose, for example, you think you need $200,000 to get your business going as planned and find you can only raise $100,000. What do you do next? You have two choices. One is to take the $100,000, get the business going as best you can in accordance with your plan and attempt to raise additional capital at a later date. Another alternative is to go back to the drawing board. Go over your business plan and try to devise a different strategy that requires only $100,000. How can this be done? You should carefully examine both the projected cash receipts and the projected cash expenditures and then try to figure out what you can do to speed up the receipts and delay the expenditures.

An important strategic decision a new business must make that greatly affects cash flow is whether to be a product company, a service company or an advice company. An example of a product company would be the manufacturer of personal computers, lawn mowers or printed circuit boards. A service company might be an accounting firm or a retail store, and an advice company would be a consultant of some sort. Many start-up businesses follow two or even all three of these options.

We faced this decision at RF Communications in developing our initial strategy. If we were to be a product company—that is, to try to have a line of proprietary radio communication equipment—we had to design the product, build prototypes, set up a manufacturing facility, get orders and make shipments before we could expect our first cash receipts. This process takes at least 12 to 18 months and requires a lot of capital. As an alternative, we could have become a service company, that is, go to the Army, Navy and Air Force and try to get development contracts and studies. Government contract business is the high-tech equivalent of a service business. We would be selling man-hours of staff time to design military products to government specifications. The advantage of this strategy is that you perform the work, send an invoice once a month and, in a few weeks, pick up a check. Not much up-front cash is needed.

To us, the major difference between a product business and a service business was timing of cash flow. The product business is capital intensive; it needs a lot of initial investment before cash receipts can be expected. With a service or advice business, positive cash flow can be expected fairly early, frequently within weeks or just a few months.

Our goal at RF Communications was to have a line of proprietary products. We believed this would result in a more profitable and stable business. We thought we could raise enough capital, but weren't certain. As a hedge, we also aggressively pursued contract work at the same time, and within a few months had several large contracts. In effect, our game plan emphasized the product business and used contract work to provide cash flow to keep the company running until our products came on-stream. From time to time, we also did consulting for other firms

as a way to generate both cash and sales leads for our products.

Even if you have a product business, there are strategies that can reduce the capital needed. A new company should buy as many components and subassemblies as possible, rather than setting up its own manufacturing facility.

One of the most successful games ever invented was Trivial Pursuit. The inventors, Scott Abbott and Chris Haney, two Montreal journalists, started their business with only a trivial amount of capital. Rather than manufacturing and distributing the game themselves, they contracted the assembly and distribution to companies in Canada, the United States and Europe. They took advantage of the capital resources of suppliers.

I suggest you do a careful job of estimating the amount of capital you need for the kind of business you want to have. If you don't like the answer, shift the strategy as much as you must to match the capital you can raise. Forecasting the capital needs of a start up is an empirical process. You may have to do it many times before you are satisfied with the result.

Now let's suppose you encounter the opposite situation, where you are able to raise more capital than you need. Suppose, for example, that you can raise $500,000 when you think you need only $200,000. What then? You'll be surprised when I say too much capital has some drawbacks. First, if you raise more capital than you need during start up, you may be selling your stock too cheap. It may be better to take $200,000, the amount you forecast. One or two years later, if you are meeting your plan, you should be able to sell stock for a higher price. This means fewer shares and less dilution will be required to raise the additional $300,000.

A second reason is that having more money than needed takes the pressure off the management of a new business. Offices will be larger, facilities will be more elaborate, salaries will be higher, more support services will suddenly appear, etc. All of these consume cash and none contributes in a meaningful way to the success of the business.

A third more subtle reason a start up should not raise more capital than it needs relates to the skills of the entrepreneurs. One of the major risks in a new venture is the uncertainty as to whether the team of entrepreneurs has what it takes to run a business. If they do, more money should not be difficult to obtain. If they do not, the sooner they learn it and stop trying, the better.

I believe there is such a thing as a right amount of start-up capital for a new venture, not too much and not too little. You want enough to give you and your team a fighting chance to achieve the goals you set out, but not so much that you either sell your stock too cheaply, spend money in an imprudent manner or try to continue the business beyond the point where it's obvious that you will not succeed.

Paul Hawken, in his book *Growing a Business*, said that he and his partner started the very successful Smith & Hawken garden equipment mail order business with $100,000, even though they had access to much more at the time. This was the amount they were comfortable with and the amount they thought necessary to do the job they had in mind.

Few financial experts are likely to agree with these comments. Almost no business failures occur because of lack of money. It is frequently the excuse, but seldom the reason. The real reason businesses fail is because of poor product selection, poor market selection, poor marketing or just plain poor management.

In discussing the financial needs of new companies in his book, *Winners*, Carter Henderson quotes Mary Kay Ash, the founder of Mary Kay Cosmetics, as saying, "It takes more than money; you must also know what you are doing."

Of all the advice entrepreneurs may seek from various specialists, the advice from financial experts will probably be the least consistent. On many occasions throughout my career, I have sought financial counsel, particularly on methods and specific problems relating to raising capital. I consulted commercial bankers, investment bankers, venture capitalists, vice presidents of finance of major corporations and other entrepreneurs. Rarely have any two been even close to giving the same advice. My conclusion from this was to always seek advice until I found someone who agreed with me, and then do what I wanted.

✒ Chapter 27 ✒

Where and How to Look for Financing

Many, if not most, entrepreneurs need outside financial support of some sort to start a business. This support is usually either a loan or an equity investment resulting from the sale of stock in the new business. The level of difficulty in getting financial support depends upon many factors, but I think it is safe to say that raising money is never easy.

Some experts suggest that raising money has a seasonal quality. For example, it is probably a waste of time to approach a wealthy individual for an equity investment either in the middle of the summer or the middle of the winter. People with large amounts of capital to invest are likely to be away on vacation during summer and in a warmer location during winter. The right time to approach them is likely to be in spring or fall.

Other experts say raising money is more cyclical than seasonal, and they are also right. A number of years ago, I did some research and found that in the upstate New York area during the 1960s, almost 100 companies raised their initial outside capital by going public. Some used an underwriter, most did it themselves.

A more recent study I conducted, which I will describe in more detail later in this chapter, showed that during the 1980s, in the same region, a larger number of companies raised more initial capital from private investors than from any other source. In the last year or two, there has been a sudden surge of Initial Public Offerings (IPOs), done mostly through underwriters both large and small.

The best place to look for outside capital during the rest of the 1990s is not yet entirely clear.

First, a course on selling

Before listing and commenting on various sources of financing, I would like to describe a recent experience I had that substantially altered my view of this important issue.

In late 1991, I spoke at an outplacement seminar at a state university in New York. Schools in the state system faced substantial reductions in financial aid and were in the process of making staff cuts to balance their budgets. This seminar, which lasted two days, was organized to help those facing termination with finding a job. My role was to describe starting a business as an alternative.

One of the other speakers was discussing making contacts, writing a resume and being interviewed. A man in the audience, very upset by his situation, raised his hand and said, "I know nothing about finding a job. I have not done it in many years. Every time I apply anywhere, there are 30 or 40 other applicants for the same job. What am I to do?"

Even though this was not my assigned subject, I could not restrain myself. I interrupted him and said that whether he liked it or not, he had just changed professions. Last week he may have been an assistant registrar or a data processing specialist, but this week he had suddenly become a salesman. And he had only one product to sell—himself. He may not like being a salesman and may not want to be a salesman, but if he wanted to find a job during difficult times, he had better get used to the fact that he was now a salesman.

His next question was, "What is the state going to do to help me?" I answered, "Probably nothing." Then he asked, "What would you do if you were me?" I suggested he do the same things I did early in my career when I made the transition from design engineer to salesman.

I would immediately find a course in selling that I could take. Go to the library where they undoubtedly have several shelves full of books about selling. Read them all. Soon you will understand that selling is a process that has well-established techniques and procedures that are followed by almost every successful salesperson, and these techniques work. Learn them and apply them. This will be an immense help in finding a job, because your competitors, the other

30 or 40 applicants, almost surely have done nothing to improve their selling skills.

Why am I telling you this complex story as part of a chapter on where to look for financing for your new business? The reason should be obvious.

When you, as an entrepreneur, decide to try to raise outside financial support for your business, you, also, have just changed professions. You are no longer an entrepreneur or design engineer or the distinguished founder of a hot new start-up company. You are now a salesperson, whether you like it or not.

The product you have to sell is a little different than in the previous example. Here you are selling your concept of a business. You are selling your management team, your idea for a product or service, your assessment of a market opportunity. In short, you are selling your plan for a business. To raise money today, you had better learn how to sell, because if you don't, your chances of success are virtually nil.

What do I mean by "selling"? Well, first you develop leads, then you separate the prospects from the leads. A prospect is someone who needs what you are selling and who can afford what you are selling. This is a little tricky to comprehend when your goal is raising capital, but it is something that must be done.

Next, you analyze your competition and plan your approach and your sales pitch. Then you figure out how to answer the objections, and negotiate and close the deal. All of these things are standard selling techniques.

They are skills you seldom learn in business schools, but you had better learn them now if you expect to raise capital, whatever its source.

Where do you look?

At last, we get to the main subject of this chapter. This discussion assumes that the entrepreneur has determined how much capital is needed to launch the new business. The question to be resolved is how to find that much money. This is another complex question for which there is no right or wrong answer. Possible sources of early capital for the entrepreneur include:

1. Personal savings and borrowing

Most entrepreneurs finance the early start-up stage of their business with personal savings. If the company is formed by a team, it is their combined personal contributions. The amount of money, though often quite small, can sometimes pay the cost of building prototypes of products, limited market research, filing a patent application, getting a service business off the ground, incorporation, and the preliminary steps of more formal financing.

Service businesses, particularly, do not require much capital, and I have seen many such ventures use only the personal savings of the founder and spouse. If you have ample personal resources available, whether to use them or seek outside investors is a decision only you can make. On one hand, you keep complete control, on the other, you reduce the financial risk and increase the potential.

Personal borrowing is also a possible source of start-up capital. However, any loans you are able to get will probably have to be secured with a personal guarantee. Many entrepreneurs become upset when they are unable to borrow from a bank to get their business underway. Another chapter of this book describes some of the things an entrepreneur can do to increase the odds of getting a loan.

Several years ago, I met an entrepreneur who had started a very successful market research firm. Unable to obtain a bank loan, she used credit cards. As I recall, she had about a dozen cards from different banks, each with a $5,000 line of credit. Five times 12 equals $60,000, a significant amount. The downside of this is that credit card interest rates tend to be very high. At that time, they were about 18 percent. When I met her, she had 15 employees and was operating at a profit. I encouraged her to try again for bank financing and suggested that if she had trouble with her own bank to shop around. She acquired a bank loan with no trouble and was out of the credit card loop.

2. Friends and associates

If more capital is needed than is available privately, the first sources many entrepreneurs turn to are family, friends or close business associates. At this point, you'll have to begin to think about some agreement with your investors. Chances are, you will need an attorney to formalize the arrangement in acceptable legal form. As you bring in more and more outside individual investors, you'll probably decide to incorporate. As we discussed, this form of business permits you to share ownership by selling stock.

3. Venture investors

There are three separate and distinct kinds of venture investors: individual venture investors, formal (institutional) venture capital funds and corporate venture investors. The amounts of capital that can be raised from these sources varies from as little as $5,000 or $10,000 up to $5 million and more. Venture investors tend to be quite sophisticated, and a later chapter is devoted to a discussion of various venture capital sources.

4. Going public

Selling stock to the public is usually not considered as a reasonable approach to raise capital for a start-up business. Almost every financial expert you are likely to ask will advise you against even thinking about this alternative. However, I suggest you do think about it, as many companies have gone public very early in their corporate lives, either on their own or using an underwriter. Here again, a later chapter is devoted to this subject.

5. Federal, state and local governments

The federal government, most state governments and many local governments have financial programs intended to encourage people to start businesses. They also provide financial support to help existing businesses grow. The purpose of most of these programs is to create jobs. Creating jobs may not be your highest priority as an entrepreneur. But that in no way conflicts with the government's

goal, because if you succeed in your business, the probability is that you are also creating jobs. Both sides win. A later chapter will cover various government programs that can provide financial assistance to a new or growing business.

There is no right answer

Which of these approaches is best? It's hard to say. There's seldom a right or wrong answer, and the best you can hope for is an answer that works.

In 1988 I conducted a study of venture capital sources in the Rochester, N.Y., area and surrounding counties. A list was compiled of all firms I could identify that raised their first outside capital between Jan. 1, 1980 and March 31, 1988. A second list was compiled of the companies among this original group that raised capital a second or third time during the same period. I included five sources of venture capital—individual investors, going public, formal venture capital funds, corporate investors and minority small business investment companies. Table I, following, summarizes how 65 companies raised their first outside capital. Table II lists how 29 among these companies raised capital a second or third time during the same period. A fairly high percentage of the companies on this list continue to operate. I don't know if the situation in other parts of the country is similar to Rochester, but I see no reason for much difference.

While this survey is not entirely up-to-date, it does gives an entrepreneur some guidance as to how a large number of new businesses raised early capital.

Table I: Sources of First Outside Capital

	#	%	Dollars
Individual Investors	42	65%	$22.5 Mil
Going Public	16	25%	30.3 Mil
Venture Capital Funds	5	8%	6.8 Mil
Corp. Venture Funds	0	0%	
Minority SBICs	2	3%	0.2 Mil
Total	65		$59.8 Mil

Table II: Sources of Later Capital

	#	%	Dollars
Individual Investors	8	28%	$11.3 Mil
Going Public	8	28%	37.3 Mil
Venture Capital Funds	8	28%	14.4 Mil
Corp. Venture Funds	5	17%	31.0 Mil
Minority SBICs	0	0%	
Total	29		$94.0 Mil

Scams

In recent years, with so many new companies trying to raise equity capital, some of these firms have become the target of unscrupulous scam artists. These vary from people who agree to raise the capital you need, but require large advanced payments, to others who in fact do sell the companies' stock, but then proceed to manipulate the stock price in ways that can seriously endanger the company for which the money was raised. Some states have begun holding seminars to advise entrepreneurs on the process of raising money. In at least one case, the manager of a seminar estimated that about 20 percent of the attendees were unscrupulous promoters "looking for their next pigeon."

The February 12, 1996 issue of *BusinessWeek* included an article that suggested a number of things a small business can do to avoid being ripped off. They are:

♦ Beware promoters promising easy venture capital or business loans, particularly if they ask up-front fees.

♦ Check references by getting written evaluations of the firm's service from former clients. Phone references may be accomplices.

♦ Beware if someone wants to sell shares or do a large stock split or reincorporate your company out of state. These hallmarks of the penny stock scam are now being applied to small cap stocks.

- ◆ Check credentials with state securities or banking regulators. Be especially careful if promoters are in another state.
- ◆ Have a lawyer read the fine print of any agreement. Some contain fees that must be paid in cash, whether or not your company receives capital; others require turning over up to 10 percent of equity.

This same issue of *BusinessWeek* describes a number of specific examples in which small companies, in desperate need of capital, have been badly hurt and even driven out of business.

So be careful.

Chapter 28

How to Obtain a Loan: Improving the Odds

This chapter was written by Victoria Posner, a Trainer and Consultant based in Rochester, N.Y. (716-461-3531: FAX 716-473-7764). Victoria has 10 years experience in commercial lending and teaches banking and finance to bankers, investment managers and other financial professionals. She also teaches a number of workshops on financial planning for small business. Victoria sits on two nonprofit micro-loan committees: the New York State Rural Venture Fund, sponsored by Rural Opportunities, Inc., and the Minority and Women's Revolving Loan Fund, sponsored by the Urban League of Rochester. She writes a monthly column for the newsletter Small Business Success. *She holds a BA from Connecticut College and an MBA from Wharton.*

Getting a loan is a hard road

Borrowing to start a business is not easy. However, the problem is often not that there is no money available, but that many people do not want to put in the time and effort necessary to submit a good package to potential lenders. Lenders ask for an awful lot of information. It takes a great deal of work to put it all together, and you may well wonder why so much information is requested. Well, lenders need to know as much as possible to make a good decision.

No lender should take inordinate risks. When banks do that, we all end up paying—remember the Savings and Loan crisis? For a lender, there is a great deal of "downside risk" and virtually no "upside" potential. If the business fails, the loan goes down the tubes; if it succeeds, the lender gets the money back with a little interest, but does not share in the profits. So, it is important that the lender be prudent, since there are no windfall profits to offset losses.

At the same time, it does not benefit you to take on any debt that cannot be repaid. A likely result is a failed business and, often, personal bankruptcy. Of course, everyone thinks that his or her idea is a sure winner. But the failure rate of start-up businesses tells us otherwise. As unpleasant and as disappointing as it may be, getting turned down for a loan may be the best thing that can happen to you. It should make you stop and think your whole idea through again. That doesn't mean that you should give up, just that you need to do more work.

The need for personal information and guarantees

Since your business is a start up, lenders rely on your ability and integrity. Therefore, they need to know as much about you as possible. Most lenders will ask you for a lot of personal information, in addition to information about your proposed business. Typically, you will be asked for a complete resume, a personal financial statement listing all your assets and liabilities, several years of income tax returns with all supporting schedules, and a recent report from a credit bureau (unless the lender can access the credit bureau directly). Many people balk at these requests, but it is basically standard procedure.

You can also expect the lender to ask for personal guarantees from you and your spouse and a lien on any major assets, such as a home. Don't be surprised; this is also fairly standard. If you want a loan, you will have to supply the requested items.

There will usually be some sort of application you must fill out. It may range from a simple one or two pages, to a long, detailed document. Many of the questions will already be answered in your business plan. You will be tempted to write "See business plan" over and over. *Don't do it!* As boring and as tedious as it is, answer each question fully and completely. While you may not understand the need for this redundancy, there usually is a good reason. For example, banks must compile information on loan applications into statistical reports for regulators.

Searching through your entire package would be very time consuming, so they ask for the needed information on the application document.

The business plan is critical

The heart of your package is your business plan. It is a constant source of amazement to me to see what people put together and call a business plan. Having a good business idea, but only some vague notion of how to accomplish it, just won't cut the mustard with lenders. Time and time again, I see applicants come to the loan committees on which I sit with what can only be described as half-baked business plans. They follow the right format, but there is no meat. Just having the right chapter and section headings does not constitute a good business plan. This may seem obvious, but it isn't.

People make the most amazing mistakes when putting together their business plan. I would like to give you some do's and don'ts that can make a big difference between success and failure.

1. Make sure it is very clear to the reader just what the business is. I have read plans that talk around it, but never say exactly what the writer plans to do. Sometimes they use a lot of industry jargon, thinking that they are being precise. But you can't expect everyone to understand. Make it very clear, in simple language, what you are doing or making and exactly who the customer is. Lenders are not inclined to approve a loan

if they can't even tell what the business is. Pretend you're explaining it to a group of 10 year olds who know nothing about the business world. That ought to do the trick.

2. Do not make broad, unsubstantiated statements, like "It is a known fact that..." If you cannot support your statements with good, solid data, don't make them. Whenever I read something like that, I know it should read, "In my opinion..." However, there is little room for opinions in a business plan. Lenders want real facts. Document, document, document. Spend time in the library doing research. Make sure you are able to support everything you say, every number in your projections. Vague ideas and shot-in-the-dark guesses just won't do. And don't rely on, "I've worked in this industry (working for some-one else) for 20 years, so I know what I wrote is true." If you really do know what you are talking about you, should be able to back up your assertions with facts from reliable sources.

3. Similarly, keep an eye on the adjectives. "There is a dire need..." A dire need? Are people dying, is the world heading for nuclear holocaust because your product or service isn't available? Negative adjectives are particularly dangerous. I had a client who made a number of negative statements about his largest competitor. That competitor had been in business for many years, so it must have

been doing something right. I had personal experience with the competitor and knew it to be a well-run operation. Knocking the competition does not build your case, so don't do it.

4. Be sure your numbers make sense. Many who start businesses are product people (engineers, for example) or marketing people. Almost everyone hates numbers. But the bottom line is that it is the bottom line that determines whether the lender gets the money back. So you have to spend time with your numbers and make sure they make sense. Here are a few classic errors:

a) The numbers don't jibe with other sections of the business plan: In another business plan I reviewed, the marketing section called for local television advertising. The financial plan showed $200 per month for advertising. This ought to buy about five seconds at 3 a.m. once or twice a month on the bowling channel.

b) Not anticipating price increases: I reviewed a set of projections where utility bills remained at the same dollar figure for three years. Even if you don't use more power over three years, it is unlikely that the rates will stay constant.

c) Presenting only annual projections: Preparing month-by-month projections for the first year is tedious, hard work but very necessary. Some people finesse this by making an annualized projection and then dividing the figures by 12 to fill in the blanks for each month. That defeats the purpose of monthly projections. Virtually every business has peaks and troughs. The lender wants to know if you can get through the slow months. If not, you're out of business and the loan goes down the tubes.

d) Not including a list of assumptions to explain how you got your numbers: The lender wants to know exactly how you arrived at your figures. This should be provided line by line, starting with a detailed discussion of your sales. You can't just pick a number. You must have good, solid reasons.

e) Numbers that don't make sense: I saw a set of projections where the Gross Profit Margin went from 35 percent in the first year to 60 percent in the third, with no explanation provided. Gross Margin in percent is defined as (Sales - Cost of Goods Sold)/Sales multiplied by 100. It's possible, I suppose, but you had better tell me how you plan to achieve that.

f) Not telling the lender how the money will be used: It is important to let the lender know how you are going to use the money, dollar by dollar. You can't just say, "inventory, equipment and working capital." You need an itemized list of exactly where all of the money will go, supported by price quotations, price lists, etc., where possible.

5. Failure to discuss risk: It's great to have a positive attitude, but you've got to be realistic, too. There is no business without risk. None. Risk is everywhere. If you don't discuss risk, then lenders are going to assume you haven't thought about risk. That scares them to death. They know, you can't possibly plan for every single contingency, but they want to know that you've thought about the major risks and of some way to manage them.

Of course, risk is not always negative. There is the risk of succeeding beyond your expectations. I once reviewed a plan by someone who was going to manufacture a sophisticated craft item. The product was beautiful and I could see where orders could well be way in excess of projections. Since it took some artistic skill to make the product, I wondered what the owner would do if that happened. Failure to meet orders on a timely basis usually means you don't get repeat orders. In the owner's plan, he/she had identified several skilled people who could be hired if the need arose. I was very impressed. The loan was granted. The business has done well.

6. Unprepared to answer questions about your plan: The applicant, whose profit margins went from 35 to 60 percent in two years, said he/she was "not a numbers person," that the accountant had prepared the projections, so he/she couldn't really explain them. The loan was not approved. If you are

going to own a business, you have to have some understanding of numbers. How else will you know how you are doing, where problems are, etc? When you tell a lender that numbers aren't "your thing" what you are really saying is that you really don't want to own a business. You are better off working for someone else. You must be able to answer virtually any question about any aspect of your business plan.

7. Excessive wordiness: Whoever is reading your business plan is a busy person. Don't waste his/her time with long, florid passages, when a few well-written sentences will do. I've read business plans that went on for 40, 50, 60 pages or more that could easily have been reduced to just 10 or 15 if only the writer had eliminated all excess language. Don't repeat yourself *ad nauseum*. People like to go on about things such as how they are going to beat the competition with better service and a more customer-centered approach, for example. That's a pretty vague statement, and repeating it on every page does not improve it. Stick to the facts, state them clearly and don't repeat them unnecessarily. The point isn't to write a long business plan, but a good business plan.

Reviewing the plan

Have your business plan read by as many people as you can. You want them to read for two purposes: mechanics and content. You would be amazed how many plans I see with gross spelling, grammar and arithmetic errors. I firmly believe that if you don't care enough about your business to do a great business plan, why should I care enough to put money on the line. Don't leave the important proofreading task to yourself alone. We all tend to see what we think we wrote, so we miss the errors. Get a couple of people to read your plan for the mechanics, even if they know nothing about business. Tell your kids you'll pay them 50 cents for each error found; it will be money well-spent.

You also want at least one person to read your plan whose business judgment you trust and who you know will give you truly honest feedback. The best person for this job is a good outside consultant—someone who has seen a number of different business plans, who has experience lending money and who won't worry about losing a friend by being truly honest. That will cost you more than a few dollars, but will be well worth it in the long run. It is important to find out where your business plan falls short before you send it off to a lender.

And now the good news

Finally, here are a few words of encouragement. There are lenders out there who want to help small businesses. There are banks that will lend to you, though you may have to search around. Generally small, local banks are your best bet, although some larger banks might have funds available under their Community Reinvestment Act programs.

You may be able to get an SBA guarantee under the 7(a) program to support a loan with a bank. In most cases, you have to go through the bank directly; the SBA rarely deals directly with borrowers, and then only under certain very specialized programs. Unfortunately, if you are truly a start-up business, the odds of getting an SBA guarantee are very slim. However, if you have been around for a while, even just a year, you may qualify. Until recently, the 7(a) program provided guarantees to banks of 90 percent of a loan up to $155,000, and 85 percent of the remainder up to $750,000. Now, however, they will guarantee 80 percent of loans up to $100,000, and 75 percent of loans above that amount. The purpose of this change is to make it possible for the SBA to guarantee a greater number of loans.

Terms are generous, sometimes allowing repayment schedules up to 10 years for working capital loans and 25 years for fixed assets. Rates must be no more than prime plus 2.75 percent. If you are interested in this type of loan, it is advisable to check with the bank you are dealing with to be sure you have the latest information.

Another SBA option is the 504 Certified Development Company program (CDC). Loans from this program must meet the purpose of job creation/retention. The minimum CDC loan is $125,000; the funds may be used for plant construction/expansion/acquisition, or for the purchase of machinery or equipment. It cannot be used for working capital. In this program, a bank lends 50 percent of the needed funds and gets the first mortgage on the property. The CDC lender provides 40 percent of the needed money, and the business must come up with the remaining 10 percent, although sometimes this requirement is waived.

If your company is exporting to foreign countries, there is the SBA Export Revolving Line of Credit program (ERLC). The SBA will guarantee 85 percent of bank loans up to $750,000 to finance working capital for products going to the export market.

Recently the SBA has streamlined the application process and has been approving/denying applications within a few days; it used to take anywhere from a few weeks to a few months. For the latest information on SBA programs, you should contact your nearest SBA office or call the SBA's free bulletin board service at 800-697-4636, using any general communication software for your modem (set your speed at 9600 baud; parity: none; data bits: 8; stop bits: 1). By the way, this bulletin board contains all sorts of information for small businesses, including a lot of downloadable software.

There are finance companies that specialize in small businesses. You must be sure to check these out carefully, since there are bogus operators in the field. If a firm asks for a significant, up-front "application fee"—run, don't walk, as fast as you can in the opposite direction. Before dealing with any of these, ask your bank or SBA office for references.

Interest rates charged by legitimate finance companies are usually higher than those of banks. But remember, your problem is access to credit—a loan at zero-percent interest isn't going to do you any good if you don't qualify for it.

Many state, county and local governments have funds to assist small businesses located within their regions. A few telephone calls may lead you to one of these sources. Look in the government section of your telephone book for offices of economic development. It may take more than one or two calls to locate these, but persistence may well pay off.

Finally, there are a lot of nonprofit organizations with micro-loan funds. These are usually loans of less than $250,000 and can be as small as several hundred dollars—to buy sewing machines for a small alteration business, for example. The SBA sponsors some of these as part of the 7(m) program; again, a call to your nearest SBA office will lead you to the ones in which they are involved. Another way to find some is through the Association for Enterprise Opportunities in Chicago (312-357-0177).

So the picture is far from bleak. If you do your homework carefully, you should be able to find some money.

☙ Chapter 29 ☙

Taking on Investors

To most entrepreneurs starting a company, the idea of raising capital from outside investors is very appealing. However, many do not fully understand the serious implications of such a move.

The benefits are fairly obvious. By using other people's money instead of your own, financial risks are reduced considerably. And by having more capital available than you can invest yourself or generate from earnings, you can adopt a more aggressive strategy and, hopefully, grow faster.

Two disadvantages of having outside investors are dilution of ownership and loss of control, which most entrepreneurs are far too concerned about. These questions are discussed in another chapter.

Another more important disadvantage, though, is that by having outside investors, you, as the head of the company, assume a substantial obligation to do all you can do to provide these investors with a return on their investment consistent with the risk, and to provide them with liquidity—that is, a way to sell their stock.

Think of your relationship with an investor as being similar to the relationship between a borrower and a bank. An equity investment from a shareholder is a liability, and liabilities must be paid back. The main difference between outside investors and a bank is that investors have different expectations and are usually more patient. Venture investors typically expect a minimum of five to 10 times the return on their investment over a period of about five years. You should not even think about selling stock to outsiders unless your venture has reasonable potential for this kind of appreciation.

In addition, you have a strong obligation to find some way for your investors to achieve liquidity, to convert their stock into cash, within a reasonable length of time. As a practical matter, the two most common ways to accomplish this are for the company to either go public or merge with another firm.

Telling your investors that they will achieve liquidity from the dividends your company will pay or that you will buy the stock back according to a formula, is a good way to make it very difficult to raise capital. Venture investors do not make high risk investments for the purpose of getting dividends. If that were their intention, they would buy stock in a public utility. And they probably will not believe you or will find the formula unacceptable when you suggest the company is prepared to buy back its stock at some future date.

What I suggest is that when an entrepreneur accepts money from an outside investor, he or she assumes a strong obligation to provide a return to that investor consistent with the risk, and a strong obligation to provide eventual liquidity. It probably requires that the company go public or merge. If you cannot accept this, do not take on outside investors.

ᚠ Chapter 30 ᚠ

The Importance of Control: Who Needs It?

Most entrepreneurs, when trying to raise capital from outside sources, seem to be obsessed with the subject of control. The 51 percent number is magic. Admittedly, it is desirable to own as much of the company as possible; however, this is not nearly as important as most people believe.

Digital Equipment Corp. (DEC) is a classic example. When Ken Olsen raised his first $70,000 of venture capital, he gave up about 77 percent of the company, keeping 13 percent for himself and distributing the rest to other founders. Today, Olsen owns less than two percent of DEC stock, but it is worth millions of dollars.

My advice in negotiating with a venture investor or an underwriter selling stock to the public is to give up as little of your company as possible in return for the money you are trying to raise. But don't panic if your share drops below 50 percent.

The bottom line here is that if you are doing a good job running the company, if your sales are increasing and you are realizing a good profit, and if you consistently meet the goals of your business plan, you have nothing to worry about, regardless of whether or not you control a majority of the stock. On the other hand, if none of the above is happening and

the company is floundering, you have plenty to worry about, even if you own all of the stock.

My point is that even the founder must earn the position of head of the firm. And you earn it only with good performance.

Assume, for example, you have to give up 60 percent of the stock to outside investors in order to raise the capital you require to start the firm. So what? When venture investors put money into your business, they are investing in you and the team you put together. A major factor in the investment decision is their evaluation of your ability to build and manage a business. Many venture investors, when asked what the three most important factors were in their decision to invest in a start up, answer, "Management, management and management." The last thing in the world they want is to run your business. If they thought that was likely to happen they wouldn't invest.

Suppose the company isn't doing too well. You should be first to suggest that someone might be better than you at running the business. Play a different role—director of engineering or sales manager, for example, rather than president. Let someone else run the show.

The management skills needed to run a successful business are different for a start up than for a $10-million company, and they are different for a $10-million company than for a $100-million company. Some entrepreneurs can make the transition—many cannot. More important in the long run for you, your employees and your investors, is that the company survive and thrive, rather than that you remain in control.

Do the best you can when structuring a financial deal. Try to keep as much of the stock as possible. But don't forget: It's more important that you have the opportunity to start the company than owning 51 percent of the stock and remaining the boss forever.

In addition, there is another more practical consideration that you should keep in mind. If you have a significant number of shareholders, say 10 or more, the likelihood of their joining forces against you is low unless you really screw up. If your stock is publicly owned, the chances of a stockholder revolution is almost nil. We all know about publicly owned, multimillion-dollar corporations in which management holds a tiny fraction of outstanding shares. Since they usually load their board of directors with friends and/or employees, they must be guilty of gross mismanagement for their job to be in jeopardy.

This has been challenged lately at Eastman Kodak, Apple Computer, IBM and several other companies where the board of directors replaced the CEO with an outsider, but that is still generally rare.

At RF Communications, the four founders first formed a legal partnership in which we were all equal. Then we incorporated and divided the stock in proportion to our expected role in the company. My reward for being founder and president was to have a little more stock than the others, or about 33 percent. Then we sold stock to the public to raise our initial capital and my percentage dropped to about 20 percent. Over the next eight years, we raised money on four other occasions, each time further diluting my share of the ownership. When we finally merged, I owned only a little more than 10 percent of the stock. But this was 10 percent of a very big pie. Had I insisted on maintaining a controlling interest in RF Communications, we could not have achieved the results we did. My personal rewards would surely have been much, much less. I can honestly say I never worried about having control.

In the long run, if the company succeeds, there will be more than enough to go around and the rewards will be great. If the company fails, it doesn't matter how much you own. Set your ownership goals high, but don't be greedy.

Chapter 31

Watch Out for the Sharks, and Other Advice for Dealing With Venture Investors

There are at least three distinct kinds of venture investors. They are:

♦ Individuals and informal venture groups.

♦ Formal, institutional venture capital funds.

♦ Corporate venture funds.

I must admit to a strong bias. I am an individual venture investor, heavily involved in a number of start ups. As you might expect, I will have some good things to say about this source of venture capital. My experience with formal venture capital funds is limited, but the results are mixed—some good, some bad. I had one experience with a corporate venture investor that was mostly good.

There are several other sources of venture capital that I have not mentioned, such as R&D Limited Partnerships and Small Business Investment Companies (SBIC). The R&D Limited Partnership seems to be out of favor because of changes in the tax laws. The SBIC is, for all practical purposes, a variation of the formal venture capital fund and need not be discussed separately.

With this as background, let's look at the pros and cons of each.

Individuals and informal venture groups

This includes individuals or small groups that invest personal money in new ventures. They are often entrepreneurs who have started their own companies and have capital that they are willing to put at risk. Individual venture investors are either willing to or insist on being closely involved with the business as directors, informal advisers or mentors. This type of investor is often called an "angel." I read an article recently about venture investing, and it said the "angels" currently invest about $10 billion a year in more than 30,000 companies nationwide.

The major advantage of dealing with individuals or small groups of venture investors is that, if the entrepreneur can catch their interest, deals can be consummated rapidly and the deals are likely to be simple and straightforward. Also, this type of investor may be more willing to finance an early start up than other sources of venture capital. In general, individual investors have goals similar to the entrepreneur. Having been entrepreneurs themselves, they have an understanding of the problems of starting a business, and their involvement can be valuable. Finally, even though individual investors and informal groups are likely to be fairly sophisticated, they often make their investment decisions intuitively, without much due diligent investigation. The deals they cut will be less onerous than those you are apt to get from a venture capital fund or corporate investor.

On the negative side, even though the total amount of money invested each year by individuals is very high, the amount they will invest in each particular deal may be limited. In addition, once having made an initial investment, individuals or informal groups may have little interest in providing a second or third round of financing. And the contacts these investors have with the investment banking community may be limited.

Individual venture investors may be hard to find. There are few formal channels available to establish contact, and the entrepreneur may have difficulty locating people with the kind of money required.

Until recently, this type of offering could be made to only a limited number of potential investors, and the company had to establish investor criteria—the minimum each investor must contribute and what income or net worth he or she must have to qualify. In effect, the Securities and Exchange Commission (SEC) permitted the sale of this type of high-risk security only to investors who are capable of fully understanding the risk and who have sufficient personal resources to afford a loss in the event the company goes under. Stock sold in private placements was also restricted, in that it could be resold only under very limited circumstances.

In 1992 the SEC amended its Rule 504, which controls this type of stock sale, substantially reducing or eliminating many of the restrictions previously in place. The purpose of the amendment was to make it easier for small companies to raise capital using this route. Among other things, it permitted a company to promote the offering more broadly, to sell stock to a greater number of buyers, made it easier for the buyers to sell the stock they purchased, and eliminated the need for the Private Placement Memorandum. It did not, however, reduce the companies' obligations under the antifraud rules of the federal securities laws.

My suggestion is that your first step in trying to raise capital from individual venture investors should be to prepare a document called a Private Placement Memorandum, even though it is no longer a legal requirement. Those I have seen are about 50 to 100 pages in length and present detailed information about the company. The information is similar to that contained in a conventional stock prospectus, but with more emphasis on the risks associated with the venture. The information in a Private Placement Memorandum must be true and should accurately describe all positive and negative aspects. Much of the information can be drawn from the business plan. An important part of this document is a description of the number of shares you want to sell, the price and what you intend to do with the money.

Because some states may have security regulations that are either different than or conflict with Rule 504, I strongly recommend that under no circumstances you conduct a private placement without the advice of a knowledgeable lawyer completely familiar with security regulations.

You may conclude from what I have said that the private placement is too complex to bother with. That is not the case. As mentioned in another chapter, in the Rochester area, between January 1980 and March 1988, 42 companies raised approximately $32 million from individual investors. I know many individuals who are interested in making this kind of investment. They understand and are comfortable with the risks. Their hope is that they may find a situation where their investment may appreciate 50 or 100 times.

Raising money through a private placement usually requires a large amount of time from the firm's senior people. Potential investors are likely to visit the company to meet the principals, see the facilities and ask questions. If you happen to include among your personal acquaintances a half dozen or so millionaires, this will be of immeasurable help. Failing this, I suggest you find one or two highly visible, successful entrepreneurs who, if persuaded to come in on the deal, may attract others.

An example of a Rochester company that successfully used individual investors for its initial financing is Ormec Systems Corp., a manufacturer of high-tech precision motion control systems used in automated manufacturing. Its customers include Eastman Kodak, for its film manufacturing operation, Johnson & Johnson, for the manufacture of pharmaceuticals, and the Harrison Division of General Motors, for the manufacture of automobile radiators.

I met two of the four founders of Ormec in an entrepreneurship class I spoke to. At the time, the two key people were engineers working for Eastman Kodak. After getting to know them and their business, I decided to invest personally and brought together a group of four other successful entrepreneurs. Together we provided $300,000 of start-up money in return for a 40-percent interest in the company. The two key founders quit their jobs, and the company was off and running. Four of the outside investors became board members.

Ormec has since raised about $1 million of additional capital in two private placements and now has about 130 shareholders. Over the past few years, they made major investments in building a large national network of distributors and representatives and in developing a new, very advanced, product line. This investment in building the business is now paying off. Sales are currently more than $10 million and growing, and they are well in the black. They hope to soon reach the point where either a public offering or merger with a larger company should be considered.

Individual venture investors can be a good source of capital for a new business.

Formal (institutional) venture funds

The venture capital industry has been one of the major growth industries of the 1980s and early 1990's. At the end of 1995, about $40 billion of investment was managed by venture capital funds. Venture funds are usually limited partnerships in which the bulk of the money is supplied by passive limited partners such as insurance companies, college endowment funds or corporate retirement funds. The investment portfolio is then managed by a general partner or group of general partners. They seek out and evaluate investment opportunities, negotiate deals, manage the follow-up activity and participate on the board of directors of companies in their portfolio.

The formal venture capital industry has structure, and there are a number of directories available that list the various funds, amounts of capital available, industry focus and addresses and telephone numbers of the managing general partners.

One such directory is *Pratt's Guide to Venture Capital Sources*, from Venture Economics, a Division of Securities Data Publishers, 40 West 57 Street, #1100, New York, NY 10102-0968 (800-455-5844 or 212-765-5311.) It includes an excellent introductory section about the venture capital industry and lists just about every venture capital fund in the U.S. and Canada and its area of specialization.

Another source of information is *Galante's Complete Venture Capital & Private Equity Directory*, available from Asset Alternatives, 180 Linden St., Ste. 3, Wellesley, MA 02181 (617-431-7353), which also contains an extensive list of venture funds and their areas of interest.

A third source is the *Vankirk's Venture Capital Directory*, which lists about 2,300 venture capital offices in 39 countries. They are located at 2800 Shirlington Rd., #904, Arlington, VA, 22206 (703-379-9200).

Each of these directories is fairly expensive, but they all contain much cross-referenced information that can save you hours of effort trying to find a venture fund that may be interested in your situation.

You can obtain a directory of Small Business Investment Companies from the Associate Administrator for Investment at the U.S. Small Business Administration, Washington, DC 20419 (202-205-6510).

Another way for a company to reach venture investors is by attending Venture Capital Forums, which are held on a regular basis in many sections of the country. They are intended to give entrepreneurs the opportunity to present their deal to groups of venture fund managers. Contact your chamber of commerce to learn whether there are any of these forums held in your area.

One of the more important advantages of dealing with an institutional venture capital fund is that they have access to large amounts of money. For example, in 1995 venture funds raised about $4.4 billion of new money, an all-time record. Except for the very small funds, their minimum investment is frequently in the $500,000 to $1 million range and they can often put together deals requiring $5 million or more. It is typical for this kind of venture investor to make second and third infusions of capital as the company grows.

Another important benefit the venture funds offer is an excellent window on the investment banking industry. At such time that the company goes public, the managers of the fund can be a valuable source of help. In general, the goals of this type of venture investor are similar to the goals of the new enterprise. However, the venture fund may be more impatient to cash out on a deal, which could force the company into a merger or public offering sooner than it wants.

Finally, the general partners are usually diligent in their participation on the board of directors of the companies in their portfolio. Because they are frequently involved with similar companies, they can be important sources of experience and expertise.

In spite of the above list of advantages, I still urge new companies seeking capital from venture funds to proceed with caution. Entrepreneurs recognize the risks associated with starting the business. They may not be familiar with the risks of dealing with venture investors.

Among the disadvantages of trying to raise capital from a venture fund is that the process can be very slow. Venture funds are typically deluged by proposals and business plans from companies seeking money, and most funds operate with a limited staff who are extremely busy and response time can be slow. Some people familiar with the venture industry say that a business plan submitted without a personal introduction has almost no chance of receiving attention.

Because they maintain a fiduciary responsibility to their limited partners, venture funds go through an extensive "due-diligence" process. Commonly they retain consultants, expert in the specific industry, to investigate the products and markets of the new venture. This process can take weeks and months to complete and can be very demanding on the time of the entrepreneur.

Another disadvantage is that venture capital funds impose some very tough conditions that many entrepreneurs consider unacceptable. For instance, it is not unusual for them to demand some form of convertible preferred stock, the purpose of which is to give them preference over other shareholders in the event of liquidation. Also, they frequently require antidilution protection if stock is ever sold at a lower price, strong representation on the board of directors, control over salary levels of managers and the latitude to take over the company if certain financial criteria are not met. These conditions are outlined in what is known as a "term sheet."

The advice I give to people beginning negotiations with a venture fund is to ask for a copy of their standard term sheet at the start rather than at the end, as this may avoid unexpected surprises and a lot of wasted time. You will likely be told that they do not have such a thing, because terms vary with the deal. Then ask for a copy of the term sheet of several recent deals, or the term sheet of an investment they made in a company similar to yours.

Most onerous, though, in dealing with venture funds is the valuation they set on the company, which determines the price they are willing to pay for the stock. My experience with venture funds is that they drive tough financial deals.

It is extremely desirable for entrepreneurs to negotiate with a venture fund at a time when they do not need the money too badly, and to have at least two sources of venture capital competing for the deal. It is not unknown for a venture fund to deliberately protract negotiations so long that the company is desperate for money, then nail them to the cross in setting a price. The expression "vulture capitalist" has some basis.

Entrepreneurs should be very careful in approaching venture funds to avoid the appearance that they have unsuccessfully approached a number of other potential investors. Communications between funds is fairly efficient, and the fact that you have shopped the deal and have been turned down by two or three may make your situation untouchable to others.

From my contact with venture funds, I have concluded that when you get past the public relations hype, many of them are really not very venturesome. Part of this results from the fact that they must report regularly to the limited partner investors, who, in turn, are managed by financial types whose performance is continually under review. Either consciously or unconsciously, they want investments that will make them look good in the short term. An entrepreneur trying to raise money from a

venture fund to finance a raw start up faces a very hard road.

Entrepreneurs dealing with venture funds had better not be thin skinned. A few years ago, a friend of mine was invited by the manager of a large, well-known fund to come from Rochester to Boston to meet with the partners at 3 p.m. the following afternoon. After being kept waiting for two hours, he was told he had 15 minutes to present his story.

If you do approach a venture fund, remember that the managers control large amounts of money, and the world seems to beat a path to their doors trying to relieve them of some. Financial power, like political power, can distort one's sense of values. Also, the general partners of venture funds are almost always incredibly busy. Typically, they travel three, four, five days a week. They're overwhelmed with potential deals, some of their past deals may be in serious trouble and they are deluged by telephone calls from impatient entrepreneurs. This frenetic existence can cause impatience and unintended slights.

My advice to entrepreneurs seeking investment from venture capital funds is to be very cautious. Talk to other entrepreneurs who have been down the same road and, of utmost importance, try to do all your money raising when you do not need the money too badly and while you still have options.

To give you the "other side of the story" about working with institutional venture capital funds, I asked a friend of mine who manages a large institutional fund to write a chapter about how to improve the odds of attracting this type of investment. It is included later in this book. I urge you to read that chapter, because it balances out some of my bias.

Corporate venture funds

The third source of venture capital is the corporate venture investor. A number of large corporations have established some type of fund, sometimes formal and sometimes informal, for the purpose of investing in new ventures. In almost all the cases that I know of, these investments are made in situations that are generally related to the main business of the investing organization.

Among the advantages of raising capital from a corporate investor is that they are a potential source of both technical and management expertise, as well as money. They often have access to fairly large amounts of capital, they can be quite venturesome, and because they have goals other than pure financial gain, they may not drive as hard a deal as a venture fund.

The major drawback of using a corporate investor as a source of venture capital is that they often want to eventually gain control of the company in which they invest. This will frequently be in the form of a buyout provision, with price based on a predetermined formula. This constraint can put a serious limit on upward potential for the entrepreneur.

An example of a company whose initial financing was from a major corporate investor is Microlytics, which was founded by a former employee of Xerox Corp. Microlytics entered the personal computer software business with products such as GOFER, a file search utility, and WORDFINDER, a spelling checker and thesaurus. Initial financing was a $400,000 investment from the venture arm of Xerox. In making this investment, Xerox required Microlytics to raise a matching amount from private investors, which the company did without too much difficulty. In addition to capital, Xerox gave Microlytics access to several advanced products originated in its Palo Alto Research Center.

Several years later Microlytics merged with Minneapolis-based Selectronics, which had a line of hand-held spelling checker/thesaurus products. Because Selectronics was a publicly owned company, they kept their corporate identity. Over two million of these hand-held spelling checkers were sold, but unfortunately, severe competition kept profit margins very low, and the company ran into serious financial difficulties. The company name has been changed back to Microlytics, and they are no longer in the hardware business. Following several years of severe ups and downs, the company is now working hard to expand its product offering and get the operation back into the black.

Xerox helped them through these very hard times with substantial financial assistance, and Microlytics had raised additional capital from several other sources. For Microlytics, the corporate venture capital route was a good approach to do its initial financing, but whether it turns out to be good for Xerox is still uncertain.

Determining the value of your business

In the early stages of a business, most entrepreneurs have a difficult time trying to determine what their company is worth. A venture investor calls this the "valuation" of the deal. In effect, what you must decide is what percentage of your company you are willing to sell for how much money. Because start-up companies have no operating history, the valuation is set mostly by estimates. The following describes the process a venture investor is likely to go through.

The first thing a venture investor will do is to look at the sales and net (after tax) profit you project in your business plan five years or so into the future. Assume for this discussion you expect annual sales to be $15 million and net profit to be five percent, or $750,000. Based on the venture investor's knowledge of the market, your competitors, your product and your management, as well as advice from consultants, he might decide that this is too optimistic. Let's say he cuts it back to $10 million in sales and $500,000 net profit.

Having determined to his satisfaction what your company's sales and net profits might be five years into the future, he then tries to estimate what the value of your company will be at that time. He estimates what a reasonable price earnings ratio (P/E) for your stock is likely to be. He will probably assume something in the range of 10 to 1 or less. So in the mind of the venture investor, the value of your company five years from now is your net earnings times the P/E ratio, $500,000 times 10, or $5 million.

Next he will ask what $5 million five years from now is worth today, or what is its present value. To do this calculation, you must assume a rate of return. Venture investors want a rate of return from 25 to 50 percent, which is high because of the risk involved. Let us use 36 percent. The present value of $5 million five years from now at a 36-percent rate of return is a little more than $1 million.

This means that in the mind of the venture investor, your company is presently worth about $1 million. If you're planning to raise $600,000 of capital, the venture investor will want to own 60 percent of your stock. Going through this process always shocks the entrepreneur by how low the valuation comes out to be.

Another factor that can affect the valuation is that many entrepreneurs in the early stages of their business make personal loans to their companies. Also, when they work for less pay than they could ordinarily expect, they often show the differential on their balance sheet as deferred salaries. Their hope is that they will be reimbursed later from the capital they raise. I always advise against this practice. When an entrepreneur puts money into the company, it should be an investment not a loan, and working for lower salary is just a way of life in a start up. Both of these practices are apt to make it much harder to raise capital because investors want their money used for future activities—not to pay for past obligations.

A business owner approached me several years ago trying to raise several hundred thousand dollars for his company. When I pressed him for the details, I learned that much of this money would be used to pay delinquent withholding tax obligations, plus penalties. As you might guess, I let that one go by.

Of the three type of investors, venture funds are likely to come up with the lowest valuation; corporate venture funds are likely to have somewhat higher valuation, because they will attribute value to other factors; and individual investors and informal venture groups will probably have the highest valuation.

✒ Chapter 32 ✒

How to Get a Venture Investment: Improving the Odds

This chapter was written by Paul S. Brentlinger, general partner in three Morgenthaler Ventures, a venture capital firm based in Cleveland, Ohio. The Morgenthaler firm manages approximately $300 million in venture capital assets, representing a wide variety of industries and types of investment. Earlier, Paul was Senior Vice President-Finance and Vice President-Corporate Development at Harris Corporation. Paul has an MBA from the University of Michigan and is a member of Phi Beta Kappa. He is a director of a number of companies in which Morgenthaler invested and is the Chairman of the Board of Trustees of the Cleveland Institute of Art.

There is a lot of money out there

If you believe the company you started can grow to a large size, and if you are willing to work in partnership with investors who own a significant share of your company's equity, you probably owe it to yourself to consider seeking capital from an institutional venture investor. Institutional venture capital comes from 600 or so professionally managed venture capital firms in the United States, plus a small amount from abroad. They manage venture-type equity investments on behalf of pension funds, foundations, university endowment funds and other institutional sources of money.

Institutional venture capital firms currently manage about $34 billion of equity capital. During 1995, about $7 billion was invested in 1100 different companies.

By comparison, it is estimated that some 250,000 individual "angel" investors invest $10 to $12 billion annually in some 30,000 companies. These "angels" are usually relatives, friends or neighbors of the entrepreneur. "Angels" have investment approaches and objectives that are different from those of institutional venture capital firms. This chapter focuses entirely on the investment process used by institutional venture capital firms, not individual investors.

Analyze your goals

The primary objective of some entrepreneurs is to build a comfortable, medium-sized company that is always subject to their personal control, that is designed to finance the family's yacht or Florida condominium, and that will provide jobs for children and relatives. These are legitimate objectives, but they are incompatible with the objectives of institutional venture capital firms.

To obtain money from institutional venture capitalists, it's important that you understand their goals. Pension funds, endowment funds, foundations and others that entrust the investment of their money to venture capitalists expect a rate of return significantly higher than the return on investment attainable from buying publicly traded common stocks. To illustrate, if the Standard & Poor's stock average has produced an annual rate of return of 10 to 12 percent over the past five to 10 years, venture capital should produce a return in the 15 to 18 percent range.

Because some venture capital investments are total failures and a number of others will produce minimal returns (these are called the living dead), the venture capitalist must see an opportunity for a very high rate of return, in the 30 to 40 percent range, on any individual investment opportunity.

With this in mind, the venture capitalists are strictly equity-oriented investors. A share of the ownership of a company is what creates an opportunity for substantial capital gains. Venture capitalists do not lend money at six points over prime rate.

Entrepreneurs seeking institutional venture capital funding must therefore be willing to share equity ownership and give up a significant degree of control of their enterprise.

Are you a candidate for a venture investment?

In general, venture capitalists prefer to invest in companies that are candidates for selling stock to the public within five years or so. In today's world, that probably means the company should have the potential to generate annual sales revenue in the $50-million range within that time frame. It's also essential that the company's products or services address markets that investors believe to be large and rapidly growing—the kinds of markets that attract attention from professional securities analysts.

Working toward public ownership requires a totally professional approach to management. This probably means a willingness on the part of the entrepreneur to work with a board of directors comprised of a majority of outsiders, including venture capitalists. Also, the company must have the ability to generate financial statements prepared in accordance with generally accepted accounting practices and audited by Big Six accounting firms, and the ability to develop an effective multilayer management team. This list is illustrative—it is by no means all-inclusive.

How to approach a venture capital firm

With all this in mind and if you believe your objectives are consistent with those of institutional venture capitalists, what is the best way to approach a venture capital firm?

It is highly desirable to arrange an introduction through a mutual acquaintance. Consultants, accountants, lawyers, private investors or friends who have a personal relationship with the venture capital firm represent ideal points of entry. Rightly or wrongly, institutional venture capitalists rarely invest in companies that make a cold "over-the-transom" approach.

The business plan is crucial

Once the introduction has been made, the submission of a business plan is a key part of the process. See Chapter 24—it is *must* reading.

In reviewing a business plan, the venture capitalist probably will concentrate on the following issues:

The business concept. What market is being addressed? Is a large and growing economic need being addressed?

Product or service. Does the product or service offer a genuine competitive advantage? Why will people buy it instead of buying alternative products or services? Will customers pay a premium price? Is there patent protection? Are there barriers to entry? Are there powerful competitors? Can the company be the low cost producer?

Management team. Are members of management experienced in the market being addressed? Do they have a track record of success—have the managers previously been winners? Is the management team totally committed to the success of the enterprise—is the team motivated and hungry? Is the team capable of growth as managers as the company grows?

Financial aspects. How much capital is needed? Is the business capital intensive? Will additional rounds of private venture capital investment be required before the company is cash-flow positive? Are the financial projections realistic?

Valuation. Will the venture capital investment buy enough shares in the company to produce the opportunity for at least the 30 to 40 percent return on investment described earlier? What is the probable exit strategy? Is the company a candidate for a public offering, and if it is, when and at what multiple of earnings? Is the company a candidate for acquisition at a high price by a larger company?

Why does the process take so long?

In a somewhat different vein, most venture capitalists like to co-invest in early-stage companies with other strong venture capital firms. By doing so, they share the workload and financial burden. You must ask if the company is one that is likely to attract an investment from other well-financed venture capital firms capable of offering constructive collaboration. The individual venture capitalist will think about whether he or she would like to put his or her reputation on the line by introducing the deal to a friend in another venture capital firm.

Once an investment opportunity gets beyond the initial screening step, a series of meetings will take place between the venture capitalist and the company's management team.

These meetings represent a critically important step. Venture capital investing involves a long-term partnership with the management team. Before an investment is made, there must be sufficient personal interaction to ensure a mutual belief that the venture capitalist and the management have the same objectives. It is extremely important that everyone concerned be comfortable working together over a period of several years to accomplish their mutual objectives.

If there appears to be a strong mutual interest regarding the investment, the venture capitalist can be expected to do a lot of reference checking regarding the management team. In many cases, the venture capitalist will also use outside consultants to advise on the technology and the market prospects. As an entrepreneur seeking venture capital funding, you have to be willing to share detailed information about your products and technology, and about yourself and your colleagues, as part of this due diligence process.

You are, of course, entitled to receive assurances from the venture capitalist that proprietary information will be held in confidence.

Upon completion of the due diligence, the venture capitalist makes a go/no-go decision. Most venture capital firms require that each partner recommend specific investments— a partner must act as a sponsor or champion. Your personal relationship with the venture capital partner looking at your company is of vital importance—the partner is unlikely to champion an investment unless he or she believes an effective relationship can be developed.

Reviewing the steps

To summarize, in order to attract an investment from an institutional venture capital firm, the following conditions must exist:

1. Your personal objectives must be consistent with those of the venture capital firm.

2. You must be willing to share equity ownership and a degree of control with the venture capitalist.

3. You must submit a business plan that presents a compelling case for your business concept, products, management team and probable financial results.

4. You must be prepared to have a lot of personal interaction with the venture capitalist in the course of an intense due diligence process. This will often require the sharing of your trade secrets.

5. You must be prepared to value your company at a level that satisfies the risk/reward criteria applied by the venture capitalist.

You get a lot of help beyond money

If your company receives funding from a group of strong venture investors, the ultimate benefits can be very rewarding. Good venture capitalists don't stop working after the investment is made—they contribute more than money. They can be helpful in such areas as arranging customer contacts, executive recruiting, shaping financial strategy and attracting strong underwriter support when the time comes for an initial public offering.

While the venture capital process may appear long and arduous, enormous wealth has been created for entrepreneurs who have successfully traveled the path. Examples include companies such as Genentech, Sun Microsystems, VeriFone, Cisco Systems and Premisys Communications.

Your challenge is to add your own company to this list of venture-capital-backed winners—you may have a chance for personal immortality by being able to put your name on the newest building of your favorite university or the latest addition to the Metropolitan Museum of Art. There is not much to lose if you try.

✦ Chapter 33 ✦

Staying Private/
Going Public

Most financial experts advise new companies not to go public too soon. I'm not sure I agree with this conclusion, and I will describe some of the benefits of going public, which can be considerable. But first, a word about the disadvantages.

One of the major drawbacks of going public with a new venture is that you will bring in small investors. Even though your offering circular or prospectus will describe the risks in great detail and with great emphasis, the typical small investor may not fully understand them. The head of a start-up company has enough problems without having to worry about "widows and orphans" among the shareholders who cannot afford to lose their investments.

A second frequently cited drawback is that it puts unreasonable pressure on management to achieve short-term profitability in its desire to keep the price of the stock up. I see nothing wrong with management being under pressure to achieve profitable operations early. My experience is that most entrepreneurs have no trouble figuring out reasons to defer profits, and pressure in the other direction is likely to be good rather than bad.

A third disadvantage is the cost of going public. Legal fees and printing costs for a public stock offering can be considerable, and if you use an underwriter to sell the stock, commissions will also be considerable. This does not worry me much either, because it's an accepted fact that the cost of raising capital can be high.

A fourth disadvantage is the time required. In most cases, you will need approval from the SEC, which can be a long and complicated process.

Finally, there's the possibility that the price of your stock will fall below the offering price, which may make it both difficult and costly to raise more capital at a later date. This should be a concern, but it is offset somewhat by the possibility that the price of your stock may increase, making it easier and less costly to raise more capital at a later date.

These disadvantages may be considered serious or not serious at all, depending upon the specific situation.

How about the advantages? For one thing, going public is a good way to avoid using venture investors. It usually involves several hundred small shareholders, rather than a handful of very large ones. The public is likely to be easier to deal with.

A second advantage is that you are almost sure to get a higher price for your stock. As I discussed in Chapter 31, venture investors drive very hard financial deals. The public is likely to be less demanding.

Another benefit is liquidity. Stock purchased in a public issue can be traded freely by outside investors. The people who help you get started are not forced to leave their money tied up for five years or more. The founders will also have greater liquidity, at least to a degree. There still remain substantial restrictions on when and under what circumstances the founders, officers, directors and/or major shareholders can sell stock. Restrictions notwithstanding, stock in a publicly owned company is somewhat easier to sell.

Still another benefit of public ownership is that the company becomes more visible. Among other things, this means that hiring new employees will be easier, and doing business with other companies will be easier. In a 1990 survey of about 100 companies that had recently gone public, more than 50 percent of the respondents listed enhanced credibility with customers, suppliers, banks, etc., as the most important benefit.

Also, for senior people in the venture, increased public visibility can result in the job being more fun. Communicating with the shareholders and conducting annual meetings are all things that can make the job more interesting, especially when the company is doing well. These may not be so much fun when the company is doing badly.

A final benefit of being publicly owned will only be realized when you decide to sell your new venture or merge it with a larger company. It is my experience, both as a seller and a buyer of companies, that the price paid for a publicly owned company is almost always higher than the price paid for a privately owned company. In the case of a publicly owned company, the price is normally the quoted price, plus a premium. If the company has done well and can catch the fancy of the investing community, the price may indeed be high. I have seen fairly large transactions where the acquiring firm paid 40 or 50 times earnings and more. In negotiated deals for privately held companies, the range is more likely to be seven or 10 times earnings. The message here is that if you are positioning your company to be acquired, going public can have considerable merit.

An interesting case

Let me tell you about my experience going public as a way to raise start-up capital. During the 1960s, Rochester, N.Y., was a hotbed of new venture activity. I researched that decade in some detail and learned that about 100 companies in the area had initial public stock offerings. The company I started, RF Communications, was one of the first.

RF came into existence during the summer of 1960. The four founders each invested $5,000 for a total of $20,000 of initial capital. We started as a partnership and incorporated several months later. The founders resigned from their full-time jobs on February 1, 1961, and on March 1, 1961, RF became an independent company. The only problem was that we were still operating on the original $20,000 investment, which was being depleted in a hurry.

During the planning phase of our venture, we considered various financing alternatives. There were no venture capital funds at the time, and we did not list many wealthy people among our acquaintances. Because of these factors, we decided to try to raise the bulk of our start-up capital through a public stock offering that we would do ourselves without an underwriter or broker. Within two weeks after setting up shop, we received SEC approval for a Regulation A Offering, which is a somewhat simplified way to sell stock to the public. Our goal was to raise $150,000 by selling 150,000 shares at $1 each—a nice round number. These 150,000 shares represented one third ownership in the company. The four founders retained the other two thirds.

Upon receiving SEC authorization, we mailed about 600 offering circulars to potential investors. We had compiled a list that included the names of everyone we could think of who might be willing to invest a few hundred dollars in our risky little deal. To our amazement, the deal caught the local investing community's fancy, and within a few days, the offering was heavily oversubscribed. We received about $500,000 from potential investors interested in purchasing shares of our stock. This was way above the $150,000 we were asking for and way above what we expected to be able to raise. Unfortunately, SEC rules permit you to keep only the amount of capital stated in the offering circular. We said we wanted to raise $150,000 and that was all we were permitted to retain. The oversubscription of about $350,000 had to be returned. We allocated the stock in a way we considered fair and sent back the oversubscribed amount.

Two small, local brokerage firms began making a market in the stock and the trading price jumped to $2 a share within several days. When it was all done, RF Communications had raised $150,000 for one third ownership, and the company was off and running.

We have often questioned whether the way we did this was smart or dumb. You could easily take the position that the mere fact that we raised so much money is evidence that we either priced the stock too low or sold too large a percentage of the company for $150,000. On the other hand, you could argue that our primary goal was to raise $150,000 so we would have the chance to prove whether the group of four entrepreneurs had the skills to create a business. We achieved this goal.

Years later, my feelings are these:

♦ We felt we needed $150,000 to run the business, and we raised that amount.

♦ The stock immediately began trading for $2 a share, so our initial investors had both liquidity and a potential profit.

♦ Two years later, when we needed more capital, we raised another $270,000 through a second public offering at $5 per share. Not bad!

◆The founders were inexperienced at raising capital and selling stock, and we had absolutely no way of knowing whether the deal would fly. It flew. If we guessed wrong, we would have been out of business in a hurry.

◆ Finally, I am convinced that selling stock works like a step function. You are either a booming success or a disastrous failure. The offering will either be oversubscribed by a mile or left struggling. It is unlikely that the last interested investor will buy the last available share of stock.

To complete the story, RF Communications followed this second $270,000 public offering with a $450,000 private placement at about $10 per share. A short time later, we had a fourth financing, raising $1 million at $16 per share through a public offering, using a New York underwriter. A year or so later, we were listed on the American Stock Exchange, and a year after that we had a final public offering at $36 per share, compared to the original $1 (taking splits into account).

And in 1969, eight years after start up, RF Communications merged with Harris Corp. RF stock was exchanged at about $45 per share equivalent. At the time, this was approximately two and a half times annual sales, five times net worth and 43 times earnings. And Harris paid about a 3-percent annual dividend, compared to no dividend at RF. You can see why I think that being publicly owned has merit.

During the late 1980s, the government made available a faster and far less complex way for small companies to raise capital by going public. It is known as SCOR, Small Company Offering Registration. By early 1992, about 21 states had adopted the SCOR registration process. I am not familiar with this type of offering, but I suggest you check whether your state is among these if you are seriously considering going public. Among the restrictions in SCOR are that the maximum amount of money that can be raised is $1 million and the stock must be priced at $5 per share or higher. This method of financing is not widely known but is likely to become more popular.

More recently, the SEC introduced a new registration process known as Regulation SB. Among other things, to be eligible to use Regulation SB, the company must have revenues of less than $25 million. Forms and instructions for using Regulation SB are available from the Securities and Exchange Commission. This and other changes in the securities regulations are intended to simplify and accelerate the registration process for going public and cut the cost of raising capital for small firms.

One final comment is that in 1995, companies in the U.S. were estimated to have raised about $29 billion of new equity by going public for the first time. This is a huge amount of capital when compared to the $3 to $7 billion raised each year by several thousand companies from venture capital funds, and compared to the estimated $10-billion-plus raised each year by about 30,000 companies from individual investors. Though 1995 may not have been a typical year for public offerings, the numbers are still mind-boggling.

Finally, a word of caution. From recent articles I have read in business publications, it seems that many companies going public during the past few years have been successfully sued for large sums by groups of their initial investors. The reason for these lawsuits is that the stock price dropped substantially a short time after the offering because of a downturn in business. The lawsuits claimed, and may well be right, that the companies should have known trouble was brewing and failed to disclose the possibility in their prospectuses or offering circulars at the time the stock was first sold.

The way to avoid this problem seems pretty clear to me. First, you must be absolutely and completely honest when you describe the business and financial situation of the company. And probably even smarter, you should go public only when you are virtually certain that the business is on an upward path that will last for a while. Try to be as sure as you possibly can that sales and earnings will continue to increase for a

fairly extended time following the offering.

Congress recently passed a law making it harder to sue companies for faulty projections. However, even with this new law in effect, my advice is for a publicly owned company to be extremely cautious when making public projections of future sales and earnings

For a new company raising capital for the first time by going public, estimating future sales and earnings is very difficult to do with any degree of confidence. If you estimate too conservatively, it will be more difficult to sell the stock. If you estimate too optimistically, you may be in for trouble if you miss your goals and the stock price drops sharply soon after the offering.

Shareholder lawsuits sometimes involve large financial judgments against the officers and directors, as well as the company. It is obviously desirable to have officers' and directors' liability insurance as a way to give some degree of protection, but this type of insurance is apt to be expensive and possibly not even available.

So be careful.

⟨ Chapter 34 ⟩

Will the Government Really Give Me Money?

To the complete surprise of many entrepreneurs, there are numerous sources of financial support available to small businesses from the federal government, most state governments and many county and city governments. These include programs that support research and development, guarantee loans, provide low-interest loans and, in some states, involve direct investment similar to a venture capital fund. Many of these programs are new in the past 10 or 15 years. Most entrepreneurs know almost nothing about them.

As you're probably aware, dealing with the government is often time-consuming and frustrating. A lot of paperwork is almost always required, and at the start, you have no assurance of a successful conclusion. But it may be worth the trouble, because for many companies, these sources of financial aid have meant the difference between success and failure.

The following will describe several federal programs in some detail. Almost every state has programs of some sort, but they may be entirely different. Some effort will be required to learn what is available in your area.

For starters, I suggest telephoning the Government Printing Office at 202-783-3238 to purchase a copy of a Small Business Administration booklet entitled, "The States and Small Business—A Directory of Programs and Activities." The document ID number is 045-000-002-57-8. I believe the latest edition is dated 1989, with no revisions planned for the near future. Even though some individuals named as the contact may have changed, the organizations and functions are likely to be the same. This book has a vast amount of useful information for anyone starting a business. I recommend it highly.

Another excellent source of information is the U.S. National Technical Information Service (NTIS), which is part of the Department of Commerce and has almost 3 million reports available describing a huge number of research programs. One report of particular interest to entrepreneurs is the "Directory of Federal and State Business Assistance, 1988-1989: A Guide for New and Growing Businesses." The telephone number is 703-487-4650, and the document ID number is PB88-101977. A description of NTIS services is available through the Internet at http:/www.fedworld.gov.

At the state and local level, almost every state, county and city has an economic development agency of some sort that can give you guidance as to the types of programs that are available and where to look. Also, your local chamber of commerce will be able to help you in your search.

Federal programs

Small Business Innovation Research program

This program, which came into existence in 1982, makes financial grants—not loans—known as SBIRs, to small businesses to support research and development activities.

In this program, 11 large government departments that sponsor research and development (R&D) must set aside a small percentage of their external research budgets for companies with fewer than 500 employees. To qualify for an SBIR, the company must be U.S. owned and must be a small business. Because the agencies involved, including the Department of Defense, have very large external research and development programs, this very small percentage adds up to a large amount of money.

The Small Business Administration (SBA) makes quarterly SBIR presolicitation announcements available to identify topics of interest. These are generally quite broad, and with so many agencies involved you should be able to find one that fits your needs. At one time, you could call 202-205-7777 to be added to the SBA mailing list for information about SBIR grants. However, I understand they are now using the Internet to distribute this information. The Internet addresses are:

1. SBA Home Page Address-http://www.sbaonline.sba.gov.
   Then go to "Expanding Your Business," which covers Small Business Innovative Research opportunities (SBIRs).

2. Or you can go directly to the SBA Office of Technology Site at http://www.sbaonline.sba.gov/Research_And_Development.

3. The National Technology Transfer Center Home Page address is http://www.nttc.edu.

4. The Department of Defense SBIR information is maintained by the Defense Technical Information Center (DTIC) at http://www.dtic.dla.mil/dtic/sbir.

I am not completely familiar with the use of the Internet for the purpose mentioned above, and have not contacted these agencies using these Internet addresses—but it may be worth a try. Contact your local SBA office for more assistance and guidance, if necessary.

The SBIR program is intended to support R&D that will later benefit the sponsoring agency, the company and the country.

I know of one company that received a grant for research in the use of laser devices to weld bowel tissue during surgery, and another company that had a grant to develop techniques for ruggedized, hand-held personal computers. The list and variety of projects is endless.

SBIR awards are made on a competitive basis. The program has several phases. Phase One can be a six-month grant of up to $100,000 to determine the feasibility of the idea.

This may then be followed by a Phase Two grant, extending over a period of up to two years, with awards of up to $750,000 for further work refining the ideas and developing prototypes. These numbers vary from agency to agency. However, in most cases, the question of when the funded program will be commercialized is receiving more emphasis than in the past.

Another resource is the publication "Writing SBIR Proposals," available from Sandra Cohn Associates at 312-648-0082. The price is $75 plus $20 for the 1993 update. Another update is planned for the end of 1996.

To give you an idea of the scope of the SBIR program, in 1991 there were about 3,800 Phase One Awards (about 12 percent of those that applied) and more than 1025 Phase Two Awards (about one third of those that applied). Currently SBIR funding is about $400 million per year, scheduled to increase to about $1 billion by 1997. Whether this increase will be approved by the present Republican Congress or after the 1996 elections is uncertain, but you can see that an SBIR is something worth pursuing.

Small Business Administration, 7(a) loan guarantees

In this program, the SBA provides guarantees to banks making loans to small businesses. This is intended for use by companies unable to obtain loans on their own. Funds may be used to establish a new business, enlarge an existing business, to acquire machinery or equipment, to finance inventory or for working capital. In its 40-year existence, the SBA loan programs have helped more than one million small business owners. SBA guaranteed loans vary in size from $20,000 to $750,000, with most in the $150,000 range. A formal application to SBA for a 7(a) guarantee can be made by the bank that declined to make your business a conventional loan.

Banks unwilling to lend to a small business because it is unable to cover the entire loan with personal guarantees and liens on personal assets are frequently willing to lend with a partial SBA guarantee. In 1995, the SBA guaranteed a total of more than 55,000 loans with a value of about $7.8 billion. However, the agency is in the process of reducing the percentage of the loan that will be guaranteed and raising fees to the borrowers in order to increase the dollar value of loans that will be covered. According to the SBA, women, minorities and veterans especially benefit from the program.

State programs

The financial aid and assistance programs of states are more diverse than the federal programs. Most are intended to create or maintain jobs within the state, to attract companies to the state or to keep companies from relocating out of the state. For New York, where taxes are high, keeping companies from moving elsewhere is an important priority.

I cannot possibly cover all programs available in all states. Instead, I will describe some available in New York to give you an idea of the scope of these programs. Keep in mind that some programs may have ended and others started.

Corporation for Innovation Development. Administered by the New York State Science and Technology Foundation and provides debt and equity capital to new technology-based businesses with fewer than 100 employees. CID operates in a way similar to a private venture capital fund, but it is willing to take greater risks. Its telephone number is 518-473-9741.

Empire State Development Corp. This agency has combined what were formerly the Urban Development Corporation and the Job Development Authority. As of this writing, they have not been funded in the state budget, so how much they will be helping small companies and what the programs will be is uncertain.

Here are some past programs. More details are available from the agency at 212-803-3100.

Direct Loan Program. Provides loans of up to 40 percent of the project cost for new and small businesses for acquisition or rehabilitation of plants, and for machinery and equipment. Priority is given to projects that contribute to revitalization of distressed areas.

Energy Investment Loan Program. This is a state loan subsidy at very low interest rates in amounts up to $1 million. The objective is to conserve energy in businesses, housing and farms.

Loan Guarantee Program. Guarantees 80 percent of the cost of loans for the rehabilitation or acquisition of plant facilities for new or expanding businesses.

Minority Revolving Loan Fund. Provides low-cost financing to certified minority- and women-owned businesses.

New York Business Development Corporation (NYBDC). A quasi-public agency that makes term loans to small businesses with varied collateral requirements and the flexibility to collaborate with or complement loans from conventional lenders. Interest rates apt to be high because of the risk involved. Its telephone number is 518-463-2268.

Regional Economic Development Loan Program. Intended to either create or retain jobs in the state.

Rural Development Loan Fund. Provides flexible, low-cost loans to small businesses located in areas with populations of less than 25,000.

Small & Medium Sized Business Assistance Program. Primarily helps finance the acquisition of land, buildings and machinery.

There are other programs administered by local governments, both county and city, either alone or in cooperation with the state, for the benefit of new or small businesses.

All involve dealing with a government bureaucracy of some sort. They are often slow, cumbersome and involve much red tape. Under no circumstances can you expect action that will help you meet next week's payroll. Get started early and you may be able to get financial assistance that is not available from any other source.

⨍ Chapter 35 ⨊

Working With Public Accountants, Bankers and Lawyers

Companies and organizations have personalities just as people do. The personality of the firm is generally determined by the personal style and values of the senior management. I do not suggest that this is either good or bad. It is simply a condition that prevails and should be recognized.

What does this have to do with public accountants, bankers and lawyers? Well, public accounting firms, banks and law firms also have personalities. Some are aggressive, others are conservative and cautious. Some are people-oriented, others are stuffy and formal. Some are willing to work with small, new companies, others consider them a nuisance. Since you will undoubtedly want a close working relationship with your public accountant, banker and lawyer, it's important that you're comfortable with the personality of the organization you select.

Determining the personality of a public accounting firm, bank or law firm is not easy. One way to start is to talk to present and former clients. Another way is to interview a number of firms, being very candid in the process. By doing this, you are more likely to be satisfied with your choice.

In addition, you must recognize that even though these organizations have unique personalities, the day-to-day relationship in all cases is based upon working with one person or a small group of individuals within the larger unit. These tend to be person-to-person relationships. You must decide whether you are comfortable with the person assigned to your account. If you are not, talk to the head of the organization and ask that someone else be assigned. If for some reason your request is refused, change firms.

The costs of these services is another complex issue. All are expensive—accountants and lawyers in the form of fees, banks in the form of interest and/or fees. In your effort to keep your expenses down, I suggest you deal with the question of the cost of these services in an open and aggressive manner. Ask for a list of hours spent, rates charged, services provided and fees charged other clients. Do not hesitate to challenge any items you consider unreasonable. Very few people do this. The minimum benefit is that they will be more careful in the future and the likelihood is that they will simply reduce the charge. In all cases, removing the irritant will lead to a better relationship.

Finally, I am frequently asked whether it is wise to ask public accountants, bankers or lawyers to serve as directors of a company. Public accountants are not permitted by their professional code of ethics to serve on the board of directors of a client firm. It is a conflict that interferes with their objectivity. Both bankers and lawyers are hired by the firm to provide specialized services. You want directors who are objective and can represent your shareholders without conflicting demands on their loyalty. No person can be expected to be a paid provider of services *and* an independent director at the same time. A banker on the board is unlikely to advise you to change banks. A lawyer on the board is unlikely to advise you to change law firms.

In addition to the conflict issue, you should not waste a board position by adding expertise that you're already buying. Fill your board with experts in marketing, engineering, distribution, finance, etc., areas mainstream to your business. Now let's get specific.

Public accountants

The relationship between a company and its public accountant is an unusual one. Even though the accountants are selected by the management and paid by the company, to a large extent they really represent the shareholders. In addition, they are required to act in accordance with well-defined professional accounting standards, because their opinions are used by outside agencies—banks, the IRS, etc.—to make judgments about the firm. They have responsibilities to others, as well as to their client. They are, and must remain, independent, and as a result, do not push easily.

In practice, the public accountant reviews the financial data of the firm—profit and loss statements, balance sheets and use of funds—and certifies that they have been prepared in accordance with accepted accounting standards. They check inventories and accounts receivable and generally mess around in the company's books. In addition, each year they give their clients what is called a management letter, which comments on internal procedures and controls.

One decision an entrepreneur must make is whether to use a major national accounting firm, a large regional firm or a small firm with just a few professionals. The big firms are likely to offer expertise in more specialized areas of accounting and have larger support staffs. They also provide substantial financial credibility, which new companies need badly. With a smaller firm, you are likely to get more attention from the senior professionals. They may be more responsive, and have lower hourly rates.

As I mentioned, good public accounting firms are expensive. However, because many understand the cash flow problems of a new company, they're often willing to work at reduced fees for the first year or so.

Some companies I know put their auditing work out to bid among several public accounting firms, with the intention of picking the lowest bidder. I advise against this. Instead, pick the firm you want for reasons other than price, then negotiate fees.

There are several other cautions in dealing with public accountants. The person with whom you deal, your main contact, is apt to be at least a manager and probably a partner. However, the person they send to your office or plant to do the work may be their most recent new hire with a bachelor's degree in accounting. And worse yet, every year it is a different person. This is a tough one to deal with, and if it bothers you, complain.

Another thing to keep in mind is that your public accounting firm may intimidate your internal controller, if you have one. The role of the public accountant is not to tell you what you should or should not do, but rather to tell you whether what you decided to do is acceptable. As a matter of principle, you should have a relationship in which you make the decisions, and then the accountant can determine their acceptability.

Finally, in dealing with public accountants, when the chips are down, they have the last say. If you cannot reach agreement with them on how some financial matter should be handled, they will simply either refuse to give you an unqualified opinion or describe their position on the issue under dispute in a note to the financial statement. Since it is important for a company to have an unqualified opinion, your only alternatives will be to either accept their position or try another public accountant.

I do not want to make it sound as if the relationship between a company and its public accountant must be adversarial. In fact, when your new company grows enough to need a controller, you will probably hire the person managing your account at your public accounting firm.

Bankers

You deal with banks in a number of ways. First, you will surely need many of the services they provide—for example, a payroll account or registrar and transfer agent for your stock. These are services for which, in some form or other, you pay a fee. Then, sooner or later, you are likely to need to borrow from your bank for working capital, inventory or a mortgage on a building. The service part of the relationship is simple. It becomes more complex when you start to borrow.

Early in my adult life, I had a hard time overcoming the attitude that a bank was doing me a favor when it loaned me money. Banks are in business to lend and unless they can find good borrowers, they will not be successful. Shake the attitude that banks are doing the borrower a favor, but remember that many bankers feel that way.

Also, remember the underlying philosophy of most banks when lending. They do not make loans when they think there may be any significant risk. Some people think that banks adjust the interest rates up and down to compensate for risk. That is not the case. If they think there is significant risk—no loan. I discussed this question recently with two bank presidents. One said I was entirely right, the other said it was not true. Test it yourself.

The next thing banks worry about is how they will be paid back. They want to see their interest covered by earnings and the principal covered by liquidation of whatever the money was used for. For example, if the loan is to finance a capital purchase, it must be paid back from depreciation. If the loan is to finance receivables, it must be paid back when the receivables are collected.

As a practical matter, you will have no trouble borrowing from most banks, provided you do not need the money very badly. In this way, the bank can be sure the loan is safe and will be paid promptly. Establish your line of credit, and perhaps even borrow when you do not need a loan and repay promptly. Sounds silly, doesn't it? But believe me, this is good advice. There is nothing like a history of good credit to make you attractive to a banker.

During the late 1980s and early 1990s, many banks experienced serious financial difficulties. The number of bank failures was on the verge of becoming a national disaster. The federal agency that insured bank deposits was forever running out of money. Many of the foreign loans made by the large commercial banks were turning bad, as were many of the more borderline domestic real estate loans. These were very hard times for the banking industry.

Recently banks have made a comeback. However, another factor has made it difficult for small businesses to get loans. With interest rates near all-time lows, banks can get almost as good a return putting their money into U.S. government securities, where there is no risk, as they can from loans to private firms

How does this effect the small company trying to get a loan from a bank? The bottom line is that it is still very hard. What could have been an acceptable loan situation five years ago may not even be considered today. I don't have any clever answers to this dilemma, other than to suggest, as is suggested in other sections of the book, that you better have a good business plan and you better be a good sales person if you want to be successful in obtaining a loan.

Victoria Posner, who consults with several government agencies that make loans to small businesses, says that many small business people are extremely naive when applying and do not present a very attractive deal to the lender. (Ms. Posner wrote Chapter 28 of this book, covering the question of how a small business person should apply for a loan.)

When lending to small companies, most banks demand the personal guarantees of the firms' officers. This means that you must pledge as security all of your savings, the equity in your home and everything else of value that you own. Their logic is that if the officers do not have enough confidence in the company to personally guarantee the loans, it is too risky a deal for them. I feel very uncomfortable guaranteeing loans and have always refused to do so. Nonetheless, my guess is that until your company has substantial sales and earnings, personal guarantees might be necessary.

It seems that new bank customers almost always get better deals than present customers, so shopping around is often a good practice. Obviously, it is not acceptable to change banks every six months. However, you can change once in a while, you can let your current bank know that it is a possibility and you might even do business routinely with more than one bank.

Finally, I have found it very difficult to determine with any degree of certainty what banks charge for their services. For instance, you borrow money at an agreed-upon interest rate and then learn that you are expected to keep a sizable balance in your account, at zero interest. We all know about mortgage loans where, in addition to interest, you must pay several points of closing costs, plus the cost for the bank's attorney to protect the bank against you.

Lawyers

There is no question in my mind that the United States has five times as many lawyers as it needs. They are all struggling to make a decent living, and we have become a litigious society in which everyone seems to be suing each other.

Be that as it may, in starting and running a business you have no alternative but to use a lawyer, and clearly, it is desirable to use a good one. The services they provide include setting up the corporation, advising you on securities regulations, assisting you in negotiations, preparing various types of contracts, counseling you on how to handle employee issues, and patent and copyright issues.

However, what constitutes a good lawyer from a business person's viewpoint is not entirely clear. Lawyers tend to be very conservative, and many are inclined to tell you why everything you want to do is not a very good idea because of the risk involved. In the company I started, we were fortunate to have as one of the founders a young attorney who had a lot of entrepreneurial qualities. He was creative and imaginative in handling the raising of capital. And during the years that RF Communications was an independent company, he was always thinking ahead and prodding us to be more aggressive. Part of this may be a result of the fact that we were personal friends before we had a professional relationship.

You sometimes hear lawyers talking about justice, that the practice of law involves trying to find just and fair solutions to disagreements and disputes. That is complete nonsense; most lawyers have no interest whatsoever in justice. All they want to do is to win! And that's the way it should be. If you ever hear your lawyer begin to talk about justice, find yourself another lawyer. You want a lawyer who works for you!

In most business situations, I suggest that you use your lawyer as much as possible for review of your work, rather than as an originator of work. You prepare the agreements and ask for their review and comments, rather than having them prepare the agreements for your comments. This will keep your costs down.

Finally, law is a very complex field. Most attorneys concentrate in fairly narrow specialties. One of these specialties is corporate or business law. By all means, use an attorney who specializes in business law, rather than divorce or real estate. Business law is complex, and your needs will only be satisfied by an attorney who is expert in this field.

These three professional groups (public accountants, bankers, and lawyers) are all very important to a start-up business. Their value will be much greater if the entrepreneur understands the relationship and deals with it in an aggressive manner.

✦ Chapter 36 ✧

Staffing Up,
Staffing Down

The ability to hire people fast when they are required—and fire people fast when they're not—is an important skill the head of any company must have. A new firm, particularly, cannot afford the luxury of putting people on staff in anticipation of need or keeping them when orders and cash flow say they cannot be afforded. Many entrepreneurs share a common fault—they are either unwilling or emotionally unable to make fast, decisive hiring and firing decisions.

Hiring is essentially a random process, while firing is very selective. Consider for a moment that most hiring is done with very little information. It is often based upon reading a resume, conducting several interviews and checking references. All of these are suspect. A resumes can be exaggerated, most references are innocuous and interviews are at best marginal, especially if a candidate has a lot of charm and personal presence.

You do the best you can in finding and evaluating a candidate, you try to be thorough in checking credentials, but when all is said and done, hiring decisions are largely intuitive. If your intuition is particularly good, you may have a good hiring record.

On the other hand, when you decide to terminate an employee, it is usually after working with the person for several years. You have had a chance to examine his or her skills first-hand and compare his or her performance to others. You usually fire only after an agonizing period of evaluation and review and after several personal interviews with the person. The process is very selective. Almost everyone does a better job in picking people to fire than they do in picking people to hire. Unfortunately, carrying out the decision to fire is as unpleasant as it is necessary.

I have heard, but have never put into practice, the suggestion that the bottom 10 percent of staff should be terminated once a year. Start by ranking everyone who works for you. Rank highest those you would least like to lose. Then fire the bottom 10 percent. It sounds heartless, but most organizations would benefit from this practice. Because of the random nature of hiring and the selective nature of firing, the overall quality of your staff would be certain to improve. The ability to staff up and staff down in a timely and decisive manner is an important personal quality in an entrepreneur.

The rest of this chapter will discuss a number of other staffing issues that new companies almost always face.

Relationships with former employers

When individuals quit a job in a big firm to start a new company, it is common for them to look upon the past employer as a source of business. Often, entrepreneurs are successful in obtaining orders from their former employers. Once having gotten the business, the new company faces the problem of hiring people to do the work. And where is the natural place to look? To the same former employer!

Obviously, this is a conflict. You cannot use the same source for both orders and new employees. I tell the start-up companies I am involved with that they must decide which is more important.

When my associates and I left General Dynamics to form RF Communications, we immediately hired a few people from our former employer, and we also embarked on an aggressive effort to secure business from them. Since we had left on friendly terms, this looked feasible. Within a few months, we negotiated a fairly large contract for product development work. The final step was for a General Dynamics attorney to send us a proposed contract. Included in the conditions was an acknowledgment that when we left we would be taking proprietary information and trade secrets with us. Apparently, he thought we were naive. We did not accept it, negotiations bogged down and we did not get the order.

In retrospect, he did us a favor. Over the next few years, we recruited many skilled people from General Dynamics at very low cost, because we had virtually no hiring or relocation expense. It was not a conscious decision at the time, but in effect, we had decided to use them as a source of employees, rather than as a source of business.

Compaq Computer, one of the fastest-growing companies in U.S. history, was founded in 1982 by Rod Canion, its first president, and two other engineers from Texas Instruments. By mid-1987, Compaq had a total of 27 vice presidents, 17 of whom were also from TI. Since TI sued Compaq shortly after it started, the question of getting business from their former employer was not an issue.

Salary policy

During our early staffing of RF, we did run into one hitch. When interviewing professional people from General Dynamics, we came to the question of salary. Our policy was to offer a 10 percent increase over their current salary. At the time, 20 to 25 percent was customary for people changing jobs, but since relocation was not required, we thought 10 percent was sufficient, and for a while this policy worked.

Then one day, we had a call from a young engineer who had been offered and had accepted a position with us. When he went to his supervisor to resign, he was offered a 25-percent pay increase to stay. He asked whether we proposed to match it. We said, "No, thank you," and wished him luck. The last thing we wanted was a bidding war we could not afford. From then on, we told people we were trying to hire that they would have to come to work for us at the same pay they had been earning—no raise. How strange! Yet it worked.

It put us under great pressure to make working for RF attractive, and to identify benefits we could offer that General Dynamics could not. This was almost like a pricing decision. We had one benefit—the stock option. Almost every professional at RF Communications received a stock option, a perk that General Dynamics was not allowed to match. So when the young engineers were offered 25 percent raises to stay, they could say no. They were not leaving because of salary, so they would not stay because of salary. This is a good example of how a small company can innovate in the area of hiring policy.

Union problems

After RF was in business for several years, we sensed rumblings among our hourly employees that some might be interested in a union. The last thing a new company, or any company for that matter, needs is a union. I had no experience or any meaningful knowledge on how to deal with the situation.

At the time, I was teaching an evening business strategy course in a local MBA program that involved inviting senior executives from local firms to speak to the class. I decided to invite the president of a labor union. During the discussion, I had a student ask the union president the following question: "If you were the head of a company and did not want a union, what would you do?" His response, almost without thinking, was: "Provide a grievance path without fear of retribution and adhere strictly to seniority, especially in firing."

Boy, was that good advice! Both are complex issues. I will discuss only the seniority question here. Whenever a company faces cutbacks because of bad business, the temptation is to use it as an opportunity to clean house. Get rid of the poor performers. Just a few paragraphs earlier, I told you the benefits of this practice. However, the time you make layoffs for financial reasons is not the time to clean house. You should, instead, lay off poor performers when business is good. Everyone in your organization knows the poor performers. The boss is the last to know. So if you terminate poor performers during good times, your people will applaud the move. Then if you must lay off because of bad business, you have at least a chance of honoring seniority.

Contract employees

Over the past few years, many companies have begun using contract employees rather than hiring regular, full-time employees. This is something you might consider, since it has a number of important benefits. Usually this is done through a contract company. The people are assigned to you to perform whatever work you give them under your supervision. Officially, they are employees of the contract firm and receive their paychecks from that firm. Their employer, not you, is responsible for income tax withholding, Social Security payments and other mandated expenses. You are then billed by the contract firm for the services provided.

At the end of 1995, it was estimated that there were about 2.2 million people in the temporary work force, most in the categories of secretarial and blue-collar workers. But this is changing fast, because in the past few years, a greater number of professionals have lost jobs than hourly workers. This means that companies are now beginning to fill more professional and management positions with temporaries.

The advantages of using contract people is that it does not require you to make a permanent commitment. If you need people only for a short term assignment or to carry you through a peak workload, you can arrange the contract accordingly. When the contract ends, the services end and it is not necessary for you to terminate the people involved.

In addition, if you eventually end up hiring the contract employee, you have in effect found a way to learn how good they are before you make the hiring decision. The short-term costs may be higher, but the long-term benefits can be great.

A word of caution is in order, since you may at some time or other retain people as independent contractors without going through an intermediary. In many circumstances, the Internal Revenue Service frowns on this practice, because it may be an attempt on the company's part to avoid the cost of Social Security and

the necessity of withholding income tax, etc. The IRS has established some very specific guidelines that define when someone qualifies as an independent contractor. Be sure you become familiar with these guidelines, since you could be subject to severe penalties if you end up in the wrong. If you are in doubt about this question, be sure to contact your lawyer for advice.

Less painful firing

Finally, on the subject of firing, I recognize that this is a difficult, even agonizing, process for many. Of all the things about being a boss that I do not like, firing ranks first place.

After RF Communications became part of Harris, my new boss, Dr. Joseph Boyd, gave me some advice I have never forgotten. It is the kind of advice I should have been smart enough to figure out for myself years earlier.

He suggested that firing should be the result of two decisions. First, decide whether the individual is good enough for the job he or she holds. If so, there is no problem. If not, the employee must be removed from that job.

After you have decided to remove the person, the second decision is how to treat that employee fairly. For a long-term employee, counseling or additional training may help, or you might change his or her job. Large companies often sweeten the retirement benefits to encourage people to leave voluntarily. This may be too expensive for the small firm. Or you might terminate the person with a generous severance allowance, and help him or her find another job.

If you make the firing process two decisions instead of one, the job will be much easier. In this way, you are more likely to make a careful, fair decision. If you remember nothing else from this book other than this two-part process, you will have been repaid its cost at least a thousand times over.

One caution is in order. It is usually smart to adhere to a formal, written procedure of informing individuals in advance that their performance is not satisfactory. Explain why and give them a specific timetable over which to improve. This may have to be done several times, in order to avoid problems with unemployment benefits or being challenged about your treatment of minorities, women and the handicapped.

Also, federal, state and local laws governing interviewing, hiring, promoting, drug and HIV testing, firing, continuation of health benefits following termination, etc., are complex and change frequently. The Civil Rights Act of 1991, for example, extends the right to a jury trial and punitive and expanded compensatory damages to victims of intentional job discrimination, and a recent Americans With Disabilities Act extends employment protection to the disabled. Even more recently, a federal Family Leave Act was passed, requiring companies to permit employees to take unpaid leave without penalty for various personal reasons. The courts must still resolve major questions on how these and other employment practice laws apply in specific cases. Seek legal counsel if you have any questions about the laws relating to any of these issues.

In summary, the staffing up and staffing down of a new business is a very tough problem. It requires the vision to see when it is necessary, and the courage to do it decisively. No one but the head of the company can decide. Of underlying importance here, as almost everywhere, is the question of limited resources and the need to aggressively manage cash flow. You will get no credit for letting a company go bust because of your inability to make difficult hiring and firing decisions.

Chapter 37

Reviewing Performance and Setting Standards

When RF Communications became a division of Harris Corp., many people thought that we would be overwhelmed by the bureaucracy and red tape of the large corporation, that we would lose our ability to react fast to customer needs and lose the freedom to be innovative and imaginative in our management. I would not be telling the truth if I said the merger occurred without problems, and some of them are described in another chapter of this book. But the relationship with Harris had many benefits for RF, because they encouraged us to do things that we should have been doing years earlier as an independent company.

One thing Harris introduced at RF was a Management Manpower Development Program (MMP). This program provided me with a number of very powerful management tools. The MMP had several different elements:

♦ Appraise the performance of all managers at least annually, using a standard form as a guide.

♦ Review the results of this appraisal with each person.

♦ Suggest to the employee how he or she could improve performance and what the company was prepared to do to help.

♦ Agree on performance goals for the coming year.

♦ Identify and evaluate replacement candidates for key positions.

Shown in this chapter is a form that can be used for individual appraisals. This is not the same form that was used by Harris. It is somewhat simplified to better meet the needs of a smaller company. Notice that it starts with basic information about the employee. The heart of the appraisal, however, includes the next three sections—results, methods and qualifications.

In the results section, the appraiser lists the accomplishments of the individual during the period covered by the appraisal. This includes quantitative measures where possible and applicable—such as growth in sales, inventory levels, profits, costs and number of orders. It should also include qualitative accomplishments, such as effective leadership or innovative ideas.

The next section, called methods, includes comments on how the employee achieved the results. This is important if the results were less than satisfactory, because the methods used may be the explanation for the poor results. Failures here might include the inability to get along with people, being overly aggressive (this has been a problem for me on more than one occasion) and failure to plan in an organized manner.

The third section, called qualifications, is important if the employee rates poorly on both results and methods. It may indicate that the person is in the wrong job, or that specific job training is needed.

The employee is then given an overall performance rating, Above Standard, Standard, Below Standard or Critical. The appraisal should also include suggestions as to what the individual should do to improve his or her performance, their potential in the organization, possible backups and goals for the coming year.

The first time I did an appraisal of the five senior managers reporting directly to me, it was an agonizing process on which I spent many hours. At the end, I met privately with each manager and explained how I rated his or her performance. Was I in for a surprise! Doing these appraisals was very hard for me. Learning the results was even harder for the five managers.

As I mentioned, RF Communications had very serious business problems for several years following the merger with Harris. These first appraisals were done during those difficult times.

I gave one individual an overall rating of standard, and I thought he was going to explode. He was one of the hardest working, most highly motivated and smartest people I have ever met, and he was very unhappy with any rating other than the highest. After a long session where we were unable to reach accord, he finally said, "All right, I will accept this rating for now, but I want you to tell me what I have to do next year to be rated above standard." I answered, "That sounds reasonable, but instead of me telling you what you have to do, why don't you tell me what you have to do to improve your rating." I added that he should give it to me in writing—one page maximum.

A week or so later, we met again and he handed me his list. I had no trouble accepting it, because he set goals for himself that I do not think he would have ever accepted from me. They were very tough. In doing this, I learned another management lesson—people will usually set more difficult goals for themselves than they will accept from their supervisor.

This approach had an unexpected benefit. A year later when I evaluated this person the second time, it was very easy. I pulled out the set of goals we had agreed on a year earlier and he either met them or did not meet them. What took me several hours the first time took about 15 minutes the second time. Obviously, his rating went up.

Another one of my managers was rated below standard. During the review, I let him know what I considered his shortcomings and told him he'd better improve quite a bit in the coming year or his job would be in jeopardy. A week or so later, the man's wife called me on the telephone and I thought, "What am I in for now?" To my complete surprise, she thanked me. I asked her why she was thanking me when I just gave her husband a bad review and told him his job was in jeopardy. Her answer was, "At last he knows how he is doing and what is expected of him. He is determined to show you how good he can be."

In a third case, where I also rated the manager below standard, the individual came into my office about six months later and asked me to do another review. I asked why he wanted this, because it was not scheduled until the end of the year. His answer was that he was very anxious to know whether he was on the right track.

In all three of these examples, the appraisal process forced me through the discipline of reviewing employees in an organized manner and letting them know the results. Instead of turning the people off, it turned them on, even though in two of the cases I rated their performance as below standard.

The last step of the process required me to meet at corporate headquarters with my boss, the president of Harris, his boss, the Chairman and an outside consultant to review my entire organization. They had each received advance copies of the appraisals covering two levels of management down from me, or a total of about 30 people. In the front of the meeting room, there was a large board to which was attached a card for each employee, summarizing his or her performance. The cards were arranged like an organizational chart. A sample of the card is included in this chapter. The cards

were color coded, blue for above standard, green for standard, red for below standard and striped for critical. This gave the group a good overview of the strengths and weaknesses of my organization.

During several hours of discussion, I had a chance to identify problems and tell what I planned to do about them. We pinpointed those people with the greatest future potential, areas where a stronger back-up manager was needed, etc. I had the benefit of the counsel and suggestions of three people for whom I had the greatest respect. Not mentioned, but obvious, was that during this meeting they were also rating me.

This process may sound complicated—and it is complicated the first time you go through it. But it is a powerful tool for running a business, and once the novelty wears off, the people involved accept it willingly, because its purpose is to help them become better at their job.

The type of formal appraisal and review process described here, or some variation of this process, is necessary to efficiently manage any business with more than a handful of people. It gives you the information you need to be sure you are on the right track. And it provides your people with helpful feedback on how you view their performance and what is expected of them to improve their career potential. How big should you be before you develop a formal appraisal and review process? It's not entirely clear, but better too soon than too late.

Management Appraisal (Confidential)

Name: Period covered:

Position: Department:

Previous position: Department:

Years in position: Years with company:

Total number of employees supervised:

RESULTS: (Be as specific as possible. Give numerical data where possible, i.e., sales, profit, inventory level, orders, etc. Compare actual results to goals for the period.)

METHODS: (Be as specific as possible. Include factors such as ability to handle people, planning skills, leadership skills, willingness to tackle unpleasant tasks, etc. If Results are less than satisfactory, try to determine whether Methods may be a contributing factor.)

**(Management Appraisal Form
Page 2)**

QUALIFICATIONS: (Describe educational background, experience and performance in previous positions. If Results are less than satisfactory and Methods do not explain the problem, try to identify whether Qualifications are adequate for the position.)

RATING: **PREVIOUS RATING:**
(Above Standard, Standard, Below Standard or Critical)

PLANS FOR IMPROVEMENT:

POTENTIAL IN ORGANIZATION:

POTENTIAL BACKUPS:

GOALS FOR COMING YEAR:

Date of Appraisal: Appraiser's Name:

Position: Signature:

Sample of card used in overall organizational review

Photo	Name:
	Position:
	Dept.:
	Years in Position:
	Number Supervised:
Rating:	Previous Rating:
Potential:	
Backup:	

Color Code

ᛎ Chapter 38 ᛏ

Who Needs a Mentor?

Every entrepreneur needs help of some sort. Few people starting a business have ever started a business before. Almost without exception, the process of planning, starting and managing a business is a new experience. Virtually everything that they do, they do for the first time.

Where do you go for entrepreneurship training? Nowhere! I suggested earlier that entrepreneurship is a vocation for which there is no apprenticeship.

Because of this, it is important and extremely helpful for the new entrepreneur to have a mentor—an individual or small group to turn to for advice and guidance. A mentor should be someone you trust, someone you can share confidential information with and who you can talk to openly and candidly. Ideally, you should choose someone who also started a company, hopefully in a business related to yours.

One way to accomplish this is through your board of directors, if you have one, or some type of advisory committee or advisory board if you do not. Directors tend to be more effective than advisers because they have power to make change, but either can be very helpful in the management of a company.

In establishing either a formal board or advisory group, pick people who bring functional experience and wisdom as well. In developing the basic strategy for your business, hopefully you will have tried to identified the key factors required for success. Is it mostly a marketing company or is your main thrust advanced technical products? If your board members have expertise in these key areas, you will have formed a powerful support group of immeasurable value.

How do you attract such people willing to spend time with you, and what compensation or reward should you offer them? One approach is to draw upon friendship. This may work for a short period or for occasional contact, but it is not a satisfactory long-term solution. You cannot be in the position of continually requesting favors.

Another approach is to turn to the investors in your company. This is perhaps the best way, because you can be assured of their interest and generally speaking, their incentive will be the same as yours. The bigger the investment, the more the interest. Or if all else fails, you should compensate your board with either money or some type of equity arrangement.

I advise people starting a new business against asking the head of a large company to be on their board. Such a person would add respectability and probably wisdom, but the likelihood is that they will be too busy to give you much time.

I have been a board member of a number of start-up companies. In each, I had either a very large cash investment, a sizable stock holding or both. With one exception, where friendship was the connection, I would not serve on a board unless I had a significant stake. I refused to be involved where my principal role was to attract investors.

In an earlier chapter, I suggested that you avoid putting lawyers or bankers on your board, or for that matter, anyone whose services you are already buying, unless friendship is a strong factor. A number of years ago, I was on the board of a large New York Stock Exchange company. The board included two lawyers and two bankers. When time came to vote on some important issue, several would almost always disqualify themselves because of conflicts. On one important decision as to whether to relocate the headquarters of a major division, all four disqualified themselves. That was a heck of a board.

Finally, I usually advise the heads of companies not to put many of the employees of the company on either the formal or advisory board. Again, the conflict will discourage them from making critical comments in front of outsiders, because it might put their own position in jeopardy.

In dealing with directors and advisers, you must be honest and candid. Seek their counsel on significant problems, especially where they may have already faced similar problems. And listen more than you talk. Nothing turns a mentor off faster than being told why everything he or she suggests has already been tried or may not be a good idea. Establish a working relationship and seek advice on key issues, but reserve the right to make your own decisions.

In the start ups on whose boards I served, I always encouraged monthly meetings. This does not take up too much time for either management or board members, yet it's frequent enough that problems will not get out of hand between meetings. I have found that meeting every two months or quarterly does not seem quite often enough. Whenever the frequency was reduced, something usually happened to make us regret it.

A board of directors or board of advisers can be a powerful asset to a new business, especially where a mentor relationship also exists. However, you should select the people for what they can contribute, not for show. And do not waste board positions on people whose services you're already buying.

✒ Chapter 39 ✑

What Is Really Important?
Operating Lean and Mean

One of the most difficult management challenges faced by the head of a new business is trying to identify those things that are critical to the success of the business and those factors that contribute little or nothing. By devoting all of your limited resources to the important factors and avoiding spending money on the unimportant things, you will be able to get much more mileage from your limited resources. Cutting back on or eliminating all unimportant expenditures is what I call running a lean and mean operation.

Unfortunately, many entrepreneurs, trained in the culture of a large company, have a great deal of trouble separating the "wheat from the chaff." I could name many things that employees of big companies become accustomed to and just assume to be a way of life in the business world. These include things such as expensive stationery, paved parking lots, pictures on the wall, private telephone extensions and numerous service and support functions. Three that I like to use as examples are the size and elegance of the facility the new business acquires, "make-or-buy" decisions and staff support.

One of the early decisions in every start up is the selection of a place of business. Many entrepreneurs envision a facility far more elaborate than is needed. Is a posh office important? Will customers visit very often? And to what extent will the elegance of the quarters contribute to getting orders? It may very well be that a fancy facility will turn off potential customers, because it raises the question of prudent use of capital and fundamental business judgment.

Another argument for modest quarters is that it sets the proper tone for the entire organization. If one person has a large office with elegant furniture, others expect the same. The attitude that I took as the head of a start-up company was to always have a small, very conservatively furnished office. Since everyone else had to be satisfied with offices a little smaller and a little more Spartan than the president's, the office situation never became a problem. When shopping for a factory or office for your new business, remember that Apple Computer and Hewlett-Packard both started in garages, and RF Communications started in a basement.

An exception to the above is a retail business, where location may be the most important early decision the founder makes. However, this is also a matter of setting values consistent with the character of the business. In this case, the character and nature of the business may require a big investment in the store location. If this is true, you will have to identify other areas of lesser importance where you can economize.

Another important issue involves the purchase of capital equipment and make-or-buy decisions. At RF Communications, our products were complex electronics devices that needed fairly expensive metal cabinets and chassis—fabricated sheet metal parts. Should we purchase these from outside sources or set up a shop with the machinery necessary to make them ourselves? There were arguments on both sides.

Our decision was to purchase all fabricated metal parts from outside vendors, because we felt that investing in new products and greater marketing effort were more productive ways to use our limited resources. Many new businesses try to do everything themselves and lose sight of their true distinctive competence. In an electronics firm, it is unlikely that skill at fabricating metal parts will ever be an important strength.

If you find you must make capital purchases, consider leasing rather than outright purchase. Leasing can slow down cash expenditures in a meaningful way. A lease has several other advantages in that it is usually much easier to obtain than a bank loan, and the value of the item being leased may not have to appear as a liability on your balance sheet.

A final example relates to staff support. When I see a company with five employees and a full-time financial manager, I am pretty sure they are doing something wrong. When I see a company with fewer than 30 or 40 employees with a full-time personnel manager, I am pretty sure they are doing something wrong. When I see a new company doing its own payroll, rather than using an outside service such as Paychex, I am pretty sure they are doing something wrong.

People in large firms are accustomed to a lot of staff support. It is very easy to forget that many of these functions can either be taught to a secretary, combined in one individual or simply ignored.

Sharpen your sense of values to isolate the functions that really contribute to the success of the business. Concentrate your resources and energy on them. Resist the pressure, which will be continuous and considerable, to spend much time and money on unnecessary trappings.

✄ Chapter 40 ✃

Patents, Copyrights, Trademarks and Trade Secrets

Mr. William R. Alexander, Esq., of the law firm Petralia, Webb & O'Connell, specializing in corporate and intellectual property law, and Ronald S. Kareken, Esq., of the law firm Jaeckle, Fleischmann & Mugel, specializing in patents and intellectual property law, both in Rochester, N.Y., provided considerable assistance and suggestions in the preparation of this chapter.

The problems associated with protecting an idea, invention or other intellectual property is one that certainly should be discussed in a book about entrepreneurship and starting a business. Unfortunately, this is a subject about which I have little knowledge and almost no practical experience. There are numerous books on this subject at your bookstore and library. I encourage you to read as many as you think you need, in order to make an intelligent decision as to whether you should secure patent, copyright, trademark or trade secret protection, or whether you should worry about the protection others may have.

Also, I encourage you to get advice from an attorney experienced in these areas. These are complex questions that require expert counsel. Sometimes the protections overlap and many are covered by both state and federal laws, making it even more difficult to be sure that what you are doing is right. Also, if you do business overseas, many countries have laws that are different than ours that should be considered. The following discussion is a brief review of the subject with comments on several related issues. The four separate areas in which protection should be considered are:

♦ Patent: A nonrenewable right granted by the U.S. Patent Office to prevent others from making, using or selling an idea covered by your invention.

♦ Copyright: Protects the work of an author or the expression of an idea—not the idea itself.

♦ Trademark: Word or design that distinguishes or differentiates a certain source of goods or services from the goods or services of others.

♦ Trade secret: Includes unpatented technology or internal business information that may give your company a competitive advantage.

Here are several examples. Polaroid protected its inventions relative to instant photography with patents. Coca-Cola is one of the most famous trademarks of all times. The formula for Coca-Cola is a trade secret, access to which is carefully limited within the company. And much of Coca-Cola's advertising and other public information about its products is protected by copyright.

Patents

Patenting an invention is a complex, frequently time-consuming and expensive procedure. It is possible, but difficult, for an individual to secure a patent without the services of an attorney. The protection you get from a patent is determined by what the patent examiner allows in your claims. The broader the claims, the better the protection—but the more difficult it is to get the patent.

Obtaining a patent can take as much as several years and a lot of back-and-forth between the attorney and the patent examiner, but in certain cases, this time period can be longer. The longest that I know of is the patent for the laser, which was issued in 1989, 30 years and $6 million after the initial filing. An interesting twist to this situation was that at that time, the 17-year protection period began when the patent was issued—not when the application was filed. Had the patent for the laser been issued promptly, it may well have expired long before the use of lasers in countless applications became as pervasive as it is today. The good news is that the

delay may have made the patent much more valuable, the bad news is that the inventor was 68 years old before it was issued.

In the United States, an inventor has one year to file an application following the first public disclosure or sale of the item or process being patented. For an individual or small company operating with limited resources, this gives them a chance to test the idea before going to the expense of trying to obtain a patent. Keep in mind, though, that in many other countries, the patent must be filed before any public disclosure or sale of the invention in order to obtain protection. However, you can wait up to one year after filing in the U.S. to file in many other countries. This makes the timing issue much more complex.

Recently, the U.S. agreed to the revisions in GATT (General Agreement on Tariffs and Trade), which changes our patent situation in several important ways. Now if a patent is issued, the protection period will expire 20 years after the filing date, instead of 17 years after the issue date.

Periodic fees are required to maintain a patent, and the term "Patent Pending" generally has no legal significance, other than to discourage copiers.

Another form of protection that I seldom hear discussed is market penetration and customer acceptance of a product. This important form of protection is unrelated to the patent. The difficulty and cost of taking a product to market may be as big a deterrent to a potential competitor as the existence of a patent.

I have seen one situation where the process of getting the maximum possible patent protection, before taking any steps to commercialize the idea, may have hurt the company more than it helped. In that case, the inventor spent several years and thousands of dollars getting patent coverage in many countries before deciding to build and sell the product. My belief is that he may have been better served filing a patent application in the United States and immediately taking the product to market, rather than using so much of his limited resources trying to get worldwide protection. This is another complex question with no right or wrong answer.

Also, be sure any patent you file is significant. I have seen one situation where an electronics company, after being informed that it was infringing a patent, spent about a day designing new circuitry. This avoided the infringement, yet did not significantly change the final product in which the circuitry was used.

A serious difficulty the individual inventor faces is that if a large company takes the risk of infringing a patent, the only remedy the inventor has may be to sue for damages. For someone with limited financial resources, the problems associated with launching and winning a lawsuit against a giant infringer may not be very appealing.

Copyrights

A copyright protects the authorship or expression of an idea. The idea itself is not protected. Copyrights can be obtained for novels, business manuscripts, books about entrepreneurship, paintings, plays, works of art, computer software, etc. Protection begins as soon as the work is fixed in tangible form.

To provide notice of copyright, all you have do is print the word "Copyright" near the beginning of the document or the letter "C" inside a circle, followed by the author's name and the date of first publication. However, I am told that registering your copyright with the Copyright Office is far better protection and well worth the trouble. The address is Copyright Office, Library of Congress, Washington, DC 20559, phone number, 202-707-9100. The Copyright Office also has several circulars with basic information about copyrights. Unlike a patent, though, the job of registering a copyright is fairly simple and relatively inexpensive. I did it myself for the first edition of this book.

Interestingly, while the contents of a publication can be protected by a copyright, the title normally cannot. That is one reason you occasionally see several books with identical or almost identical titles. Titles to some works, such as periodicals and computer software, can sometimes be protected as trademarks.

Trademarks

First, you want to protect the words or designs that distinguish your product or service and, second, you want to be sure that your trademark does not infringe upon or duplicate someone else's mark.

Trademark rights are generally established by use. However, it is better that they be registered for maximum protection. Trademarks used in interstate commerce can be registered with the Patent and Trademark Office, U.S. Department of Commerce, Washington, DC 20231. They have a pamphlet entitled "Basic Facts About Trademarks." In some areas, it may also be advisable to register a Trademark at the state level, especially if the mark is only used in one state.

Also, you may be able to file an application to register on the basis of a "bona fide" intent to use a mark in commerce.

In the one case that I registered a mark, I used an attorney. It was not very expensive and I saved myself the time and trouble of learning how it was done.

I often think about an amusing situation I encountered many years ago when I worked for the Radio Corporation of America as an engineer just out of college. Their trademark were the letters RCA and they protected it with a vengeance. As I recall, two organizations gave them fits, because they apparently used the letters R, C, and A before the Radio Corporation of America even came into existence. One was the Radio Club of America and the other the Rodeo Cowboys Association.

Trade secrets

Consider for a moment the things that you believe may give your company a competitive advantage. This could include a secret formula, manufacturing techniques, customer lists, pricing information and similar things that your competitors would

like to know about. These are your trade secrets. Like any other secret, the best way to protect this material is to avoid disclosing it to anyone. However, that may not be a practical solution. Trade secrets can be protected by a variety of agreements between a company and its employees, customers, licensees, contractors and others to whom the information is disclosed. Sometimes the law will help even if you do not have agreements, but don't count on it.

Most large companies have written agreements with their employees requiring them to assign their inventions to the company, preventing the employee from competing for a given period of time after they leave the company, and requiring that the employee not divulge any confidential information to outsiders or make use of the information for their own benefit, either during or following their employment. Anyone in a technical business or in a business where internal information may have value or may provide a competitive advantage, should consider using such an agreement. Many companies learn too late that without an agreement, they may have no protection or rights to inventions of employees who leave.

In addition, confidentiality agreements are usually required from anyone retained by the company as a consultant or independent contractor.

Also, when you divulge information to another company, such as a potential customer or possible strategic partner, it is worth trying to get them to sign a confidentiality agreement. However, this may not be possible in every situation. For instance, I spend a lot of time with entrepreneurs who are either thinking about or who have already started a business. They come to me for general advice, to review a business plan or to just test an idea. Occasionally they ask me to sign a confidentiality agreement, and I always refuse. My reason is that I have a lot of involvement with new businesses and have no way of knowing whether someone was in to see me yesterday or may come in to see me tomorrow with exactly the same idea. Obviously, I am protecting myself, even though I am extremely careful to treat everything I see or hear during these discussions as confidential, even without an agreement.

Patents, copyrights, trademarks and trade secrets are complex issues. They may or may not be important in your particular situation, but in some cases, they can be the most valuable asset a company has. Early-stage companies should give serious consideration to implementing some type of intellectual property protection program covering all of the valuable information that may be important to their long-term competitive position.

◆ Chapter 41 ◆

Two Plus Two Equals Five— No, Two Plus Two Equals Three: The Theory of Acquisitions

I mentioned earlier that the management skills needed in a small firm are substantially different from those needed in a large firm. Managing a small business is much more of a hands-on proposition. Managers who make the transition from a large organization to a start-up business often have a difficult time adjusting.

The skills needed to manage an acquisition are also substantially different. Most businesspeople do not give this issue sufficient consideration. This is one reason many acquisitions turn out badly. The risk, difficulty and complexity associated with the acquisition process is widely underestimated.

If the company you start is successful, sooner or later you will be faced with the decision of whether to buy another firm in order to grow faster or improve your product and/or market position. My advice here is to proceed with the utmost caution, because it may turn out to be a much harder process than you would think.

The following discussion is entirely from the viewpoint of the acquirer, or purchasing company. The problems associated with selling a business, or being acquired, are entirely different. The four principal reasons one company might acquire another are:

◆ The company wants to offer a new product line or enter a new business. Even though it may have the skills and resources to develop the product, the objective is to do it faster by acquisition. Buying another company, even though much more expensive, might save several years or more. An acquisition buys time.

◆ The company can reduce the risk of developing a new product or entering a new market by acquiring another business. The other company is already there. No matter what your skills, there is always more risk doing it from scratch.

◆ There is the hope that synergism will be achieved. Synergism suggests that the whole is greater than the sum of the parts. Two plus two equals five, so to speak.

- Finally, when a company acquires a much smaller firm, it is believed that the hot new start up will give an infusion of entrepreneurial spirit.

Now for the other side of the story. Through the years, I have been personally involved in the acquisition of four companies. They all turned out badly. In each case, within a few years, the acquired firm was either sold at a loss or permitted to just disappear from sight. Here are a few of the factors that make the acquisition process so difficult:

- Managing a small acquisition is a very time-consuming proposition. It takes a disproportionate amount of effort and energy, especially if the new company is in a remote location or in a substantially different line of business. And the time it takes is usually the time of the senior people. The acquirer will often try to delegate responsibility to a staff or a lower level of management. This tends to flood the acquired firm with red tape and bureaucracy.

- Some people in the acquired company will either leave or lose interest. I had a conversation with a senior manager of a company that had just paid a handsome price to acquire a successful small business. He said several unanticipated problems had developed. Both senior people and lower-level employees were leaving, creating big holes in the operation. I said that neither should have been a surprise.

For the senior people, the acquisition in all likelihood made them rich and liquid. They did not have to work anymore. Sure, they had contracts, but a contract is always more binding on the company than on the employee. You can require people to come to work every day but you cannot force them to do a good job.

For lower-level employees, the situation was a bit different. If they had wanted to work for a larger company they would have. So after the acquisition, there was a drifting away, as they found jobs more to their liking.

- What was previously a very profitable small company is likely to become less profitable after it is acquired by a larger firm. There are several reasons for this. First, the employees of the acquired company become uncertain about their future with the new owner. Work is no longer as much fun as it was before. The tendency is for everyone's commitment to decline.

- Another reason is that small companies tend to be lean and mean, while large firms are not. This may be the main reason the smaller company is profitable. In the acquiring company, offices are probably larger, support staffs larger, fringe benefits more generous, and so on. The natural result is for the smaller unit to emulate its new owner, so everything becomes more expensive. Also, there is an overhead administrative cost imposed on the small unit, to pay for the management services the new owner provides.

The acquired company has to absorb its share of the headquarters staff, the company plane, the president's salary, etc. This can be in the range of 5 to 10 percent of sales, a burden that will have a detrimental effect on profits.

♦ Finally, and perhaps most importantly, there is the possibility that the only reason the owners agreed to sell was that the future no longer looked so bright. Their products were no longer quite as competitive, they had lost some key players, their competitors were suddenly giving them more trouble, etc. The business looked like it was in for some serious problems, and it was time to sell the store.

So it is my belief that two plus two seldom, if ever, equals five. You will be fortunate, indeed, if two plus two equals four, but the likelihood is that two plus two will equal three or less. Charles Exley, retired chairman and CEO of NCR, describes most acquisitions as being like "Two manufacturers of left shoes getting together to build on their combined strengths."

Even very large companies that you would think would have the skills and resources to handle acquisitions in areas unrelated to their core businesses, are often unsuccessful. Many are forced to take immense write-offs in the process of withdrawing from those businesses.

A number of years back, Eastman Kodak Company made a major move entering the pharmaceutical business. As its core photographic business began to have problems, they removed the Chairman and CEO from his position and hired George Fisher, then president of Motorola. One of his first moves was to sell off the drug companies and lead Kodak back to its core business, and he is succeeding.

Another example is Xerox Corp., which several years back acquired Kohlberg, Kravis, Roberts & Co., a large casualty insurer. Reports in the business press are that Xerox's insurance business is now up for sale, and they may have to take a billion dollar write-off in the process.

There are, of course, exceptions. Gannett, one of the country's fastest-growing newspaper chains, and Teledyne, a notable high-tech conglomerate, were each built on a long series of successful acquisitions. My guess is that in both cases, they organized their own firms so that the acquiring process became a distinctive competence, to which they devoted major effort. Acquiring was an important strategic thrust. The following chapter describes what might be done to improve the odds of an acquisition program succeeding.

Another exception is when you purchase a separate, discrete product line rather than the entire business. It will be much easier to integrate the new activity into your operation, thereby minimizing many of the drawbacks of the outright purchase of an entire company.

You will not get an idea of how difficult and risky the acquisition process is by reading corporate annual reports. All you hear about are the acquisitions that work. The bad ones attract little attention.

So be careful.

Chapter 42

Making an Acquisition Work

This chapter was written by Douglas H. McCorkindale, Vice Chairman and Chief Financial & Administrative Officer of the Gannett Co. For more than 20 years, he has been responsible for the very successful Gannett acquisition program. Before that, he was a partner in the New York law firm of Thacher, Profitt & Wood. Doug is a director of Gannett and a number of other organizations and a graduate of Columbia Law School.

Bill Stolze suggests that most acquisitions do not work because the people acquiring do not know how to manage an acquisition, or they make acquisitions for the wrong reasons, or the sellers are selling for the wrong reasons, etc. Bill may be right about many companies, but at Gannett, acquisitions have been an important and successful part of our growth strategy. That's probably why he asked me to write this section of his book.

When Gannett went public in 1967, we had revenues of $110 million and owned 28 newspapers. At the end of 1995, we owned 92 daily newspapers, a variety of nondaily publications, 15 television stations, 13 radio stations, 460,000 cable subscribers, more than 100,000 alarm security services, an entertainment programming unit and the largest outdoor sign company in North America, as well as many other related businesses.

Have all of our acquisitions been successful? No, but it is not an exaggeration to say that more than 90 percent of them have been.

What does Gannett do differently? First of all, we do not buy companies we do not know how to fix if the game plan goes wrong. It's very easy to make acquisitions in an inflationary market with no competition and brag about how successful you have been. The challenge comes when you make acquisitions in markets with a lot of competition during periods of low inflation.

It is Gannett's experience that an acquisition must be analyzed from several different viewpoints. First, and very fundamental, is the question "How do you get the seller to agree to sell?" We spend a lot of time making sure the seller feels at home in Gannett, making sure the seller will stay to run the business (we do not have an excess of managers to run every acquisition) and making the seller's employees feel positive about their future, big-company employer. If the seller wishes to talk about taking Gannett stock as part of the acquisition purchase price, we also try to make them feel comfortable that the stock is a worthwhile investment.

Assuming the seller is ready, Gannett has developed an internal process for analyzing acquisitions and making them work. As we acquired more and more properties, we built a statistical data base to compare the operations of the potential acquisition against our existing properties. We can quickly decide where expenses are too high, where revenues are too low, where the body count is high or low, where rates look out of line, etc.

We combine the analysis with what we think we can give the property in terms of "help from corporate." Help from corporate includes purchasing equipment and supplies (mostly newsprint) at significant discounts.

Gannett does not have a planning department to review acquisitions. They are analyzed by the people who are on the firing line in operations, production, marketing, finance, etc. It's part of their day-to-day job to look into the acquisitions being considered and decide where they fit and how much money they could make if they were part of Gannett. Each operating group gets a chance to provide input. Once we have the overall picture, the pricing decision comes into play.

For almost 30 years, Gannett has used a simple formula—the purchase price must be such that the acquisition should make a contribution to Gannett's operating profit within three or four years. We estimate the long-term cost of money and calculate what the operating profit must be to exceed the cost of money plus the goodwill write-off, if any. There is generally a large goodwill write-off in media acquisitions. If we can find a way to obtain the necessary operating profit in the required time frame, all the customary equations and calculations used to analyze financial performance generally fall into place.

Over the years, the formula has worked reasonably well in all lines of business, but some lines of business are less predictable than others, and more care must be taken. Newspapers and, until the 1990s, the outdoor sign business, have generally been the easiest to predict. Television is somewhat more risky, so the game plan must get us to No. 1 or No. 2 in local news in the particular market. Local news is where success starts. The radio business is even more volatile and, accordingly, the success ratio has been more challenging.

On the people side, once an acquisition is completed, the opportunity is almost unlimited within the Gannett Co. We make that known to the employees at acquired companies at a very early stage. If the employees, or even the seller who decides to stay on, want to move up, the opportunity is there. A number of present Gannett senior executives came to the company as a result of acquisitions.

Finally, an additional factor that has made Gannett's acquisition program successful is that we don't have many "rules" that "must be followed." We don't argue over fringe benefits that are important to sellers. We just consider them part of the purchase price. We don't say we will only do a deal in one form. We're flexible and try to meet the sellers' needs. We'll use stock, cash, notes or any combination of the above.

We don't try to nickel and dime sellers so that they feel like they have been taken to the cleaners. They generally sell only once—we buy often. It's a very difficult experience for the seller, and we understand that.

Having said all that, however, if the economics described above don't work, then we simply pass on the opportunity. We do not have any "need" to do an acquisition just for the sake of doing one. As a result, we passed up many acquisition opportunities in the late 1980s, when prices got out of control. Some of the properties were re-offered to us by buyers who paid too much, who assumed the world would always be a better place and that inflation would cure their mistakes.

At Gannett's corporate office, we strive to remain financially strong so we can take advantage of acquisition opportunities whenever they become available. We have learned that we cannot plan for a certain number or certain size of acquisitions to happen every year. We have to be ready to act when the opportunity strikes. For example, in the mid-1980s, we completed $1.2 billion in acquisitions in about 18 months. A number of properties we thought would never be available all came on the market at the same time. In December of 1995, we closed the $2.3 billion acquisition of Multimedia—a company we had been following since the early 1970s. We manage our finances always keeping in mind that the next big acquisition may be just around the corner.

So, it is possible to succeed in the business of making acquisitions. But we have found that it is necessary for it to be part of the basic strategy of your company, to which you commit considerable resources. You must be prepared to make a move when the opportunity occurs, and you must understand that you cannot expect 100 percent success.

⟨ Chapter 43 ⟩

Selling the Rest of the World: Exporting as an Opportunity

Very few start-up companies that I am acquainted with seem to put much effort into selling their product or service outside of the United States. One reason for this is that the process appears to be hopelessly complex and expensive to someone unfamiliar with exporting. By failing to pursue the international market, the entrepreneur may be missing an extremely valuable business opportunity.

An example of how important the international market place has become is that between 25 and 30 percent of all goods manufactured in the U.S. is now sold outside of the country. In recent years, the combination of the poor economic conditions in the U.S., together with political changes that have taken place in Europe and the former Soviet Union, have greatly increased the attractiveness of world markets.

At RF Communications our main product line, long range radio equipment, had a natural market in lesser developed areas of the world. However, very few things in a start up happen easily, and it took an aggressive and dedicated effort to capitalize fully on this opportunity. And what an opportunity it turned out to be!

Our first order, two weeks after starting RF, was a simple electronics assembly contract from the University of Rochester. Our second order, three weeks later, was a $50,000 order for 20 radios from the government of Pakistan. Within a few years, we shipped equipment to more than 100 different countries. (To give you a feel for this, try to list the names of 100 countries without referring to an atlas. My guess is that not one person in 1,000 can do it.) In some years, more than 80 percent of RF Communications' sales were to customers outside of the U.S. Had we not gone after this market as aggressively as we did, it would surely have become an entirely different and much less successful company.

RF Communications realized another important benefit from such strong participation in the international market. Historically, the international market seems to be contra-cyclical in nature to the U.S. Government market (another important group of RF customers). When U.S. Government sales are down, export sales have usually been up, and vice versa. Through the years, this helped RF avoid large swings in sales revenue as economic conditions changed.

Selling outside the U.S. is another subject to which we could devote an entire book. My goal is to cover some fundamentals and to give you enough information to encourage you to consider the international market more seriously.

There are two basic approaches to international business. One is to consider business outside of the U.S. as icing on the cake. Not much effort and very little risk would be involved, but the result may be an increase in sales of five or 10 percent. Handled well, this approach should be profitable. The second approach is to make a genuine commitment, with the goal that business outside the U.S. should become as important as domestic business. This is the strategy used by large companies such as Boeing, IT&T, Xerox and many others. It was our strategy at RF.

Some of the alternative ways available to develop international business are shown in the chart in this chapter. The U.S. company is on the left, the overseas customer is on the right, the ocean in the middle. As we move from top to bottom, the investment required and accompanying risk increase, but the opportunity is correspondingly greater.

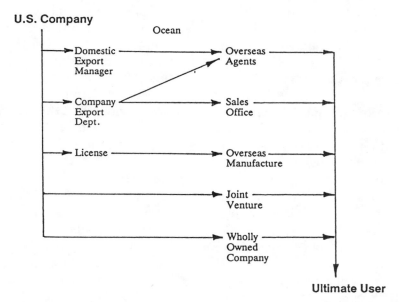

At the top, a company employs the services of an independent domestic exporter or consultant to handle its overseas sales. The exporter typically gets information about products from the company, and then offers them to the ultimate user through a network of independent agents located in various countries, with whom the exporter has a working relationship.

Incidentally, I use the term "agent" in the generic sense. Depending on the area of the world in which you do business and the nature of your product line, the term distributor, representative, dealer, etc., may be more appropriate.

In an ideal situation, the exporter will handle a number of complementary lines that are combined into a more attractive offering to the end user. When orders are received, they normally come to the exporter who, in turn, places them with supplier firms. Since your orders are from another U.S. firm, you are relieved of the problems of securing export licenses, arranging shipment, dealing in other currencies and the complications of collection. The credit risk is another U.S. company, rather than an overseas buyer.

The exporter expects a fee of 10 to 15 percent of the purchase price, and the overseas agent or dealer also expects anywhere from 10 to 25 percent. Even though these markups appear high, if the exporter and its agents do a good job, this arrangement could, in fact, be a bargain.

A little further down on the graph, the next approach is for the U.S. firm to do its own exporting and deal directly with the overseas agents. The markup of one middleman is eliminated, but the company assumes all of the exporter's functions and expenses, which are not trivial. However, neither are they onerous, and this approach has many advantages for a small company trying to emphasize international business. An important benefit of doing your own exporting is that it speeds up communications between the company and its overseas agents and customers, because a middleman has been eliminated from the process.

The major challenge is to find the best possible agents to represent you in as many countries as possible. As in using external channels for domestic sales, you must work hard at finding agents, training them and supporting them aggressively in every possible way. The selection of top-quality agents is absolutely crucial if you want your export business to be a success. The qualities to look for are:

♦ Technically qualified to understand your product.

♦ Not already committed to a competitor.

♦ Financially strong.

♦ Politically well-connected.

♦ Ambitious and motivated.

♦ Willing to set up service facilities if needed.

♦ Able to install your products and train the customer.

In addition to the above list of qualities, what separates the "super agent" from a "good agent" is when someone in their organization is familiar with people at all levels in their customer's organization—from elevator operator to the most senior general, for example. Their information-gathering potential will then be very great, and your ability to make informed sales decisions will increase dramatically. Agents such as these are few and far between, but if you find one, they are worth their weight in gold.

For a highly technical product, how many people with these skills do you think can be found in places like Tanzania, Bahrain, Venezuela, Morocco and Nigeria? Not many, you can be sure. In the beginning, we found that the better qualified agents were all committed to competitors. However, the combination of hustle and the strength of our product line soon permitted us to build an agent organization second to none.

In dealing with agents and customers from other countries, Americans often fail to realize how different the culture and customs are in other parts of the world. In order to develop strong, long-term relationships, it is important to be sensitive to these differences.

One piece of advice I always give business people is to be sure to treat their visitors to the U.S. the same way they are likely to be treated when visiting other countries. For example, some years ago, I visited an agent in a Middle Eastern country where we had sold a good number of radios over the previous few years. I was going there from Stockholm and was scheduled to arrive about 8 p.m. Our agent, a man in his mid-70s, said he would meet my plane. Unfortunately, the flight was delayed and I arrived about six hours late at 2 a.m.

To my surprise, as I walked off the plane, our agent and his wife were at the gate. They whisked me through customs and drove me to a downtown hotel. Earlier that day, the wife had inspected the room and registered me in advance. They saw that I was comfortable, arranged for pickup the next morning and left me to catch up on my sleep.

They really knew how to welcome someone to a strange country. How many Americans would treat a business visitor in this way? Also,

you may have noticed that I never use the word "foreign" to refer to either people or places.

The mechanics of handling export shipments also tends to intimidate U.S. businesspeople. It is not quite as simple as calling UPS or FedEx, but neither is it all that complicated. Almost everyone I know who exports directly uses a forwarding agent of some sort. This is a service business, located in most major U.S. cities, devoted entirely to handling the complexities of export shipment. It will often arrange for packaging and crating, schedule shipment via ship or plane as specified by the buyer, provide evidence of shipment for use in securing payment, and generally take over most of the onerous technicalities of exporting. The charge made by the forwarding agent may be as low as $25 or $50 per shipment. This is incredible, considering the problems it takes off your hands. You might ask how the agent can do so much for so little, and the answer is, "They can't." In addition to the fee you pay, the forwarder covers some of its costs by commissions from the carriers that transport the shipment.

When a company acts as its own exporter, one area of risk it must manage is getting paid. In general, the less developed the country to which you are selling, the greater the risk. For RF Communications, the best answer was to require payment by confirmed, irrevocable letter of credit (LC) through a major international bank, whenever possible. LCs are the equivalent of a check, issued to you by a bank, that can be cashed when you show evidence of shipment. They have become more difficult to obtain in recent years, but other things you can do to minimize the risk are to require large down payments or ship C.O.D.

Another issue that has become more common in recent years is a thing called "offset." This is where the country buying your product requires that you offset part of the cost, either by doing some local manufacturing or with unrelated purchases from sources within their country. This may involve things completely unrelated to what you are selling, for example, in order to sell radios you may have to buy apples. Offset usually applies only to very large purchases. However, when it does, it is often possible to find another U.S. company willing to work with you that will take the offset material off your hands.

The U.S. exporting firm can also consider putting its own employees overseas to either sell direct, manage the agent relationship or both. As your export business grows, this is something you will almost surely consider doing in regions where your market is strongest. I am not sure it is always a good idea.

We, at one time, had a company-employed salesman, residing in his native Portugal, whose territory was southern Europe and Africa. Two problems developed. One was that a field salesperson simply will not travel 100 percent of the time. Anyone with a family will always figure out how to be at home at least half the time. This being the case, home should be the company's headquarters, where the individual can interface with the organization during these periods. Travel time from Rochester to most of Africa was not much longer than from Portugal. A second problem, which we did not realize until later, was that Portugal is a former colonial country and it's citizens were not especially welcome in many parts of Africa.

The next example, going down the graph, is an arrangement where the U.S. firm licenses one or more overseas companies to build and sell its products, in return for up-front licensing fees plus royalties. These are fairly low-risk approaches, but hard to control.

The final example is where the U.S. firm establishes an overseas manufacturing and marketing subsidiary, either alone or as a joint venture with a non-U.S. partner. I have been involved in several such overseas manufacturing arrangements. The results ranged from mediocre to bad. It was our good fortune that all the deals were small. The following is an example of how naive we were in one undertaking.

We were asked by our distributor in Mexico City to set up a joint venture to manufacture one of our products for sale in Mexico. They had represented us for a number of years, importing from the U.S. and reselling. The relationship was generally good . The arrangement they suggested was to set up a jointly owned company, with the ownership and investment divided 51 percent for them and 49 percent for us, a requirement of Mexican law. The first signal of future problems developed when they wanted to borrow their part of the investment from us, secured by a commission that would be due them on an order expected to ship several months in the future. Unwisely, we agreed.

Shortly after the business was set up, we learned that one of their first purchases was a company car and that the president of the new company was a son of one of our Mexican partners. The son had no experience in the radio business, or any business for that matter. From there, the relationship deteriorated. Considerable fault lies on both sides, but the result was that we both lost our investment, and our business in Mexico went from a modest amount of exporting to zero.

Manufacturing in another country under any arrangement is more difficult than exporting and should be approached with caution. This may be an area where large firms have a natural advantage, and it probably represents excessive risk for a small enterprise.

As I mentioned, the further down on the graph you move, the greater the opportunity and the greater the risk. A young company would be well-advised to achieve at least some success in exporting before it spends very much time worrying about overseas manufacture.

The most important advice I can give the entrepreneur entering the international market is to do it with a high degree of commitment. Do not just dabble. In the changing world we now live in, the international market cannot be ignored. In many situations, business outside of the United States can be an immense opportunity.

⨎ Chapter 44 ⨏

Help! Help! Where Do I Go for Help?

When I started a company in 1961, there were very few places I could go to for help. Today, there are countless places and people that offer help, counsel and guidance. It is no longer a question of whether there is help available, but more a question of which sources of help to use. This chapter lists some that I consider to be of potential value. They are almost certain to give you answers to many questions—and give you greater confidence in your program for becoming an entrepreneur.

Other entrepreneurs

Perhaps the most valuable help you can get in planning or managing a new business is from someone who has already started a business. I am approached constantly by entrepreneurs and potential entrepreneurs to discuss every imaginable problem related to going out on their own. I seldom refuse to see them and rarely charge a fee. In almost every case, I can help them in some way.

You may wonder why I do this, and I often ask myself the same question. At one time, I was actively seeking investment opportunities and did, in fact, invest in about a half dozen of these situations. But today,

I no longer make venture investments and still see about 100 entrepreneurs every year. It is something I enjoy, and it gives me satisfaction in being able to help others.

What I am suggesting is that you should get to know a few successful entrepreneurs in your area and spend time with them. Make it clear that you are seeking advice, not trying to raise money or sell them anything. You'll be surprised at how often they are willing to see you, and almost invariably, they will be able to help you in some way and not expect to be paid.

College courses

Until about 15 years ago, very few colleges and universities offered formal courses in entrepreneurship and small business management as part of their curriculum. Today, more than 500 in the United States offer such courses. In some schools, entrepreneurship and small business management are major concentrations. Some universities have entrepreneurial centers devoted to teaching and academic research. A number have endowed chairs in entrepreneurship.

In many of the programs, the courses are taught by successful entrepreneurs who teach part time. These entrepreneurs are willing to devote considerable effort for small compensation to help students along the road to starting a business.

In almost all of these courses, the term project is the preparation of a business plan. I taught entrepreneurship in MBA programs for about 12 years. Most of my students were young people with little or no business experience, individuals who did not yet know whether they wanted to go out on their own. However, when a student either had already started his or her own business, seriously planned to do so or was employed by a small company, I strongly encouraged him or her to write a plan about their own business.

You should consider taking one of these courses. In doing so, you will probably be forced through the discipline of writing a real-life business plan and, in all likelihood, get a detailed critique of the plan, either from the faculty or other students.

In many of these courses, entrepreneurs are invited to address the classes. This is a good way to establish contact with a business owner you can network with later on your own.

Small Business Administration (SBA)

SBA offices are spread all across the country. They have countless publications and programs in which you may have an interest. The SBA has a Small Business Answer Desk (800-827-5722) that can answer general business questions, including the location of the SBA office

nearest you. They can also provide a list of the many publications and videos available to small businesses at very low cost that may be of value to an entrepreneur.

Recently, the SBA began using the Internet to provide a great deal of information about its various programs. The main address I have is http://www.sbaonline.sba.gov or you can check with your local SBA office.

Small Business Development Centers (SBDCs)

This is another program of great value to small business owners that is supported by the Small Business Administration. SBDCs are usually associated with a community college or state university. They each have a small group of business specialists who will counsel and advise you on a one-on-one basis, and who conduct seminars, programs and courses for entrepreneurs. Often, the SBDCs have a library of books, pamphlets and other material. In some cases, they publish newsletters with articles of interest to entrepreneurs. There are about 800 of these centers around the country. You can contact the Association of Small Business Development Centers in Washington, D.C., at 703-448-6124, or your local chamber of commerce for the location of the SBDC in your area.

Of special interest is a publication called the *Small Business Forum, the Journal of the Association of Small Business Development Centers*. It is published by the SBDC at the University of Wisconsin Extension in Madison, Wis. (telephone,

608-263-7843). I recommend this publication, because it contains articles on a wide variety of subjects that are very practical in nature and that can be of great value to entrepreneurs and small business owners.

Business incubators

A business incubator is an organization that provides low-cost space to new companies on a leased basis. This usually includes low rental charges, small units of space when necessary, short leases and the availability of shared services that most new businesses cannot justify having on their own. Sometimes business incubators are publicly supported and sometimes privately financed. The types of shared services available will vary, but are likely to include a conference room, copier, FAX machine and secretarial services. I have seen one where a law firm and public accountant were among the tenants. Finally, the sponsors of the incubator may also be able to provide the new companies with general business guidance and counseling. A list of incubators can be obtained from the National Business Incubation Association, 20 East Circle Drive, Suite 190, Athens, OH, 45701, 614-593-4331. Your local chamber of commerce may be able to guide you to business incubators in your area that are not associated with the NBIA.

Service Corps of Retired Executives (SCORE)

This is a free program sponsored by the Small Business Administration in which retired businesspeople agree to devote time counseling small business owners. In many cases, SCORE chapters are associated with a local chamber of commerce. You cannot always choose your adviser, but in almost every case, you will benefit from the opportunity to discuss your problems with a knowledgeable person.

Books, tapes and videos

Books, audio tapes and videos on the subject of entrepreneurship have become very popular in recent years. For example, this book, which I first self-published in 1989 and which is now published by Career Press, has sold almost 50,000 copies in the first three editions. At last count, it was used either in small business programs or as a text in more than 50 colleges and universities.

I read, listen to and watch many of these books, audio tapes and videos about starting a business. Some I find to be extremely informative, and some are interesting but a little short on useful advice. In any case, I advise you to go to your bookstore or library and read, listen to or watch as many as you can find. You may end up a little smarter, and you may garner advice and suggestions that will be of great value.

Small Business Councils

Many chambers of commerce have subgroups called "councils." In Rochester, the chamber has an International Business Council, a Sales Executives Council, a Minority Business Owners Council, a Small Business Council (SBC) and others.

The SBC in Rochester has more than 250 members, mostly owners of small and not-so-small businesses. The council runs seminars on entrepreneurship, occasional breakfast meetings devoted to a wide range of specific problems faced by small firms and monthly evening meetings, where extensive networking is encouraged. Also, they organize small groups of owners of noncompeting businesses into advisory boards that meet monthly to discuss mutual problems. These SBCs can be a valuable resource for an entrepreneur. Check your nearest chamber of commerce to see what is available in your area.

Small business seminars

Seminars are available on almost every imaginable subject of interest to a small business owner. Check the events list in the business section of your local newspaper for information about what is happening in your area. Sometimes these cost hundreds of dollars and sometimes they cost very little, depending on who organizes and runs the seminar.

Several years ago, a woman business owner and I organized and conducted a seminar for women entrepreneurs. It drew about 100 attendees. The fee was $75, and a local bank and public accounting firm provided some financial support. We ended up with a $5,000 profit that we used to set up a small scholarship fund for women business owners in an area business school. Seminars of this type can be a valuable source of information and networking for an entrepreneur.

Entrepreneurial magazines

There are number of specialty magazines devoted to entrepreneurship and small business management. Some have huge circulations, such as *Inc.*, *Entrepreneur* and *Home Office Computing,* while others are smaller and more focused, such as *Midnight Engineering* and *InBusiness Magazine.* All try to include articles, book reviews, case histories and other material of interest to entrepreneurs. I make a habit of reading as many as I can and almost always find information that is both interesting and useful.

Professional service organizations

Many public accounting firms, law firms and banks have various kinds of written information and publications that they make available to entrepreneurs and small business owners. Those that I have seen are mostly in the form of pamphlets and small booklets on a variety of subjects. Specifically, I have copies of material put out by Ernst & Young, Price Waterhouse, Arthur Young and KMG Peat Marwick, all large national accounting firms. They give them to clients free and charge little or nothing to others. Most of this material is very good.

Venture capital clubs

These groups provide a forum to which entrepreneurs can present an outline of their business plans, usually for the purpose of raising outside capital. In Rochester, we have two such groups, which meet up to 10 times a year. Typically, there are two or three presentations at each meeting. Sometimes the entrepreneur is successful in raising money, other times not. Recently, it has become more difficult. At worst, these groups can be the source of contacts, at best, a source of interested investors.

Networking

Then there is networking—meeting and speaking with others who have problems similar to yours and who have knowledge that may be helpful. How do you find people with whom you can share problems and gain useful advice and counsel? Take seminars, attend association meetings, take advantage of everything mentioned here and make a habit of asking for one or two more names of other possible sources of help whenever you talk to anyone about a business problem. Doing this may get you a personal introduction that will make it easier to gain an audience with your next contact. The value of networking will be increased if you are well-prepared in advance. Be sure to have at least a good outline of a business plan available and a list of questions or problems you would like to discuss.

Professional associations

Finally, there are a number of national associations whose main purpose is to help various categories of small businesspeople. Several are:

♦ The Council of Growing Companies. An organization of the heads of small- and medium-sized companies, it provides lobbying, seminars and conferences for its members. Its address is 7910 Woodmont Ave., Ste. 1206, Bethesda, MD, 20814 (301-951-1138).

♦ National Association of Self-Employed. This group represents about 320,000 entrepreneurs, most of whom have only a handful of employees. It has a number of publications, including the *Small Business Resource Guide*. Its address is 2121 Precinct Line Rd., Hurst, TX, 76054 (800-232-6273).

♦ National Federation of Independent Businesses. This organization has about 600,000 members and, in addition to lobbying in Washington on small business issues, it has a monthly publication. Its address is 600 Maryland Ave., SW, Washington, DC, 20024 (800-634-2669).

When I decided to add this chapter to the later editions of *Start Up*, I was surprised at the long list of people and places an entrepreneur can go to for help. Most are available at little or no cost and most can help you identify and solve problems that would have been much more difficult to do on your own. Gaining access to some of these sources may require you to be pushy and aggressive from time to time, but the benefits are almost sure to justify the effort.

৵ Chapter 45 ৵

Entrepreneurship for Women! Is It Different Than for Men?

Up until 15 or 20 years ago, there were not many women entrepreneurs. Those who did manage to start a business often started either service businesses, such as bookkeeping firms, or small local retailers, such as gift shops. This is definitely no longer true. Near the beginning of this book, I mentioned that the 1990s is the "Age of the entrepreneur." The 1990s might also be described as the "Age of the woman entrepreneur."

Evidence confirming this fact is clear. The February 19, 1996 edition of *U.S. News & World Report* indicated that between 1990 and 1994, the number of American firms owned by women increased from a little over 5 million to almost 8 million. The article also stated that sales generated by woman-owned businesses in the U.S. increased from about $800 million in 1987 to almost $1.4 trillion in 1994. Is this progress for women? You'd better believe it is.

To achieve this growth, woman-owned businesses are hiring new employees at a much higher rate than larger companies in the U.S., many of which are going through extended periods of massive downsizing.

Woman-owned companies employed almost 15.5 million people in 1994. Between 1991 and 1994, woman-owned businesses with more than 100 employees grew at about twice the rate of all other companies. Many analysts consider woman-owned businesses as one of the hottest growth sectors of the U.S. economy.

Why has this happened?

First, I want to mention a few of the reasons I think this dramatic change has taken place. There are still a number of obstacles faced by women who start businesses that men do not face. I will discuss some of these later in this chapter.

Back in the 1970s, when I first began teaching in a prominent graduate business school, there was almost never a woman student in any of my classes. This is no longer the case.

In recent classes in MBA programs to which I lectured, mostly on the subject of entrepreneurship and small business management, anywhere from a quarter to half of the students were women. These women are at least as capable as the men students. This means that women entering the business world over the past few years are as well-trained in business skills as men and, in general, are able to get just as good jobs.

Also, even in spite of the "glass ceiling" that still exists in some large organizations, women are holding more and more responsible positions today than in the past, and when they make the decision to go out on their own they are more knowledgeable, more experienced and much more likely to succeed.

A second factor that I also think drives many women into the business world is the need for two incomes in many families. The Bureau of Labor Statistics estimates that almost 50 percent of all workers now come from married, dual-earner couples. Because of this large increase in the number of married women entering the work force, many may decide the best way to increase the family income is to start their own business and go it alone.

Third, the trend in the U.S. is for better-educated married couples to have fewer children. This makes it possible for women to take jobs at a younger age than in the past and with fewer family responsibilities. Because the willingness to work hard, long hours is an important personal quality of successful entrepreneurs, fewer family responsibilities may also be a positive factor.

And finally, because of remaining family and home obligations, once having decided to go into the work force, the flexibility a woman has in setting working hours is much better for an entrepreneur than it is at a company with a time clock. Women entrepreneurs are better able to match the demands of their business with the responsibilities of family and home than would be possible in a "normal" work situation.

This category should probably also include divorced women, who must support themselves and their children and are unable to get financial assistance from their ex-husbands. They sometimes have to enter the work force for the simple purpose of survival. Some will decide to start their own businesses, and time flexibility could be an important factor.

For these reasons and probably others of which I am not aware, we are in the midst of great change in the U.S. business world.

What are the differences?

Over the years, a woman entrepreneur faced a much tougher road in many ways than a man. There were probably a few things in which women had the advantage, but not many. Today, many of these bumps in the road for women have disappeared, but some still remain. I think a few are the fault of the women themselves and some because many men simply are still uncomfortable working with or working for women.

My personal experience, knowing and having taught and counseled many women business owners, is that they tend to be much more fiscally conservative than men. For example, over the years, I have gotten to know about 100 women business owners and only one of these has taken outside equity investors (this comment does not include assistance from husbands). This kind of fiscal conservatism has some benefits in that there have been fewer failures among women business owners in recent years than men. Women's financial obligation to outsiders is much lower—they have fewer loan obligations, less commitment to equity investors, etc.

One of the reasons for this fiscal conservatism, I believe, is the fact that it was probably much harder to get the business underway in the first place. Therefore, women, in general, are more reluctant to share the ownership in their enterprise with others. I also think they tend to have a greater fear that outside investors may try to take over their business, if it ever became possible.

I think this is an unwise attitude for several reasons. First, by having outside investors and sharing the ownership of the business, the risk of entrepreneurship can be greatly reduced. Starting a business using other people's money clearly has less risk than putting everything you own on the line.

Another reason I think women should have outside investors is that it gives them access to much more capital with which to run the business. This means greater opportunity to grow a much larger and more successful business than would be the case using only one's own limited personal resources. A final reason is that many outside investors are willing and anxious to serve as directors of the companies in which they invest, thereby providing an excellent and knowledgeable source of guidance and advice.

The question of control is also one that I believe many women consider

to be far too important an issue. Chapter 30 of this book discusses this in some detail. The compulsion to own 51 percent of the business forever will also limit growth opportunity and make it much, much harder to find outside equity investors.

I should also mention the difficulty many women business owners still face getting bank loans. This situation is changing, but has by no means been completely eliminated. In discussing this problem with one woman entrepreneur, she said "Were you ever asked by a bank loan officer, does your wife know you're here?"

On the plus side, I read a recent article in *The Wall Street Journal* that described an interview with the head of the Small Business Administration. He stated that the number of SBA guaranteed loans to women business owners was more than $1.4 billion in fiscal 1995, an increase of more than 84 percent from the prior period.

In mid-1995, I discussed the difficulty women entrepreneurs have had raising equity capital with two friends who manage venture capital funds—one a very large fund, the other a medium-sized fund. They both said they were about to make their first equity investment in women-controlled businesses. My guess is that this trend will become more prevalent in the coming years, much to the benefit of the more aggressive woman entrepreneur.

How about preferences?

Preferences are a complex issue. In the past few years, the federal and many state governments have started to eliminate or reduce preferences of all sorts for many minority groups. I must mention that I personally oppose business preferences. There are several reasons for this, but the most important is that if the business you start depends on a preference, there is a good chance that your idea for the business and the strategy you are following may not be strong enough to stand on its own feet. Sooner or later, most preferences will probably disappear and without them, your business could be in big trouble.

However, if you ask me whether or not people should take advantage of any preferences that are available, my answer would be, "Absolutely yes." This position goes back to the time I read of an interview with Milton Friedman, one of our country's best-known free market economists. He was asked how he could, with a clear conscience, possibly live in a rent-controlled apartment. His response was that people should make decisions that maximize their own personal well-being. If any local government is dumb enough to institute rent control, anyone who can benefit from living in a rent-controlled unit should do so.

My counsel to women entrepreneurs is to take advantage of every preference you can find, but don't forget that sooner or later your business will have to operate without these and your fundamental strategy must be good enough to accomplish this: To stand on its own feet.

Some examples

Throughout this book, I include many examples of what I view as very successful woman-owned businesses. Here are a few more.

Mary Kay Ash, a great-grandmother and founder of Mary Kay Cosmetics, started her business after a successful career in real estate sales. At first, she planned to operate her business with her husband, but he died just before it started in 1963. She went ahead on her own and in 1984, when Mary Kay went from a publicly owned company to a privately owned company, their annual sales were more than $280 million.

Louise Woerner is an early graduate of the Business School at the University of Chicago. Initially, she worked as a management consultant. Later she founded HCR Rochester, which provides home health care in competition with Visiting Nurses. HCR is a privately owned, for profit company. Louise now has about 500 employees and has achieved national recognition as an entrepreneur.

At the other end of the size spectrum, I am acquainted with a woman named Nancy Carlson who, about 11 years ago, purchased a small toy shop named "Kaleidoscope" located in a Rochester suburb. The store was in a poor location and not very successful. Nancy came to me for advice on raising outside capital, and I suggested that in her situation it would be difficult if not impossible.

I asked her how she was doing with Nintendo which, at the time, was a very popular electronics game. Her answer was that it was a terrible product for her, because her cost was very close to the selling price at major toy retail chains, which meant she could not make a profit.

I then asked what products she had that the larger toy stores might not have. Her answer was christening dresses. This surprised me. She pointed out that christening dresses were bought mostly by grandparents, they were not widely available and price was not an important part of the purchase decision. Kaleidoscope soon moved to a new location, introduced an extensive line of children's wear for ages 0 to 5 or 6, children's toys and books for ages 0 to 9 or 10, and featured attractive gift wrapping at no extra charge.

Not long ago, I saw her again and asked her how business was going. She answered, "Very good." Then I asked how she was doing with Nintendo, and she said they no longer carried it. In addition to being an excellent example of a successful woman-owned business, Kaleidoscope is also an excellent example of finding a unique niche and sticking to it.

Interestingly, Nancy is now in the process of liquidating her business. Her two children are now adults, and she and her husband both decided they were ready for a major change in lifestyle. They plan to move to another state, where he has a job opportunity with great potential.

I asked about her future plans, and she said her first goal was to just relax for six months or so. Then she added that owning her own business is probably in her blood, and that within a year or so, she will probably again become an entrepreneur.

Home offices

Because many businesses started by women are still small service type businesses, it is sometimes possible to operate the business from the entrepreneur's home. Rhonda Abrams, an independent consultant based in Palo Alto, Calif., said in a recent Gannett news article that 10 years ago, when she started her own home-based business, people generally believed it was because she could not afford an office. Now, she says, people envy home-based workers.

However, before doing this, determine whether zoning codes in your neighborhood permit home-operated businesses, and whether you can have other employees of the business also work from your home. Some of the reasons home-based businesses have become more prevalent in recent years are the availability of FAX machines, cellular telephones, inexpensive copiers, the Internet, e-mail and personal computers with which you can exchange all kinds of files with others using a modem. These technologies have made operating from one's home a practical reality.

If you decide to operate your business from your home or simply have a home office, there are a few guidelines you should remember. These are very important, especially if customers are likely to go there to carry out their business.

First, and perhaps most important, be sure your office is isolated from the rest of your home, and if possible, has an entrance from the outside so that visitors do not have to go through your living room or kitchen. Also, be sure it is used exclusively for business purposes.

At the present time, three of my six children operate all or part of their business activities from their homes. One daughter is a tax accountant, a second daughter is a financial analyst for a large West Coast health care organization, and one son is a salesman for a major instrument company. Two of these are examples of the fact that even large companies are either permitting or requiring that their employees operate from home offices.

In summary, it is important that the office in your home be just as professional as any other place of business.

Where to look for help

Another chapter of this book lists many sources of help available to all entrepreneurs and small business owners. Those listed here may also be of specific interest to women:

♦ The Spring, 1995 issue of *Small Business Forum*, the national publication of Small Business Development Centers, published a very interesting article entitled "What Is the Most Important Difference in Management Styles Between Men and Women?" The article describes a study conducted by the National Foundation for Women Business Owners. Included in the same issue were the reactions of eight specialists to the conclusions of the study. This article is well worth reading for a woman considering becoming an entrepreneur. You can reach the SBDC at 608-263-7843.

♦ National Association of Women Business Owners (NAWBO). NAWBO represents women business owners of all kinds in all fields of endeavor (1100 Wayne Ave., Ste 830, Silver Springs, MD 20190, 301-608-2590).

♦ National Foundation of Women Business Owners. This group has about 7,000 members, publishes a monthly magazine and holds management retreats, among other things (1100 Wayne Ave., Ste. 830, Silver Springs, MD, 20910-5603, 301-495-4975).

♦ Office of Women's Business Ownership (WBO). This office provides information to women regarding federally funded programs for small business owners. They can be reached through your Small Business Administration District Office.

♦ The complete Census Bureau report on woman-owned businesses ("1987 Women-Owned Businesses") may be obtained by calling the Superintendent of Documents at 202-783-3238. The document number is 033-024-06949-1.

What does all this mean?

What path women entrepreneurs should travel is not entirely clear and depends upon the nature of the business they are trying to start and their personal goals. Today, however, the opportunity for women to own their own businesses is greater than ever before in history.

❦ Chapter 46 ❧

This Is How It Should Be Done!

Valerie Mannix and Mercury Print Productions, Inc.

Mercury Print Productions is a woman-owned, full-service printing company located in Rochester, N.Y. It was founded by Valerie Mannix in 1968 in the basement of her home in order to support herself and her two small children following a divorce. Today, Mercury Print Productions occupies two plants, has about 138 employees and annual sales of $10 million.

Mannix is a graduate of a Rochester high school, but does not have a college degree. Before starting Mercury, she worked in various jobs, starting as a comptometer operator and eventually managing a small print shop for a local manufacturing company.

The following is a transcript of discussions I had with Valerie in early 1996, following her selection as the winner of the prestigious Vanden Brul Entrepreneur of the Year Award by Rochester Institute of Technology (RIT).

As you read this section, think about the strategies Valerie followed

and the problems she faced as a woman entrepreneur, and how they compare to the strategies and operating principles suggested in earlier chapters of this book.

Q: What is your educational background and how come you did not get a college degree?

A: As a high school student, I wanted to become a lab technician, but I hated math. My school counselor said I wouldn't really need it, so I didn't take any math classes. Well, you can imagine what happened when I came to take the entrance exam at RIT. The first page, and most of the rest, was all math. I closed the exam book and left.

Q: What did you do then?

A: After leaving RIT that day, I came home and found a flyer in my mailbox for a training course on a comptometer machine. It said I would be guaranteed a job when I finished, so off I went. Now if many of your readers know what a comptometer is, I would be amazed. It was a machine that performed calculations in such a roundabout way that it soon became obsolete.

Q: Did you get a job as a comptometer operator?

A: I did get a job as promised, a job I couldn't wait to get out of! If my story so far doesn't sound much like "How to become an Entrepreneur for Fun and Profit," you're right. I never started out planning to one day own a multimillion-dollar business. But I did have determination, the ability to work hard, and I did have confidence in myself.

To my dismay, that first job landed me in the payroll department of a small company, and needless to say, I hated it. I went to the personnel department and said, "I'll do anything else, anything." They told me they were buying a printing press and would train me to run it. I learned how to operate that press, often came home covered with ink and loved it.

Q: Did that job change your goals?

A: I loved finding ways to do the impossible on that small press, like a nine-color printing job on a machine that could only print one color at a time. I have always loved the adventure of a new challenge.

Q: How long did that job last?

A: A few years, but when that company left Rochester, I started a new job and became assistant to the manager of an in-house printing operation at a much larger company. After just three months, the manager left and I was given his position.

Now a woman printer was definitely not the norm then. It's still not common now, but I didn't worry about whether being a printer was a "right" career choice. I just knew it was something I wanted to do.

Q: How did you handle the new job?

A: I developed more work for the in-plant print shop by talking with people throughout the company about the forms they used in their departments. I created enough work for two shifts in the print room, while saving the company a lot of money in the process. Then in the early '60s, I became pregnant and took a maternity leave. It sounds like a cliché, but the company put a man into my position who knew nothing about printing. They knew, of course, that if a woman could do a job, then certainly any man could do it just as well.

Q: What happened when you returned from your maternity leave?

A: When I returned, I was told that he would stay in charge of the print room. Working under someone who knew nothing about a job I knew very well was just not possible for me. I resigned, knowing it was time to start my own company.

Q: Did you have the financial resources to take such a step?

A: You won't be surprised to hear that not a single bank would lend me the $800 I needed back in 1969 to buy my first printing press and various supplies. I had to ask my ex-husband to cosign a loan for the money I needed to get started. But finally, my basement business was born, and I named it Mercury Forms. I chose the name Mercury because it represented someone who was very fast and very efficient, and for the practical reason that I already had a piece of artwork to serve as my logo!

Q: How did you sell your services in what was a very competitive business?

A: I began to build my business by making sales calls during the day, printing the jobs I got at night and saving every penny I could. Thanks to my replacement, my former employer closed its print shop. I bought all their equipment for $3,000, paid in cash from the money I had been saving. At this point, my basement was full, but I was still just learning.

Q: Learning! What do you mean by that?

A: There are many ways to get an education. Formal training and college courses are certainly two good routes to take, but my own road to success was to learn by doing and by listening to others who knew more than I did. My business continued to grow and in 1979, I moved out of my basement and into a building near my home.

Q: How did that work out?

A: New challenges, overhead and more employees! My next major obstacle was learning that one of my major clients, Xerox Corp., would no longer be available to me. My ex-husband had begun to work in the department that bought their printing services from me, and my company was now perceived as having a "conflict of interest."

Not wanting to lose this important client, I gambled by investing in some typesetting equipment. This meant I would still be able to get Xerox business through another department, diversifying my business at the same time. My strategy worked, and the gamble paid off. In fact, I soon had three typesetters and several artists working for me, as my company continued to grow in this new direction. Printing actually became a smaller percentage of our workload.

Q: So you still had Xerox as a major client?

A: Then as fate would have it, my former husband was moved to the typesetting department at Xerox, and my company again faced a conflict of interest problem! Determined to keep doing work for this major customer, I rented more space and bought a bigger press. I was soon calling on their print buyers again. But now my growing business wouldn't fit in that new building, so it was time to buy one where it would fit!

Q: Things were going well again?

A: Yes. We moved to another plant in the city and Mercury Forms was really on its way. But we also had an identity problem now. We weren't doing mostly forms any longer. We were doing a variety of printing jobs for a wide range of customers. My company became Mercury Print Productions.

Within just six years, this plant couldn't hold us any longer, and I sold it. I bought another building three times bigger, and I was sure we would have plenty of room, which we did for about a year. Two years later, I was looking for a larger facility again. Rather than trying to find an existing building, I decided to build one.

Q: How did you manage this and was being a woman a factor?

A: I applied for and received financial assistance from the City of Rochester and the County of Monroe partly because I was a woman, in addition to having a successful business track record. I didn't need a man to cosign for me this time and the amount far exceeded that first $800 loan by a few million dollars.

My company continued to grow. We added more shifts, more equipment and more staff. However, at this point, I could see that new technology for high-volume copiers would soon replace most of our black and white printing.

Q: Did this mean you had to shift your strategy?

A: If you look in Webster's Dictionary, an entrepreneur is defined as "a person who organizes and manages a business undertaking, assuming the risk for the sake of the profit."

To fit the definition, I started thinking color. My strategy was to quote 4-color work as if we had a 4-color press. But we had to run it on a 2-color press twice. Not too profitable. When 25 percent of our workload was color, it was time to look for a full-color press. I finally bought a used 5-color press in England, because

European printers run fewer shifts and work their equipment less than here in the United States. On December 1, 1994 our Heidelberg press arrived, a machine that wouldn't fit in my entire house when I started, let alone the basement.

Q: This really represented a major step forward, didn't it?

A: It certainly did. Over the past 27 years, the small company I started so that I could make enough money to support myself and my two children has moved four times to larger quarters that could hold more equipment and a growing staff.

Mercury Print Productions now occupies 30,000 square feet in a custom-designed facility. Our previous building is also still in use; as a satellite facility for our high-speed copier division, and now I'm looking to add on to our current building sometime in 1996.

Q: Have these moves and rapid growth affected the quality of your work?

A: No, rapid growth has never resulted in reducing the quality of our work. We met quality control standards to become an approved printer for Xerox Corporation in 1988—we were certified by Xerox in 1995. In fact, Mercury is the only printing company certified world-wide. We're now working to achieve the international ISO 9000 standard. Our goal is five years.

Q: Your record as an entrepreneur has been outstanding. How do you feel when your think about these accomplishments?

A: At a recent Quality Control meeting for our staff, I stood at the podium and looked out over 87 employees gathered in a hotel conference room and couldn't believe it. Where did all these people come from? I now employ 113 people full time and another 23 part time. In 1994, we did about 5 million in sales. In 1995, we reached $10 million—three years sooner than our business plan had projected!

Over the years, rapidly changing technology in the printing industry has kept me challenged. There are so many more choices to make when doing a print job now, and the needs of our customers have certainly changed over this past quarter of a century.

Q: Please comment on what you think it requires to be a successful entrepreneur?

A: I think that I have always been able to spot an entrepreneur. There are certain qualities that just give them away. For example, being willing to take a calculated risk is one. Knowing how to focus on a long-range goal and to envision the steps needed to get there. But most important of all is to really love what you're doing.

You must be passionate about your business and know that the first success is never the end of the road. An entrepreneur is always driven to accomplish something more. To be successful, you must be willing to dream, but not be satisfied with just generating ideas. You must plan and organize for the future, as well. The entrepreneurs working for me all have initiative, dedication to a goal and the drive to achieve.

Q: Is that all?

A: Loving your business is not enough. You must know every aspect of it. Get to know your competitors. Know where their weaknesses are. Get to know their business strategies, their customers, the niches they succeed in. Know where to look for opportunities for your own business and learn from others how to spot problems you may face yourself one day.

Very often, I find college students expect to go right into a job that pays them 40 to 60 thousand dollars a year. That may lead to a comfortable lifestyle, but if you are an entrepreneur at heart, it won't be enough.

Q: Thinking back, what were the most important factors that drove you to go out on your own?

A: I didn't get into business to get rich, I just needed to support myself and my children. But believe it or not, running your own business can almost be compared to being on vacation. There are always new adventures and interesting people to meet. Also, there are bonuses, the excitement of success and the satisfaction of overcoming failure. Don't get me wrong, I have bad days just like everyone else. But as I look back on my career, I realize that the moments when I had butterflies in my stomach taking a chance on something were the most rewarding and exciting times in my life.

Q: How has all this affected your personal life?

A: On the personal side, we entrepreneurs are not easy to live with.

There were times when personal relationships kept me from growing. And I have learned that the significant people in your life can't be threatened by your success. I was never in a hurry to reap rewards from my earliest business efforts. I put every penny I made back into my company. It was 15 years before I allowed myself the luxury of taking more than just a wage to live on.

Q: Do you have any advice for people thinking about starting a business?

A: To all entrepreneurs out there today, I urge you to do the same things I did. Take only a small salary at first and invest your profits in your own business dream. The rewards will be much greater in the long run. Take small steps, but always move forward. And don't be afraid of failure. Welcome it! If you fail at something along the way, okay it happens. Do everything you can to correct the situation and learn from it. Learn the lessons that no one, not your parents, not your most respected professors, etc., can teach you.

Just know you won't make the same mistake again and you have a lifetime to get it right! To me, retiring may mean cutting back to just three days eventually, maybe taking a month off to travel once in a while. I don't think I could do it "cold turkey." If I did, I'd probably go out and start something else, but I still love what I'm doing now.

Q: Any final comments?

A: Yes, I want to thank my family and friends for their support over the years, especially my mother, my husband, Jim, and my son John, who is my vice president and right-hand man, and my daughter Jackie. Both of my children work at Mercury. I also thank all the employees who have helped my company to grow. While I provided the vision and the leadership, they became the ones to help carry it out.

Finally, I want to challenge all of the readers of your book, Bill. They should never settle for a job well-done, they should always look for the next challenge, and if it doesn't already exist, go out and create it!

Thank you, Valerie, for your candid, complete and very knowledgeable comments about your experiences starting Mercury Print Productions. I'm sure they will help all the readers of the 4th edition of Start Up, *both women and men, in achieving their goals of becoming successful entrepreneurs.*

⨍ Chapter 47 ⨂

Managing a Turnaround

There are a number of reasons turnaround management may be important to an entrepreneur. The first is that sometime during the life of your business, you may face a situation where everything seems to go bad for any number of reasons. A second is that companies go through stages of growth, and sooner or later, reach the point where they must make the transition from a founder-dominated operation to one that is more professionally managed. As was discussed in an earlier chapter, failure to do this can cause very serious business problems. A third reason is that buying a business is one way to become an entrepreneur. Buying a business in trouble, or even in bankruptcy, that needs a turnaround, is a way to buy a business at a bargain price.

When RF Communications was about seven years old, I left to take a faculty position at an area business school. About a year later, RF merged with Harris Corp. During the next two and a half years, the business situation at RF Communications deteriorated badly. Sales dropped by about one third, there had been large staff reductions and they were experiencing substantial losses.

One of the other founders, who succeeded me as president, had left the company, and another founder, who had succeeded him, also announced his desire to leave. This left Harris, the acquirer, with a serious problem. They had paid a very high price for RF Communications, all of the founders had left the company and everything seemed to be going wrong.

Harris invited me to return full time to head up the company again, and I accepted with many reservations. I no longer had any financial need to take such a demanding job, and I was uncertain whether I had the skills to turn the situation around. Managing a turnaround turned out to be the most difficult and challenging business experience I ever had.

I spent much time thinking about why things went so bad. It was in the early 1970s and the U.S. was in a modest recession. Additionally, defense spending, which represented an important part of our business, had been reduced. Also, RF had just gone through two and a half years becoming part of a much larger company. This was a very disruptive process. Perhaps more important, though, RF never made the transition from a founder-dominated company, where the four founders made all the important decisions, to a professionally managed company with more structure and more formal control and review procedures.

After returning and spending the first few weeks looking around and talking to people, this is what I found:

♦ Many employees were demoralized. There had been a number of substantial staff reductions and everyone was worried about his or her job.

♦ Orders were drastically down.

♦ There were two product lines, unrelated to the core business, that were a financial drain on the company.

♦ A former vice president of marketing and several other employees had left to form their own company in direct competition with RF.

♦ There were poor controls throughout the organization. Inventory levels were skyrocketing and even though orders were down, most shipments were late because of parts shortages.

♦ The company seemed unable to make a decent sales forecast as little as one month in advance, yet a senior member of management spent almost a third of his time doing the forecasting.

There were other problems, but this gives you an idea of what I faced. Anyone who has managed a company during a turnaround is certainly familiar with this list. It is a perfect example of a situation where if anything goes bad, everything goes bad.

Here are some of the things I did:

One of the first problems I tackled was to try to improve morale. I decided to personally visit every department in the company and speak to every employee. RF had about 600 employees. I met with groups of 15 or 20 people at a time, right in their work place, and spoke for 15 or 20 minutes. It took two whole days.

The approach I used was to tell the truth. I told them exactly what I had concluded about the problems we faced and asked for their help. I said business was bad, there would be no salary raises for the foreseeable future and that in all likelihood there would be further staff reductions. When I finished, in most cases, the people applauded. I was astonished. When I asked why they were applauding when all I told them was bad news, their answer was, "At last somebody understands the problem." This was a real lesson for me. Communicating honestly with your employees, as close to one-on-one as you can, almost always pays handsome dividends.

I addressed the orders problem by making myself the head of marketing. Almost every problem we had would have been less of a problem if we had more orders. For almost a year, I spent half to three quarters of my time working on the problem of getting orders. As mentioned many times in this book, the head of the company is almost always a most effective salesperson.

I immediately did things to cut expenses, such as banning first-class air travel, eliminating raises, walking around in the evening turning off lights and pulling out soldering irons, and ending all charitable contributions. But the fact is, while these efforts were highly visible and may have looked good, they had little effect on profits. In most situations, the only meaningful way to cut expenses is to reduce the number of employees. This I also did quite aggressively, mostly at the management level. I reorganized operations and within six months had reduced annual expenses by about $400,000, which was almost enough to reach breakeven.

We had two products outside of our main line of business that seemed to be going no place. Even though each had taken a sizable investment, I decided the best approach was to terminate them and concentrate on what we knew best. One I sold to another company for about half our investment, and the other we transferred to another division of Harris.

Another major problem resulted from the fact that we had always been founder dominated, and never took the trouble to introduce formal management review and control procedures. I knew this was a problem, but did not know how to deal with it. So I visited two of the people I considered the most effective division managers in the entire Harris organization. I spent a day with each, observing how they ran their operations. I learned a lot and put much of what I learned into place at RF.

The most important step I took was to establish formal, monthly review meetings. During one week in the middle of the month, we spent about a day going over every active program, a day reviewing marketing opportunities, a day on financial review and sales forecasting, and a day on *ad hoc*, in-depth review of new research and development projects. At first, all of the people reporting to me complained that they could not afford the time. It soon became apparent that these meetings were an invaluable aid for us in keeping on top of what was going on and learning about problems before they became serious.

I remember one situation vividly. During a review meeting, I learned that on one especially complex product, we were getting back about half as many units as we shipped each month. I discovered that the units were being shipped to customers without instruction manuals. I blew my stack. I was told the publications department was busy and the manual would be ready soon. My reply was, "All right, no more shipments until an instruction manual was ready." The answer I got was, "You can't do that, our customers will get mad." My reply was, "I certainly can do that and our customers will not get half as mad as they will if they have a problem with the equipment and no instruction manual to help fix it."

I am almost embarrassed to tell this story, because it sounds so ridiculous. How long this situation would have lasted without the benefit of the formal review meetings, I have no way of knowing. This same disciplined review process also helped correct the problems of accurate sales forecasting and excessive inventory.

As I look back, these review meetings helped take the company from being a founder-dominated organization to a being professionally managed organization—a long-needed move.

How did all these changes work out? Just great! The first quarter after my return we had another huge loss, the second quarter we cut the loss almost in half, the third quarter we broke even and the fourth quarter we had enough of a profit to almost break even for the year. The following year, RF ended up in a tie for the award as the best-performing division within the entire company.

I mentioned earlier that buying a bankrupt company is one way for an entrepreneur to go into business at a bargain price. In preparing to write this chapter, I came across the January, 1992 issue of *Inc.* magazine which had an article about another interesting turnaround. It describes the situation at Elyria Foundry, in Lorain County, Ohio, where in 1983, a man named Greg Foster purchased the company from the former owners at a very attractive price. Since then, he turned a bad situation completely around, and the company is profitable again and successful in a very tough industry. The article describes a long list of problems generally similar to mine. But in addition to these, Foster also had to deal with a union. Eventually, the employees decertified the union, which helped him immensely. But boy, did he have his hands full for a while! Anyone facing a turnaround situation would do well to read that issue of *Inc.*

ᒥ Chapter 48 ᒣ

<u>When Should the Entrepreneur Step Aside?</u>

The goal of almost every entrepreneur is both to get their new business successfully off the ground and to make the new business grow into a large business. However, I have tried to emphasize many times in this book that the skills needed to manage a start-up company are substantially different then the skills needed to manage a large company. Herein lies a dilemma. If the entrepreneur succeeds in getting the start-up company off the ground, they must then decide whether they still have the skills needed to continue as head of the company, or if they should step aside and let someone else take over. Some entrepreneurs have the skills, but many do not and should not try.

When an entrepreneur understands this issue, they will willingly step aside when the time comes. They realize they can probably continue to contribute to their company in other ways than being the boss. Become the head of engineering or the head of marketing, for example. Starting the business has probably been an exciting and challenging experience loaded with "fun." Managing a large business will probably not be nearly as exciting for them and, almost surely, not as much "fun."

Ideally, the founder and his or her board of directors or board of advisers should try to make the change with as little disruption as possible. An important decision is whether to select someone to head up the company who already works there and seems to have the necessary skills, or to recruit someone from a larger outside company.

Several years ago, I read an interesting example of how one established company resolved this problem as the company grew. John Walker, founder of Autodesk, Inc., the very successful producer of AutoCad drafting software sold to architects and engineers, stepped down as president on his own initiative to return full time to programming. He apparently concluded that his programming skills would be of greater value to the company than his administrative skills.

Perhaps the management transition that was done with the most fanfare and most publicity in recent years happened at Apple Computer. About a decade ago, Steve Jobs, one of the founders of Apple, was replaced as CEO by John Scully, who was recruited from PepsiCo. Jobs continued with the company as chairman of the board.

All I know about the situation at Apple is what I learned from the business press, but it seems that they did not get along very well. A short time later, Jobs left to form NEXT, another start-up computer company.

In early 1993, Scully stepped down as head of Apple and since then, there have been several other CEO changes and much turmoil among its senior management.

Whether Apple was better off under Scully's leadership than it would have been under Jobs's leadership is impossible to say. Even though the Macintosh personal computer that Jobs created before he left the company has been quite successful, conventional wisdom in the investment community is that Apple now faces some challenging problems over the next few years.

My strong advice is, if you find it necessary to make a change such as this, try very hard to avoid the kind of turmoil that they had at Apple.

I have been personally involved in several management transitions, where the board of directors took the initiative for the change. All were difficult to handle. In one situation, the company was doing poorly. A person already employed there was promoted. The company continued to face hard times, and soon after, went bust. In another, a new CEO was hired from the outside. Here the company survived the change, but there was a fairly long period of adjustment for everyone involved.

Obviously, it is better for the entrepreneur to accept the necessity for a move such as this, and actively participate in making it work. An entrepreneur, who successfully started a business and built that business to a substantial size, should not be embarrassed to step aside to make room for someone with skills they do not have. The fact is that they will almost surely be doing themselves a favor. It is likely that much of their personal net worth is still in the form of stock in the company they started. Doing the things needed to help that company continue to thrive can only be good.

The main message I have is that everyone involved, both the entrepreneur and the board, should address the situation well before it becomes a serious problem.

⟡ Chapter 49 ⟡

Cashing Some Chips or Getting Out

This chapter is about the problems entrepreneurs face in converting their ownership in a business into liquid form. The business that you own, in all or in part, may be the most valuable asset you have, but it may be a paper asset. Sooner or later, you will surely want to use some of that asset for things such as buying a more expensive home or to pay college tuition. Or it may be that your interests have changed, and you just decided to withdraw entirely from the business and move on to other things.

Your goal will be to convert "worth on paper" to a more liquid, spendable form known as "worth in the bank." Unfortunately, this is a difficult subject to discuss, because so much is affected by your specific situation. As I've mentioned so many times, "It all depends."

My goal in this chapter is modest. I will describe the process of "cashing some chips" in general terms and then describe some personal experiences. Hopefully, it will give entrepreneurs an idea of some of the possibilities available and some of the obstacles they may encounter.

But first, let's set the stage. Assume, for the sake of discussion, your venture is five to 10 years old, it had substantial growth in sales during that period and in recent years achieved an acceptable level of earnings. Chances are, you will find yourself in the following situation:

- You're no longer working 80 hours a week (probably only 60 hours).

- Your share of ownership in the business has achieved value, but remains almost completely non-liquid.

- You are becoming nervous about having all your eggs in one basket and, as a result, are more cautious in running the business.

- You are becoming bored. The excitement and thrill of running the business is beginning to wear thin.

- The personal interests of the team of people who started the business with you are changing.

- Your salary has reached a level that is about proper for the job.

- Your family is becoming restless.

- Your children have reached college age.

- For the first time in your life, you have written a will and have started doing estate planning.

♦ The business has reached the stage where it must make the transition from being founder dominated to one that utilizes more formal, disciplined management practices. (This is a very difficult hurdle for many entrepreneurs.)

Which of these applied to my situation after starting and running a company for seven years? Every one of them applied—where else would I have gotten the list?

Your ownership situation is the most important factor in how you approach achieving liquidity. Three possibilities are:

♦ You own the business yourself, or have one or more partners active in the operation of the business.

♦ You have a number of passive shareholders, probably as a result of raising capital through private sale of stock. However, all shares are restricted and there is no public market.

♦ The company has gone public and the stock is openly traded, probably in the over-the-counter market.

Before suggesting how you can sell all or part of your share of the business, I advise you to seek counsel from experienced securities and tax lawyers. Securities laws are complex— especially regarding the sale of stock by officers, directors or principal owners of a business. They change from time to time, and are often confusing and hard to interpret and understand. In addition, these types of transactions can have serious tax implications, and the tax laws are also complex and changing continually.

Some main alternatives are:

♦ Going public if you are not already.

♦ Selling part or all of your ownership to one of your partners or an outside investor.

♦ Selling the entire business.

The pros and cons of going public have been discussed in some detail in another chapter. Depending on whether you use an underwriter and the specific circumstances of the offering, you may be able to sell some of your own stock as part of an initial public offering. When the company sells stock, it has the purpose of raising money for the business. However, if you include some of your personal stock in this offering, it has the purpose of raising money for you. These are conflicting goals that make some investors nervous.

When founder stock is sold as part of a general offering, it is called either a "secondary" or a "bailout," depending on how kind your underwriter wants to be. Frequently, underwriters will refuse to include founder stock in a public offering, but even so, going public may be your best approach, because it sets the stage for you to sell your founder stock more readily at a later date.

In closely held companies, selling all or part of your share of the business to one of your partners is a way to cash some chips. It is fairly simple legally, but the drawback is that you may have to take much of your money on the installment plan. There are also tax implications you should look into.

Selling all or part of your share of the business to an individual not already associated with the company may be more difficult to arrange, because in addition to the financial aspects of the transaction, you must find an investor who is acceptable to the other owners.

If your company is not publicly held but already has a number of outside investors, the sale of all or part of your stock to another outsider can also be a fairly simple transaction, provided the buyer is willing to accept the same restrictions that you have. But under any circumstances, restrictions tend to make for a lower price.

Barter, or trading stock for other things of value, may be a legal way to achieve some degree of liquidity. I know of one entrepreneur who used restricted stock to pay an orthodontist to straighten the teeth of two of his children. Also, I have used restricted stock as security on loans for fairly large real estate transactions.

A common way to cash all your chips is to sell the entire business. for cash or in exchange for stock in the acquiring company. Each has advantages and disadvantages. If you sell for cash, all the uncertainty of the transaction is removed, but your profit may be taxable immediately. If you take stock in the acquiring firm, it may be possible to defer taxes on the gain, sometimes permanently. But the long-term value of the deal will vary, depending on the performance of the acquiring company. One way to look at a stock-for-stock transaction is that it is simply another way to go public. Whether you keep the new stock becomes an investment or tax decision, rather than a business decision.

Finally, if you decide to sell your business, you have the difficult task of determining its value. This is another issue that could be the subject of an entire book. Sales, net worth or earnings are often used as a guide or market value if the company is already publicly owned. As I mentioned earlier, my experience as both a buyer and seller of companies is that the price is almost always higher with a publicly owned company than when negotiating a private sale.

Which way or combination of ways you use to achieve liquidity depends on the specific situation. The best advice I can give is to plan for it well in advance and get expert advice, because you want at least a fair chance of maximizing your return—and minimizing your taxes.

Chapter 50

This Is How It Should Be Done!

Tom Golisano and Paychex, Inc.

Paychex, Inc., is a payroll service company specializing in providing services to companies with between one and 200 employees. It was founded in 1970 by B. Thomas Golisano and has since grown to become a company with more than 4,000 employees. Paychex has 70 processing branches in 34 states and the District of Columbia. Its sales exceed $300 million and it serves more than 225,000 clients. As part of their service, Paychex prints paychecks for their clients, and they now print more than two million checks a week.

Golisano is a graduate of Alfred Tech., with a degree in business. Before starting Paychex, he worked for Burroughs Corporation, published a business newsletter for New York State companies and was sales manager for Electronic Accounting Systems.

The following is a transcript of a taped interview I did with Tom on November 11, 1993. All numeric and financial data, such as number of employees, sales volume, etc. has been updated to the Spring of 1996. Otherwise, the rest of the interview is unchanged. At the end of the chapter, I have added several comments about Mr. Golisano's activities since the interview and some of Paychex's more recent product offerings.

Paychex is an incredibility successful company. I suggest that when you read this interview, think about the strategy Paychex followed and how it compares to the strategies and operating principles suggested in earlier chapters of this book.

Q: Tom, please describe the factors that caused you to start Paychex. What things drove you?

A: I think the most important thing that drove me to start Paychex was the nature of my prior job. At the time, I was sales manager for a payroll processing firm called Electronic Accounting Systems (EAS). Like the traditional payroll processing providers during the mid-60s and early 70s, most of EAS's marketing and sales effort was directed at companies with between 50 and 500 employees. I think their rationale was that the larger size the client, the better the revenue and profit potential for the company.

However, it seemed to me that if you drive down any street in the U.S. today and look at the businesses, you certainly get the impression that most of them have less than 50 employees. One day I went to the library and found a publication called *County Business Patterns*. It was put out by the federal government based upon payroll tax returns. I learned that about 98 percent of all American businesses have fewer than 100 employees, and 93 percent have fewer than 50.

From this I concluded that there was a market niche out there in which no one had an interest.

Q: Was it necessary to modify the services offered, in order to succeed in this new market niche?

A: Yes, I concluded that in order to be successful addressing this small company market, you had to do three things differently.

The first was to make it very easy for small companies to transmit their payroll data to the processor each pay period. Up until that time, it was customary to have the client fill out a complex computer input sheet. It was an error-prone procedure that required skills most small businesses did not have. In addition, it was necessary for the client to either hand deliver or mail the data sheet to the processor.

Instead of having the client fill out the complex computer input sheet, I decided that it would be great if they could just call in the information on the telephone. A payroll specialist would read the name of each employee, and the client would tell them how to process that person's payroll. If it was a salaried person, they would just be paid. If they were an hourly employee, the client would tell how many hours they worked. Any changes in wage rates or exemptions, marital status or address could also be verbalized over the telephone.

A typical client with 20 employees can complete this chore in three or four minutes. Very simple for the client and they can do it from anywhere. It is not necessary for them to even be in their office or plant.

The second thing that had to be done was to provide the client with payroll tax returns. Only one company in the country provided that service at the time. In the U.S., employers are unpaid tax collectors. They are required to collect taxes from their employees and remit the funds to federal, state and local governments on a timely basis. The fines and penalties for nonpayment are severe. So I concluded that this could be an important adjunct, or addition, to the preparation of paychecks. To give you an idea of what a difficult chore this is, remember that in New York State, a company with five employees must file a minimum of 42 payroll tax returns each year. This is a very onerous task for small firms.

And the third thing is that costs had to be controlled. Payroll processors at that time had a very high minimum processing charge. For example, if you had five people on your payroll, the minimum charge was something like $24 a pay period. This was a large burden for a very small company. My belief was that we could substantially reduce the minimum processing charge and sell our service to many more very small companies. In fact, when Paychex started, our minimum charge was $5 for the first five employees. Today it is only $8.50.

Q: Did you suggest that Electronics Accounting Systems enter this market?

A: I put these three ideas together and went to the management of Electronic Accounting Systems with a proposal to go after this low-end market. They rejected my idea. I think they were concerned that certified public accountants, the CPA community, would look unfavorably upon a payroll processing firm that prepared payroll tax returns.

My intuition was that they were wrong and that CPAs would look favorably on our doing payroll tax returns. These tax returns had to be filed in a timely manner, putting the CPA under time pressure. And payroll tax returns done manually is very tedious, time-consuming work. In some cases, CPA firms were not even able to recover their costs. So I thought the CPA community would welcome our relieving them of this task.

Well, when Electronic Accounting Systems told me they were not interested in this concept, I left my job there to start Paychex.

Q: When you started the company, what were your goals?

A: I must admit, I always wanted to be an entrepreneur and have a

business of my own. It was in my bones.

Q: You started a business once before, did you not?

A: I did. During the time I was working at Electronic Accounting Systems, I published a report called "Bidders Guide." It came out three times a week and listed all requests for quotation from municipalities and school districts throughout the state.

In New York, there are laws that require all proposed purchases by municipal agencies and school districts over a certain dollar amount be advertised in a newspaper weekly and put out to public bid. My little company subscribed to all of the daily newspapers in the state, and three times a week, put out this publication, which listed forthcoming procurements. When I decided Paychex was a viable business opportunity, I sold Bidder's Guide and used the proceeds to pay off all my debts. This left me with $3,000 that I used to start Paychex.

Q: So deep in your body for many years was the desire to have your own business?

A: I think I had that desire when I was in early college. I felt that the best environment for me was working in a smaller firm, where I had much more control and could use my talents better.

Q: Do you think one of your incentives was to prove that you had the skills to do it?

A: Oh, absolutely—the job I had before Bidders Guide was as a sales rep for Burroughs Corporation. In that position, I got to talk to and know many business owners in the area. In the normal course of events, I had the opportunity to continually size up their skills as entrepreneurs. I came to the conclusion that I had a skill set that could compete with these people. Many of them were very, very successful, and I think that encouraged me to want to become an entrepreneur.

Q: Where did you get the capital you needed to start your business?

A: Starting a business, even in 1971, with only $3,000 was probably impossible. If I had to do it over again, I probably would not do it, but I felt so secure in what I was doing that even though I did not have enough money, I started anyway. The $3,000 lasted about 30 days. Then I found myself in a situation where I was borrowing money using consumer installment loans from several banks, I borrowed money from relatives, I even used my credit card to meet our payroll on a few occasions. I did all the things undercapitalized companies must do to survive.

Q: So at one point, you were up to your ears in debt?

A: Absolutely, and I did not get out of that debt until 1977 or 1978.

Q: How long did it take you to get your first customer?

A: It only took me a couple weeks to get my first customer. Quite frankly, I found a friend who had a business that really needed our service, and he was my first customer.

Getting customers was not as big an issue with me as it might be in other cases, because I had two years experience in selling payroll service, and I knew the market was there. The credibility issue was a bigger problem, because here I was starting out as the new payroll pro-cessing company in town with zero clients. That was an issue during the first three to six months. But after we got past that threshold and had 30 or 40 clients, it became much easier.

Q: How long did it take before you could say you were making a "decent living" from the business?

A: I did not begin to make a decent living until 1977 or 1978.

Q: You mean seven or eight years?

A: I started in business in November, 1970. But you have to realize that during the time period between 1974 to 1978, I was plowing back a lot of the proceeds from the Rochester operation to start other new Paychex operations in cities around the country. Consequently, all of the money that Paychex made locally was being used to open new locations. My standard of living did not start to improve until after that.

Q: Did you have a wife and children at the time?

A: Yes, I had a wife and two children.

Q: So this was a sacrifice for everybody?

A: Absolutely it was, and I would be less than honest with you if I did not tell you that the financial sacrifices, as well as the time commitment, really wore on us as far as our marriage was concerned.

Q: I've read that the stress and strains and time demands of starting a company have wrecked many marriages. I know that you were divorced and remarried. Was this a factor in your family situation?

A: I would say it was a factor. I do not know whether it was the major factor, but it certainly was a contributing one. I do not know if you heard the story, but one night I came home and my wife said to me, "I think you love Paychex more than you love me." I said, "Well, that might be true, but I love you more than I love football." But there is no question that my life was consumed by Paychex during those formative years.

Q: I am amazed at the parallel between your life and mine. One time my wife said to me, "Bill, your six children were brought up without a father." I don't think they were really brought up without a father, but she may know better than me.

A: I've heard that line.

Q: Your first office was here in Rochester, and it took a number of years to become established and operate anywhere near a profit. When and how did you go about putting offices in other cities, and how did you raise the capital to accomplish that?

A: It was not until 1974, and the way it happened was that a friend of mine who worked at Electronic Accounting Systems with me walked into my office one day and said, "Tom, it looks like Paychex is going to be successful. How can I get involved?" I came up with the idea that we could each put in some money and start a corporation in which we each had 50-percent ownership. It was to be located in Syracuse, New York and patterned after Paychex.

Q: It was a joint venture?

A: It was a joint venture partnership—a separate company. A few months later, an employee of one of our clients walked into my office and said to me, "This service is terrific—it can be sold in other cities. I want to go down to Miami, Florida, and start a Paychex office there." I said, "That's great, I would like to be partners with you." He said, "No, I don't want to be your partner, but I will be your franchisee." So we put together a very loose franchise agreement, and he moved to Miami and started a Paychex operation down there. After these two offices got going, I could see that it could be done and represented an opportunity. Then I began the process of going out and finding people to start Paychex offices in other parts of the country.

Q: You mean it became a deliberate part of your strategy?

A: Absolutely, over the next four years, it evolved into 11 joint ventures and six franchise operations. All the people but one had lived in Rochester and moved to other parts of the country to set up these operations.

Q: The services Paychex provides requires a fairly sophisticated computer program to do the calculation of the tax payments. When you move to another state, the computer program may not be transferable. Was that much of a problem?

A: It's a lot more transferable than you would think. Basically, there are only seven methods of calculating state income tax, even though there are 43 states that have them. And the concept of unemployment insurance is basically the same. The experience rates and the taxable wages may change, but conceptually it's all the same. You are right in saying that our payroll software must be very sophisticated, but we grew at a rate that the software was able to grow with us. Right now, we have several million lines of code in our payroll software. But in the first two years that we had the system, there were only 30,000 or 40,000 lines.

Q: Are you telling me that when you expanded outside of Rochester through the use of joint ventures and franchises, you discovered a way to do it without any outside capital?

A: In the case of the franchises, yes, but in the case of the joint ventures, I had to either provide 50 percent of the capital from existing company resources or borrow the money. It was a combination of both.

Q: In the early days, how much money would an individual have to raise to start a Paychex franchise or joint venture? What kind of resources did they need?

A: The total cost on the average was between $35,000 and $50,000 to get the operation going and to reach a break-even point. If it were a franchise, the franchisee had to pay all of it. In the case of a joint venture, we split whatever amount it turned out to be. The people in Washington, D.C., got it going for $22,000, that was the lowest. The highest was more than $100,000. It was a matter of capability and how fast sales volume could build.

Q: At some point, you decided that you wanted to have a single integrated company and bring your joint ventures and franchises back into the parent. Why did you decide to do that?

A: I think there were a number of factors. The first thing I began to realize was that even though these people that I got involved with were very entrepreneurial and very aggressive, I started to notice a difference in their ambition level. Some of the people were very aggressive in opening multiple office locations, and others only wanted to open one and rest on those laurels. That began to bother me, because I started to see some undeveloped territory.

The second thing I realized was some of the people were very good in the sales side of our business, but not very good operationally, and vice versa. So we were not doing a very good job of skill matching.

The third reason was that these individual corporations, even though they were working, were very weak. It was very difficult for them to buy computers, it was very difficult to upgrade offices, it was just a weak environment in which to operate.

And fourth, no one had given any thought to how they would cash out when the appropriate time came. I think many entrepreneurs never think about this when they start their venture.

Q: It seems to me, you faced a very difficult challenge. How did you go about integrating these joint ventures and franchisees back into the parent company?

A: Well, the first thing I did, of course, was try to reduce their resistance. You have to remember, it was just three or four years earlier that I convinced these people that they should be entrepreneurs and own their own businesses. What I did was write a business plan and send it out to the group in early December of 1978. It was an outline for a consolidation of the 18 separate Paychex operations.

The plan was a five-year strategy outlining what we should do. It included spending three years building the sales organization to open new markets and the next two years concentrating on building profitability. The end goal was to either become a publicly owned corporation or to merge. Of course, when I presented this plan, it created a lot of consternation and generated many telephone calls, because the people really did not understand my rationale. Just a year or two earlier, I had encouraged them to become entrepreneurs, and now I was suddenly telling them we should consolidate. I was suggesting

we should combine into one larger company and that we should all be shareholders and employees of that company.

In February 1979, we all met around a big table down in the Bahamas and spent an entire day discussing the virtues and downside of this kind of consolidation. The next morning, everybody came into the room at nine o'clock. We sat around the big table again, and I went around the room asking each person whether or not they would agree to this consolidation. They all agreed to it.

One key question they all had was how much stock each one of them would receive for their contribution to the new corporation. That was done by formula by myself and two others. We actually sat in a motel room in Buffalo, New York, and came up with a formula. Then we were either smart enough or lucky enough to decide that using the formula was okay, but we had to make some adjustments based upon what we thought would be some subjective feelings. The final point, though, was that once we announced how much stock each one of the individuals were gong to get in this new corporation, we did not allow any negotiation.

Q: It was either this or nothing?

A: I knew as soon as I allowed one person to negotiate and change their stock allocation, every one of them would be standing outside the door, and the thing never would have been accomplished. I just decided I was going to stand firm, and it was going to be take it or leave it.

Q: Did they have the option of continuing on their own if they chose?

A: Yes, they did. If a person decided they did not want to become part of this new venture, we guaranteed them we would not open a Paychex branch in their city. However, in the case of the joint ventures, one of the realities was that they did not know who their partner might be the following week, because I always had the option of selling my half to someone else. Fortunately, they all agreed.

Q: Many people starting new businesses have great ideas for products and services, but completely overlook the fact that to succeed it is necessary to find a way to sell that product or service. Paychex seems to have overcome this problem. Can you tell how you accomplished this?

A: Well, I will tell you it is not something we learned on day number one. It evolved over time. For example, Paychex was started here in Rochester, New York, and for the first four years, my average sales volume was something like 40 new clients a year. Today, the Rochester branch of Paychex sells over 1,300 clients a year. The average sales rep in the Rochester area sells 180 new clients a year. I used to sell 40. So you can see that it really evolved over a long period of time.

You can also see that if there is one thing that Paychex did well, even from day one, it is that we do a very good job networking both the CPAs in our community and existing clients. Today about 75 percent of new business comes to us because of referrals from either of these two groups. But I can tell you that the level of expectations and the achievement level of our sales people has changed dramatically over the years as our visibility and credibility have grown and as our skill set has grown.

Q: Would you describe some of the marketing and selling programs you are now following? Where do you get your new customers? Do you advertise, use direct mail, use agents, etc.?

A: We do all of those things, Bill. We telemarket, we use direct mail, we do some institutional advertising, but I can tell you that 98 percent of our marketing budget is in our direct sales organization. We now have 500 sales people nationally, plus the management to direct this sales force. And on average, each sales person brings in about 140 new clients a year.

Q: Do your sales people spend a lot of time getting to know the CPAs in their area and working with them?

A: Yes, our sales people have a geographical territory for companies, and they have a named account list for CPAs. Each CPA in an area is assigned to a sales person and it is up to that sales person to develop the relationship.

Q: While Paychex was growing, were there any people outside the company whom you leaned on for advice and counsel and who were especially helpful?

A: I think that up until 1981, the answer to that question was no. In 1981, however, the University of Rochester and the Hambrecht & Quist Venture Capital Fund bought substantial stakes in Paychex. This was before we became a public company. Those two organizations had people in them, namely Phil Horsley at the U of R and Grant Inman at H & Q, who became members of our board of directors. They have been and still are a tremendous help to our organization.

Q: Are they both still on your board?

A: Yes, they are. In addition to their expertise in the area of general management, they had great expertise in the area of finance and going public. Their relationship with Wall Street and stock analysts has been extremely helpful to us.

Q: So from then on, the additional capital you needed as Paychex grew came from conventional sources, rather than from your credit cards?

A: Actually, the money that the U of R and H & Q invested to get a stake in Paychex did not go to the corporation. It went to existing shareholders.

Q: You mean they bought stock from individuals and not from the company?

A: Yes, the real benefit was that it gave some of our shareholders liquidity before the public offering. That was very important, because many of us had gone for many years without any way to cash in, if you will.

Q: But what did you do for additional capital as the company grew?

A: We never had any additional capital before we went public. We borrowed money from banks, and at one point, our loans were even classified.

Q: So you used every method available to raise capital?

A: I think if you add them all up, Bill, we did. Everything from home equity loans to family borrowing to borrowing from banks to borrowing larger amounts from banks to venture capital to going public. I think we used them all.

Q: Is it accurate to say that during the first 10 years or so of Paychex's existence, you were at considerable personal risk every minute?

A: Absolutely, absolutely.

Q: There is no easy street.

A: No, there wasn't at Paychex.

Q: In 1983, Paychex became a publicly owned company. Why did you take that step?

A: We did it for a number of reasons. Obviously, most important was to provide liquidity for our shareholders. By then, we had approximately 85 or 90 shareholders with varying stakes in the company. This included the original joint venture people and franchisees who each owned from two to six percent of the company. The other outside shareholders had been very patient and very supportive, but it was time to do something to give them their rewards.

Another reason we went public was that we were able to raise about

$7 million for the company, which we immediately spent in developing an online computer system. This gave us a great economic advantage in offering our payroll services. Up until then, we were using relatively uneconomic computer systems.

The third reason was it gave us more visibility and more credibility with our customers.

Fourth, being a public corporation made it easier to recruit key employees. A publicly owned company gives the perception that you are more stable and will probably have a longer existence. You also have the additional benefit that you can give employees more visible incentives, such as stock option, which are very important.

To this day, I never regretted the decision to go public.

Q: What were some of the problems of being a public corporation? Did you find any unanticipated difficulties?

A: None that were important. Some people say that dealing with the Securities Exchange Commission is a problem. Fortunately, we have a Chief Financial Officer, Tom Clark, who is responsible for maintaining a good relationship with the SEC and making sure we are always in complete compliance.

Also, we always looked at the Wall Street community as providing us with a sense of discipline. You hear a lot of CEOs tell how burdensome it is to run their company on a year-to-year, quarter-to-quarter basis. We have never looked at it that way. We think the outside investor market gives us a structure and discipline and makes us focus better on our responsibilities. Frankly, I have never felt that being a public corporation had any negatives. We have tried to take those perceived negatives and turn them into positives.

Q: When you started the company, there were few if any other companies following the same strategy. Today, there must be many Paychex clones going down the same road and selling their services at lower prices. How has this impacted your business?

A: You are right about your observation that there are many more payroll processing companies out there serving the low end of the client base than there were when we started. And you are also right in that they usually price their services about 10 or 15 percent lower than Paychex. For whatever reason, we have become the price setter, and others keep working their price around us. The competition that this offers us has a positive effect. There are so many companies now considering using computerized payroll processing that it actually makes our marketing easier.

Q: You mean people are more likely to accept the concept?

A: Yes, 10 years ago, when you tried to sell payroll processing services to a company with 14 employees, their perception would be, "Not for us, we can't afford it, it's too complicated." Today, it's exactly the opposite, because our average client is a company with only 14 employees.

So those other payroll processing companies, even though they are competitors, have done a service to us and others in the industry. They help market the concept by educating the public that such a service is available, comprehensive and very low in cost.

Q: Is the market becoming saturated?

A: I don't think so. If you add up all the companies doing payroll processing in the United States, combined they have less than 14 or 15 percent of the total market. The rest of the market is either still doing their payroll manually or have some sort of in-house system.

Q: So this remains almost virgin territory?

A: Right. Paychex, with 225,000 clients, has about three percent of the markets we serve, and seven years ago, we had three percent of the markets we served. Remember that many Fortune 500 companies are downsizing. People are starting small companies today who would not have considered it 10 or 15 years ago. Even though Paychex has a great track record of client growth over the last 10 years, we are only growing at about the same rate that the market is growing.

Q: I have been of the opinion for some time that the 1990s has become the age of the entrepreneur. Do you agree?

A: I would say so and, quite frankly, I think it will continue for the rest of the decade.

Q: For a number of years, Paychex was a very focused company, computing payrolls, printing checks and preparing the required reports for your clients. Is this too much concentration at this stage of your development?

A: Well, let me tell you what has evolved. We are in the process of change. Up until about three or four years ago, we considered ourselves to be a payroll processing company. In an effort not to be myopic, and in an effort to take advantage of other opportunities, we like to think of ourselves as a provider of employee administrative services. Let me tell you what the difference is.

First of all, we still continue to do payroll, and that is the core product that represents over 90 percent of our volume. But the other things we now offer include employee handbooks, Section 125 Cafeteria Plans and administration of health, workman's compensation and disability insurance. We offer other employee-type products even so basic as writing job descriptions and the posters that go on the company billboards regarding state labor laws.

All of these items somehow involve the relationship between the employer and the employee. We think we have broadened our horizon to be much more comprehensive in our product offering, while still not losing our focus on the small employer. Even with these additional services, our target market niche has remained the same, namely, companies with between one and 200 employees.

Q: You mean you are expanding your offering, but you have not changed your market focus?

A: That's right. If you look at our financial numbers over the last three or four years, you can see that our client growth has been 11 or 12 percent, but our revenue growth has been substantially higher. That is because we are now selling incremental products and services to the same customers that we were just selling payroll service to four or five years ago.

Q: I view Paychex as being a niche-based company—you concentrate in your offering and you concentrate in your target market. I think if you analyze all the great companies of the world, you will find a similar quality. How important was the niche, the idea of focus, in your developing a strategy.

A: I think it was very important, and I will give you some examples. We made the decision years ago, as we consolidated the franchisees and joint ventures, that we would focus on geography with current payroll products. Rather than diversifying into other services, we knew we could establish more branch offices selling the same product and make money at it. So the theme was to do it in as many geographic areas as possible and build the distribution network. Then we would have a client base that we could sell additional products and services to.

I think with the benefit of hindsight, that was the best decision we could have made. If we had become a multiproduct company too early,

we could have gotten bogged down in product development and drifted away from the geographic expansion. The ability to sell additional products to existing customers is a lot easier than selling new products to new customers, but we tried to find the right time to make that move.

Q: Paychex has a reputation for spending a great deal of effort training all of its employees. Would you describe the program, and why do you think it is so important?

A: We are in somewhat of a technical business. We have a responsibility to our clients and to the CPAs who refer clients to do payroll processing in such a way that it is accurate and timely. The preparation of tax returns requires that we have a very high level of competence. It demands that we be as good at it as we possibly can. The thing that differentiates payroll processing companies is the confidence the client has in your work and in your people. The best way to get client confidence is to be technically competent.

Now I will tell you the extremes we carry it to. All new sales people and all new payroll specialists that come into Paychex come to Rochester for training. Payroll specialists, incidentally, are the people that provide the day-to-day service to our clients. They answer the phone, take employee information, etc. We have about 1,100 of those people. Every new payroll specialist and every new sales person receives two weeks of comprehensive training. At the end of that time, they are given a technical competency test. If they pass the test, they stay with the company, if they fail the test, they are not allowed to become a payroll specialist or a salesperson.

Q: It's up or out?

A: Yes, up or out. Then on a continuing basis every three or four months, the payroll specialists are given another exam in their branch office which tests them again on their ability and knowledge regarding payroll tax law and their ability to interface with our software system. This is not a pass/fail test—it is more a management tool to determine where our people may need to improve in certain skill areas.

Also, at least once each week, every branch office must conduct a three-hour training program for all of their payroll specialists. This curriculum is provided by the corporate staff, so we know that it is happening every week in all of our branches.

Q: How big is your corporate training department?

A: We have a corporate training department of about 30 people located right in the headquarters building. We bring into Rochester between 1,200 and 1,400 people a year. Out of 4,000 employees nationwide, that is a very big percentage. We do computer training, teach people quality service skills and we have a lot of management and supervisory training courses. On an average, we invest between $15,000 and $20,000 in training for every new sales person and payroll specialist.

Q: This certainly distinguishes you from 99 percent of your competitors?

A: Hopefully, it does. We have just made a decision to carry it one step further. We are going to have a receptionist training course here.

Q: I told you sometime ago that of all the telephone calls I make, the ones I make to Paychex are the most pleasant experience. I once spoke to your advertising manager, and she told me her first assignment when coming to Paychex was to prepare a video telling people the correct way to answer the telephone.

A: The telephone is a key issue here, but even if it were not, we would still go to the same effort. That initial telephone call presents an image of a company.

Q: I am sure you are as offended as I am when a machine answers your call and says, "If you want product information, press 1, if you want to speak to a sales person, press 2, etc., etc.

A: I am not an advocate of mail boxes for telephones.

Q: Recently, you seem to have become involved in a number of activities unrelated to Paychex's main business, such as starting a third national political party, becoming involved in community antidrug and teen pregnancy programs, and investing in other new businesses. Why have you decided to do this, and don't you think the distraction might have a detrimental effect on your business?

A: To answer the second part of your question first, there is no question that you can become involved in a lot of outside activities that could greatly impact your ability to do your job at the company where you earn your living. Fortunately, we have a staff of people that allows me to have more time away from the company than might be considered normal. But the reason I have gotten involved in these other activities may also be the result of my strong entrepreneurial leaning. When you see an opportunity to improve things, you just want to do it.

You mention substance abuse and teen pregnancy. We have major problems in this country in both of these areas. They are causing much misery among our people and costing the country tremendous amounts of money. I happen to have gotten involved in an environment where I have learned about these problems. I guess my "pot stirring" philosophy of life caused me to want to go out and see if I can do something to improve the situation.

Q: So you suggest that Paychex is somewhat self-sufficient, independent of you?

A: I hate to use the words "independent of me," but let's say, less dependent on me than they used to be.

Q: In thinking back through the whole history of the company, what do you believe were the smartest things you did, and what you think were the not-so-smart things? You notice I did not say "dumb."

A: I can give you a dumb one later. I think the smartest things we did relate to the market niche we choose and the fact that we stayed very focused on the payroll product as long as we did. Also important was that we were able to pull those 18 separate entities into one and become a serious company. For the people involved, this was very rewarding financially, and from the viewpoint of our clients, this made Paychex a far better company.

Now I will tell you what I think was the dumbest thing we did. We went public in August 1983, and right after that we made the announcement that we were planning to start a new service in Boston, Massachusetts, called Jobline. The function of Jobline was to find employees that were looking for jobs and find employers that were looking for certain types of employees. Then we put these two things into a common data base and created a service, whereby we could provide the names of potential employees to potential employers. This was an alternative to putting ads in newspapers or using recruiters.

You can say this is consistent with our payroll business, but I can tell you that it is not. It was really not for us. We got involved in a business that we did not understand, knew very little about and were unfamiliar with the dynamics of the market we choose, namely Boston. Consequently, the project lasted about nine months, and we spent about $750,000. It was a total loss. Doing that right after a public offering was about the dumbest thing we could have done.

Fortunately, we recovered over time, but with hindsight, we would never do something like that again.

Q: You are now past 50 years of age and have certainly achieved financial independence. What are your personal goals over the next few years?

A: Right now, my vision for myself is to do more of the same. Paychex has achieved some notable objectives. We passed the $300 million mark in revenue, our market valuation, i.e., the market price times the number of outstanding shares, exceeds $2 billion. This makes me very proud. But I realize that even at $300 million, Paychex has barely scratched the surface. We believe we have a formula for growth that will serve us well over the next four or five years. We think that if we can continue that revenue growth, we will continue to increase our profits by about 20 or 25 percent a year. And I want to see that happen. We are a $300-million company and should be a $500-million company. If we achieve that, we will probably want to be a $1-billion company.

Q: Now this is no longer for your personal financial gain?

A: I think I am long past the goal of increasing my personal net worth. This is no longer an issue with me. I think the thing that keeps me coming to work every day is the fact that I enjoy what I do and still feel challenged.

Q: This is the entrepreneurial instinct causing you to want to create something with impact?

A: Exactly. It is like someone who falls into the boat syndrome. You buy your first boat, which is small, and all of a sudden you are looking for your next bigger boat and next bigger boat yet.

Q: If you were advising an entrepreneur on the verge of quitting his or her job and starting a business of their own, what are the three or four most important pieces of advice you can give them?

A: The first piece of advice I would give is to make sure that, whatever their family relationships are, the people involved are knowledgeable about what you are doing and are supportive.

Secondly, I think I would be very concerned about my capitalization. I have seen too many good ideas fall by the wayside because the entrepreneur either overestimated their ability to sell their new product or service or underestimated how much cash they would need. Selling is a major, major part of starting a business.

Third, I think before I got involved in my new enterprise, I would try to learn as much about that business as I possibly could, whether it be marketing or product/service development. I came out of one payroll processing company and started another. The strategy we followed was different, but I really understood the market and the needs of the users of the service we proposed. I think that is the best possible scenario. Build your business on a strength. It is very undesirable to try to learn a new business at the same time you try to start a new company.

Thank you, Tom, for your candid, complete and very knowledgeable comments on your experiences starting Paychex and your suggestions about starting a new business. I'm sure this will be of immense help to the readers of the 4th edition of Start Up.

Comments: *Mentioned in the interview is the fact that Mr. Golisano is one of the founders of the Independence Party in New York State. In November 1994, he ran for governor of New York against Mario Cuomo, a Democrat, and George Pataki, a Republican. There were a total of six candidates. George Pataki won and became governor. Tom Golisano placed third, with a total of about 217,000 votes. This means that the Independence Party will hold the fourth row in voting machines for the next five years, which was one of his goals for being a candidate.*

Since the interview in November of 1993, Paychex has added the following services to its product offering:

- ◆ *401(k) Administration.*
- ◆ *Pay-as-you-go Workman's Compensation Insurance.*
- ◆ *Long Distance Telephone Services.*

Notice that all of these services are directed to its target market of companies with between one and 200 employees.

Chapter 51

25 Entrepreneurial Deathtraps: Avoid the Classic Mistakes

This chapter was written by Frederick J. Beste, CEO of the General Partners of NEPA Venture Funds, L.P., based in Bethlehem, Pennsylvania. NEPA specializes in seed and start-up stage venture capital investing. Beste has seen many successes and many failures among start-up companies. These Death Traps are the things he considers the most important common mistakes made by entrepreneurs. Previously, he was CEO of Kentucky Highlands Investment Corp., a venture development firm in London, Kentucky, and vice-president of Greater Washington Investors, Inc., a venture capital firm in Washington, D.C. He has been a venture capitalist since 1968.

Entrepreneurs face all kinds of potential adversity—some can kill them, some merely set them back a little. The saddest failures I have seen are those that should have been predictable and should have been avoided. As senseless as some of these death traps seem, they can be very difficult to avoid. Some of them appear in the form of well-worn paths, which logic, greed and even common sense might suggest taking.

How tragic that some take entrepreneurs over the cliff, time and time again.

Even though none of these traps is certain to be fatal, they have been for many new companies. Each should be avoided or tempered, if possible. The following are, in my opinion, the most serious hazards faced by new and small businesses (not necessarily in order of importance):

1. Over-reliance on one or two customers. Getting a telephone call from a very large customer telling you that they are planning to bring the work you have been doing back in-house can be a devastating experience. Suddenly you find yourself running a $1-million business that has a $3-million break-even. I strongly recommend that you do everything possible to build up other parts of your business to reduce your dependence on a single large customer or two.

2. Three (four?) (five?) musketeers. Three friends start a business. They split the ownership absolutely equally, they draw identical salaries and they plan to make decisions by "consensus." One, perhaps the oldest, reluctantly becomes president.

This arrangement has three drawbacks. First, the company has no leader, no one with ultimate responsibility for its success or failure. Second, sooner or later there is sure to be an honest disagreement among the principals with no one to resolve the impasse. And third, the president will almost inevitably see himself or herself as "a little more than equal." The others will resent it.

The solution? Pick a leader from the start and treat that person as the leader. He or she should have the largest equity position and the largest salary.

✓ **3. 50-50 partnerships.** This is similar to the "Three Musketeers" with all the same problems, plus one— a stalemate of power. It implies distrust. These marriages almost always turn sour or end in divorce.

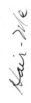

✓ **4. "Mousetrap" teams.** A handful of brilliant engineers spend six months in the basement designing an absolute gee-whiz prototype that should set the world on fire. They have created a "better mousetrap," however, the world does not beat a path to their door. No one on the team has ever commercialized a technology. Doing it is as hard or harder as creating the product. It is imperative that at least one member of the team has been down this road before.

5. Underpricing. A start up that adopts a lowest-price market strategy is roughly analogous to Liechtenstein insisting on settling a dispute with the U.S. with ICBMs. I would add that the statement that causes me to lose my last meal fastest (always accompanied by big smiles, no less) is: "We're going to have the best product at the lowest price."

✓ **6. Insufficient start-up capital.** Even though detailed cash flow projections have been made, the reality is that sales and margins do not meet expectations in 90-plus percent of new businesses for many different reasons. If each founder initially chipped in the limit of his or her resources, it may already be time for the fat lady to sing. Do not start a business if you can't come up with more capital than you think you might need.

Need income for a year for me—

✓ **7. Failure to consider the downside.** Three critical factors drive the cash needs of a business— <u>product development time</u>, <u>sales and gross margins</u>. Most entrepreneurs are too optimistic on all three. Look at the downside in advance. Developing fallback plans is the only effective medicine for failed initial assumptions.

✓ **8. Failure to look at industry norms.** Most entrepreneurs who fail, blame "undercapitalization" as the culprit. <u>Overoptimism is again the real villain.</u> Do not project margins of 30 percent in an industry where 10 percent is considered as doing well.

✓ **9. Lack of focus.** A new venture's most precious resource is talent. Doing one thing well from scratch is an enormous challenge. Tackling three or four is inviting disaster. Sort out the opportunities before you start to determine the best market and product opportunity. Pursue the daylights out of the best.

10. Bringing on the vulture. The bad news is that while all money is green, it is not all equal. There really are vulture capitalists out there and they do not all work for venture capital firms. They're obstructive, controlling, heavy-handed and mistrustful. The good news is that there are also investors out there who are *gems*—experienced, constructive, supportive—and they don't all work for venture capital firms.

How can you tell a jerk from a gem, *before the fact?* Do two things. One, ask around among the service providers—the lawyers, the accountants, the bankers. They know who the good guys are and who the bad guys are. Two, ask for a comprehensive list of phone numbers of CEOs of companies the firm or individual has backed, after which, call them and grill them mercilessly as to what kind of partner the investor has been.

11. First class from the start. Show me a start up in fancy quarters with elegant furniture and management salaries matching their last position, and I will show you a prescription for failure. Most of the successful entrepreneurs I have seen have an uncanny ability to spend a nickel in six places. They not only realize that adequate cash spells life, but that the lack of it spells death.

12. Diversification into the unknown. There are many reasons this is done: an initial failure in one field, "the grass is greener" syndrome, whatever. If you do not know the marketplace—not the technology, the *marketplace*—and the competition, you are asking for trouble.

13. Emotional litigation. I am virtually allergic to litigation for small businesses. Justice is all too often not achieved. Lawsuits are expensive, outrageously distracting, emotionally stressful and often end up with all parties ultimately agreeing to drop the action. There are some circumstances where such action is needed, but most of the time, entrepreneurs should bite their tongues and get on with the business. Talk to your peers who have been down this road—horror stories are in abundance.

14. Product never ready for market. Many engineers simply will not show their baby to the world until they achieve perfection. This is an unattainable goal. When you have your product to the point that it represents a clearly superior choice, freeze the design and hand it over to the sales force.

15. Low barrier to entry growth industry. Video retailing, oversized chocolate chip cookies, quick-change oil franchises and others burst onto the scene virtually overnight. In many of these, there has been a tremendous shakeout of the Johnny-come-slightly-latelies. If industry visibility is high and the barriers to entry low, the growth rate of supply will, in all probably, exceed the growth rate of demand all too quickly.

16. Inadequate market research. A book could be written on this phenomenon alone. Suffice it to say that failure of the entrepreneur to get out there and research the marketplace and talk to at least a dozen prime potential customers *before* committing to a product is asking for trouble.

17. Failure to segment the market. The U.S. tent market is $100 million. Your product is a high-end backpacking tent, and you hope to sell $5 million annually in five years. All you need is five percent of the market—right? No sweat.

Wrong—circus, funeral and special events tents take 20 percent of the market, the military represents 20 percent and backyard family tents are 20 percent. And the two largest backpack retailers controlling 20 percent of the market own captive suppliers. That leaves 10 percent as your opportunity, so you really need 50 percent to achieve your goal.

18. No reason for the customer to change. The best entrepreneurial efforts I have seen have flowed from the development of a competitive matrix, i.e., a comparison by vendor (competitors) of all factors influencing the purchase decision. If you cannot find good reason for potential customers to switch to your product, they probably won't.

19. Payback can't be calculated. If you intend to sell your product based upon saving your customers money, make sure the savings are easily calculable. A claim that you save on scrap is easy to demonstrate, a claim that your product will cut down on back injuries is not. The latter is a much tougher sale than the former.

20. Failure to admit a mistake. Psychologically, one of the most insidious death traps is the one entitled, "We have too much invested in this to walk away now." Do not hesitate to admit a mistake. The right question to ask is, "Would we invest in this now, knowing what we know, if it were presented as a new opportunity?"

21. Step function growth. Every once in a while, a venture grows by leaps and bounds. When such a happy event occurs, be sure you don't succeed yourself into bankruptcy. Some pitfalls include failure to check credit, poor quality control, hiring unqualified people and bad customer service. Keep a careful eye on the business and adjust to your success accordingly.

22. Betting the ranch. Contrary to legend, entrepreneurs are not high rollers. They are not afraid to take moderate risk that is largely under their control, but they would never bet the ranch, whether on an acquisition, a new product or anything else. They will not risk all that they have, even on a "sure thing."

23. Ignoring the handwriting on the wall. Holding on to old ways, continuing to rely on original, bedrock assumptions in the face of mounting evidence to the contrary, can take even a healthy company down in an amazingly short time.

Several years ago, the stuffed toy industry began to shift to offshore production to reap the benefits of lower wage rates. One domestic manufacturer reacted to an eroding market share by cheapening its line and offering lower quality. Obviously, this did not work. The firm ultimately abandoned stuffed toys entirely and redirected its efforts into other businesses.

24. Spiraling costs. As you expand from your garage into an industrial park, hire a chief financial officer or install a new computer system, your break-even point will creep, maybe even gallop, up and up. Before you increase expenses by these kinds of moves, plan carefully and develop fall-back positions before going ahead.

25. Silliness phase. This does not need to be a company jet; lesser gluttonies can have the same effect. "If they can have a leased car, why can't I?" "Maybe I have earned a country club membership?" And other such extravagances can inflict major damage to work force morale and divert management energy, sharpness and desire.

As you build your business, keep this list in mind. It may sound strange, but you cannot succeed if you do not avoid failure. Entrepreneurial human nature is to just be on the offensive; but even in building a business, defense is critically important. Avoid making these classic mistakes and you can be sure that you have substantially increased your chances of winning the game.

✧ Chapter 52 ✧

The Personal Computer and the Entrepreneur

Without question, the introduction of the personal computer (PC) 20 years or so ago caused a revolution in entrepreneurial activity in both the hardware and software areas. A number of today's finest companies started because of the popularity of the PC. Who would ever have predicted companies like Microsoft, Compaq Computer, Intel and hundreds of others coming into existence and thriving over such a short period of time?

This chapter is about the idea of using the PC as a tool to help you in the management of your business, whatever it might be.

Anyone starting or managing a new business would be well-advised to become skilled in the use of a personal computer. You do not have to be a programmer or hardware expert, but by learning and using some inexpensive, readily available, off-the-shelf programs, you can save many hours in the operation of your business and probably do a better job, as well.

Software

Described below are a number of software applications where using a PC will almost surely make your job easier. I mention, as examples, several popular programs that you might consider in these applications. Even though most of these programs are good, this chapter is not intended to be a quality rating of PC software.

I believe it is more important to use programs with which you are familiar than more modern programs, loaded with features you are unlikely to ever need. Several of the more important programs I use I have had for five or six years and am completely familiar with their operation. This is much more desirable than changing to more modern programs that are complex and must be learned over from scratch.

A second issue is the subject of upgrades. Selling upgrades is an important source of revenue for software companies. They seem to come out almost once a year, and the temptation to upgrade is frequently very persuasive. My policy is to buy the first one or two upgrades, because in addition to offering new features, they are often correcting errors and bugs in the original version. After that, I usually no longer purchase upgrades, because again, they are frequently more complex, have features I will not use and often take up much more memory.

Spreadsheets. I used a spreadsheet to do the cash flow examples in Chapter 25 of this book. Programs such as QuattroPro, Excel or Lotus 1-2-3 can be of immense value in doing financial projections, cash management, scheduling and other similar tasks. A spreadsheet helps you organize your thoughts and performs arithmetic and mathematical calculations automatically as you change the data in the model.

Word processors. These programs let you compose letters, reports, memos, etc. They check spelling and grammar and let you modify and change the material without retyping the entire document. The high-end word processors include Microsoft Word, WordPerfect and others. They are all extremely versatile.

Data bases. I used a data base to maintain lists of thousands of potential and actual buyers of the first edition of this book, which I published myself. And it helped me do many focused mailings, based on these lists. The names and addresses were mostly obtained from the membership directories of various professional associations.

When you buy your word processor and data base programs, be sure they include a capability known as "mail-merge." This is a system for writing a single letter and sending it to all of the names you select from your data base. The final document will have the recipients name and address printed on the top of the sheet, which makes the letter appear personally typed. There are many excellent, high-quality data base programs available.

Financial accounting. I have not personally used any, but I am told that several low-end, inexpensive accounting programs can be of great value to the small business owner. Your accountant may be able to advise you on which program is best for your particular situation.

Telephone and address books. This is the program you will probably use more than any other. It keeps a file of names, addresses and telephone numbers, similar to a Rolodex. And it will automatically dial numbers if you use a modem. Some programs also provide a calendar and have the capability to organize your daily appointment schedule and keep track of "to-do" lists. I use a program named HotLine, which is simple, versatile and easy to use. It may be that there are newer programs with added features, but once you enter 500 names, telephone numbers and addresses, etc., into a program that does an acceptable job, it is hard to persuade yourself that a change is worthwhile.

Desktop publishing. This is similar to a word processor, but is designed specifically for the preparation of brochures, catalogs, promotional material, etc. There are several available, costing about $100. Using a program such as this can substantially reduce your publication costs.

Presentation programs. If you do many presentations in the course of managing your business, you might consider a program that can be used to develop overheads and slides that combine words with icons and graphics.

Utility programs. If you use a PC a lot, you will find the need for a utility program to use in managing files, making backups, searching for viruses, cleaning up your hard drive and various other tasks. Caution is advised because programs designed for DOS sometimes are incompatible with more modern operating systems, such as Windows 95. Be sure the utility program you choose is compatible with the operating system you use.

Information services. If you need information about almost any imaginable subject, subscribe to a service such as CompuServe or America Online. They can help you with information searches, weather forecasts, airline schedules, stock quotes and countless other tasks. The cost is only a few dollars a month and the value can be great.

Some offer "forums," which are groups of people interested in a particular specialized subject. I use a number of these, including Entrepreneurs Forum (for my business) and Photoforum (for my hobby). I've sold a fair number of books through contacts made on CompuServe.

Windows. This is an operating system introduced by Microsoft and it is available in several versions, most recently Windows 95. I use Windows mostly for special applications, however, if you use it for more than that, try to buy the Windows versions of the above mentioned application programs.

Integrated software. There are also programs available that combine a number of the above functions (such as Microsoft Works). Some include in a single package word processor, data base, spread sheet and communications capability. These might be applicable in your situation, cost less and have the benefit of a common feel. For a beginner, or near beginner, the advantage of using integrated programs is that they should shorten the learning process and will assure compatibility between functions.

Focused software. Depending on the business you are in, there may be programs available designed for your specific situation. I know of programs for retail stores, service stations, restaurants, dry cleaning businesses, doctors, dentists, lawyers, consultants and many others.

Other. As your company grows, consider using a computer for things such as production control, inventory management, employee records, etc. One place to look is in the publications of the professional societies related to the subject of interest.

Hardware

The following are some suggestions about hardware:

Desktop computers. You have many choices—personal computers are now almost a commodity. I use IBM clones at my office and at home that have Intel 486 microprocessors and 480 megabyte hard drives.

So far, these have served me well, but with software programs becoming more complex and more demanding of memory, I am beginning to feel the need for more powerful machines. Prices are now low enough that a machine with greater capability may be worth the investment. Whichever machine you purchase, be sure it is equipped with a mouse and a high-speed modem.

Laptop computers. These have capabilities generally similar to a desktop machine, with some limitations. However, they weigh only a few pounds, operate from batteries and are small enough to be carried on business trips or back and forth between office and home. If equipped with a modem, messages and files can be sent from a hotel room or over a cellular telephone back to your office. Be sure the machine you buy has floppy disk capability.

Printers. By all means, use a laser jet or ink jet printer. They provide high quality output that looks almost as if it were typed on an IBM executive typewriter with proportional spacing. Good printers of this type now start under $500. They can print graphics and give you a choice of type fonts and sizes, as well as other features. There are also printers with color capability.

CD-ROMS. This is a fairly new addition to the list of PC capabilities. I believe they were originally intended to be used with games, but there are now CD-ROMS available to help in many tasks an entrepreneur faces.

Several CD-ROM programs that I use regularly are an encyclopedia and two programs that sell for under $20 each that list 100 million individual telephone numbers and 10 million business telephone numbers. More than 90 percent of the time, what I am looking for is there, and it is much faster and less expensive than using an information operator.

Other examples of the impact of CD-ROMS are in accounting, law and any other activity that requires frequent updating of complex rules and regulations. My daughter, the CPA, specializes in taxes for small businesses and individuals. Up until a few years ago, she had to have about 20 volumes of tax regulations. They were updated monthly, with about 100 additional pages of supplements.

Now, she has all of this information on four CD-ROMS, one updated annually, two quarterly and one monthly. In addition to the space savings in her office, she has better search capability. The cost is about the same as the printed volumes.

Scanners. With a scanner, you can feed in a printed document and it is converted to a computer file, without the need for retyping. At least two major computer manufacturers are offering a scanner as an integral part of the keyboard. I've used scanners from time to time, but would undoubtedly use one more if it were part of the machine.

Special applications

Two other relatively new applications of the PC that are likely to be used extensively in coming years are the Internet and e-mail.

The Internet. This is a computer application that makes it possible for the user to obtain information and communicate with others world-wide on almost every subject known to mankind. Information about practically every company, educational institution and countless other groups is now available on the Internet, as is access to libraries and information sources of every conceivable kind. To use the Internet, you need appropriate, inexpensive software and must subscribe to an access service, which costs in the range of $15 to $30 per month. Internet capability is now also available through CompuServe and America Online.

Despite the enthusiasm about the Internet, it is not yet entirely clear what the long-term impact of this service will be. But it is certain to be great.

E-mail. This is a service that I am convinced will be popular in the long term and of great value to almost every business. It is a system for sending messages electronically to anyone with an e-mail address, in a very short period of time, at virtually no cost. It can be done through CompuServe, America Online and other information services or through the Internet.

I had an interesting experience with the use of e-mail. One of my granddaughters, aged 18 and whose home is in Berkeley, California, just started college at Brown University in Providence, R.I. As she grew up, I would see her perhaps three or four times a year, and because she is a quiet person, I never got to know her as well as I would have liked. I don't think I ever sent her a letter—only birthday cards.

Now that she is at Brown, I send her an e-mail message every week or so and, since she has a computer in her room, she responds almost immediately. These messages are just a few paragraphs. I tell her what her grandmother, uncles, aunts and cousins are up to and my current activities. She tells me about how she is doing in school, her activities as a member of the basketball team, etc. Through e-mail, I have gotten to know her better in four months than I got to know her in 18 years.

Every businessperson should have e-mail access, probably through one of the services previously mentioned.

Networks. As the PC use in your company increases, you are almost sure, at some point, to consider using a network of some sort. By using a system that ties PCs together, people in your organization can share data and communicate with each other. I have not used networks and am not familiar with the details of their use. Here, I recommend you consult a computer professional to get expert advice.

Other things you decide to do with your PC will depend on your specific needs and your specific skills. However, using a computer for day-to-day applications can save the new business much time and money and do the jobs better as well.

By the time you read this chapter, the information will be at least partly out of date. I have purchased new PCs on about eight different occasions over the years, and in each case, six months or so later, I concluded that perhaps I should have waited. I recommend you get the machine that best meets your needs at this time and accept the fact that, a few years from now, you may want to reconsider your choice and upgrade to a more powerful machine.

✒ Chapter 53 ✑

In Search of Excellence
and the New Venture

In 1982, a book entitled *In Search of Excellence* by Thomas J. Peters and Robert H. Waterman, Jr., (Harper & Row) hit the bookstores. Since then, more than five million copies have been sold, making it one of the best-selling books ever on the subject of management.

In examining more than 300 U.S. companies, mostly large firms, Peters and Waterman identified eight qualities, which they called *findings*, that seem to be present in the most excellent companies. The attributes are:

1. A bias for action.

2. Close to the customer.

3. Autonomy and entrepreneurship.

4. Productivity through people.

5. Hands-on, value-driven management.

6. Sticking to the knitting.

7. Simple form, lean staff.

8. Simultaneous loose-tight properties. Excellent companies are centralized and decentralized.

I look at this differently. I suggest that these qualities also accurately describe the situation that exists in most successful entrepreneurial start-up companies. If you carefully examine successful new ventures and try to identify qualities that most contribute to their success, I believe you could end up with an identical list.

I urge the readers of this book to race to your local bookstore and buy a copy of *In Search of Excellence*. Read it carefully from cover to cover. If you already own the book, read it again.

But do not read it from the viewpoint of the manager of a large company, who wishes to do things that will improve the performance of their organization compared to other large companies. Read it from the viewpoint of an entrepreneur whose organization probably already has most of these eight qualities. Try to think of things you can do to incorporate these principles as key parts of your basic business strategy. Try to think of things you can do to avoid losing them as your company grows.

❦ Epilogue ❧

In writing this book, I have tried to include as much of my personal knowledge and experience as possible to help those who are really interested in becoming entrepreneurs and in having a business of their own. The information was generally of a practical nature, and included example after example to illustrate the points I was trying to make.

My goal was to identify and discuss the key issues that will help improve the chances of your business being a success. Some things I did not include I considered as being too elementary and obvious. If I guessed wrong, refer to other sources to get more information.

This fourth edition includes two revised sample business plans, two new chapters on entrepreneurship for women, updating of all chapters and expansion of many, and the addition of a chapter about the use of computers in a new business.

It also includes a number of chapters written by others. I did this for two reasons. First, some of this new material covers issues on which I do not have too much personal experience. The people who contributed are all more expert than I and their comments more valuable. The second reason is to present the other side of certain issues where I have a strong bias that is sometimes in conflict with conventional wisdom. This, I believe, makes *Start Up* a better book.

Remember that there are very few right or wrong answers to the problems of starting a business. The best you can hope for are answers that work, and you will never know whether another approach would have had a better result.

Hard work and persistence are important qualities in almost every successful entrepreneur. Somehow or other, they find ways to meet and overcome adversity. No one in their right mind will suggest that starting a business is easy. It is not easy; it is hard. But it can be the most exciting business experience of a lifetime, and when and if you succeed, can have rewards beyond belief. These rewards can be professional, emotional and financial. Also, being an entrepreneur gives you infinitely more freedom to control your own life and your own destiny.

If you found this book helpful, please tell your entrepreneurial friends to read a copy if you think it will be of value to them.

In closing, I wish all of you who start a business of your own the best possible success. I hope this book has helped. Please contact me if you have suggestions, to help make future editions more valuable. I can be reached through the publisher. Good luck to all of you.

⟡ Appendix I ⟡

Sample Business Plan:
SmartSafety Systems, Inc.

SmartSafety Systems, Inc.
"Innovations for Your Safety"
The KidSmart™ Vocal Smoke Detector

The following, prize-winning, business plan was developed as a course project in the MBA Class in Entrepreneurship and New Venture Formation, taught by Dr. Charles Hofer, Regent's Professor of Strategy and Entrepreneurship, Terry College of Business, at the University of Georgia.

This is a very well-written and well-organized business plan for a product business. The founders are in the process of getting the business started and hope to have it in operation by late 1996.

As *Start Up* goes to press, the SmartSafety Systems team is preparing a videocassette presentation of this business plan. For further information, contact Dr. Charles Hofer, University of Georgia, Terry College of Business, Brooks Hall, Athens, GA 30602.

The plan was prepared by:
Ann Mooney
Cyriac Roeding

with the assistance of:
Trevor Knott, Indu Arora, Velma Davis, Melinda McCalla, S.M. Chapman

The inventors of KidSmart™ are Larry W. Stults, Ph.D., Esq.,
and Brent E. Routmann, Esq.—patent (U.S. No. 5,349,338).

SmartSafety Systems, Inc.

"Innovations for Your Safety"

The KidSmart™ Vocal Smoke Detector

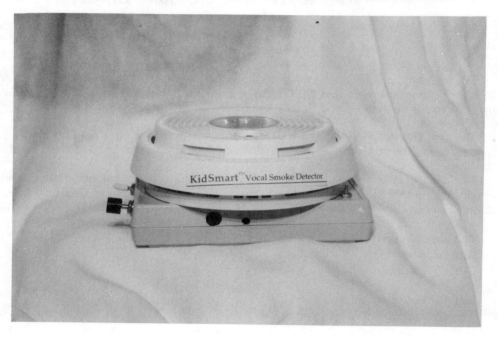

SmartSafety Systems, Inc.

P.O. Box 888903
Atlanta, GA 30338
706-542-3724

Table of Contents

I. SmartSafety Systems Executive Summary

Long-term Vision and Mission

SmartSafety Systems will develop and market new safety-oriented products to provide consumers with protection from residential safety threats, especially fires. Within 10 years, SmartSafety Systems seeks to become a leading developer and marketer of high-end special-application home fire-protection systems.

Our Products: KidSmart™ Vocal Smoke Detector

It is a tragic fact that despite the presence of functioning smoke detectors, more than 150 children die and thousands more are injured every year in U.S. household fires. According to safety experts and psychologists, a familiar voice, especially that of a parent, helps a child overcome panic in unfamiliar or traumatic situations. SmartSafety Systems will market a new product, the KidSmart™ vocal smoke detector (U.S. Patent No. 5,349,338), to address this important problem. *KidSmart™ is a vocal smoke detector that allows parents to record personalized, life-saving instructions to their children, which are broadcast in the event of fire.* These instructions can be customized to meet the needs of each child in the residence. Specific instructions may also be recorded for different areas of the residence to aid the child's escape from smoke or fire-filled rooms.

KidSmart™ will incorporate three additional features to provide the maximum possible protection. *First, KidSmart™ will have a system whereby a long-life backup battery will give a vocal warning ("Battery Needs Replacement") every hour, so the primary battery can be replaced as soon as it runs low. Second, KidSmart™ will have three types of alarms—a buzzer, horn and siren— so parents can test which is best at waking up their child. Third, KidSmart™ will have a testing button and a set of instructions so that parents can easily conduct fire drills with their children.*

Because of these lifesaving features, KidSmart™ won the Inventors Club of America 1996 New Product Award and 1996 Environmental Safety Product Award. It was also one of the top 10 new inventions featured at the 1995 Inventor's Exhibition, sponsored by the U.S. Patent and Trademark Office.

Start up Goals

Within two years, SmartSafety Systems seeks to achieve two primary objectives: 1) leadership in the high-end, residential smoke detector market, and 2) a 100-percent return on its founders' investment.

Start up Strategies

SmartSafety Systems will market and distribute KidSmart™ to the U.S. residential market. Distribution will be primarily through high-end specialty retail catalogues and stores. *Parenting Concepts, a catalogue received twice a year by 70,000 parents nationwide, has agreed not only to carry KidSmart™ but also to make it the featured product of their Fall 1996 catalogue.* SmartSafety Systems is currently negotiating with several suitable manufacturers of KidSmart™. In *the future, SmartSafety Systems will develop and market advanced versions of* KidSmart™, such as KidSmart™ Complete Home System, which will be an integrated set of detectors located throughout the house. Start up and growth strategies are built on the following competitive advantages:

♦ **KidSmart™ is a superior product that can help save children's lives,** by reducing the "panic response" that young people experience in crisis situations.

♦ **KidSmart™ has strong support from fire experts and child psychologists.**

♦ **SmartSafety Systems has an exclusive licensing agreement with Child-Life Products,** which holds the patent and trademark protection on KidSmart™.

♦ **The KidSmart™ patent (U.S. 5,349,338) is effective through 2013.**

Socially Responsible Policies

In order to enhance the use of smoke detectors through all elements of society, a $10 rebate will be provided to customers who donate existing smoke detectors to local charities and fire departments for distribution to needy families.

Financing

SmartSafety Systems has almost completed the process of raising the $100,000 needed to fund its final prototype and its initial legal incorporation fees and marketing expenses. An additional $400,000 in start-up capital will be sought from private investors after the prototype is complete. Working capital loans will be used to finance early operations. In the future, venture capitalist financing will be sought in order to rapidly introduce new products and expand into new markets.

Investor Returns

SmartSafety Systems' initial investors will not receive a Return on Equity in the first year of operations, but will receive an average Return on Equity of 61 percent over the next four years. These will be reinvested in order to support and accelerate growth.

SmartSafety Systems projects the following financial results for the first five years of operations:

Fiscal Year* (in thousands)	1996-7	1997-8	1998-9	1999-2000	2000-1
Sales	$ 260	$ 1,000	$ 2,000	$ 3,500	$ 5,000
COGS	104	300	500	770	1,000
Gross Margin	156	700	1,500	2,730	4,000
Operating Exp.	156	150	246	348	462
Income Taxes	0	154	351	667	991
Net Income	*$ 0*	*$ 396*	*$ 903*	*$1,715*	*$2,547*
ROE	*0%*	*57%*	*67%*	*65%*	*53%*

*SmartSafety Systems' fiscal year runs from July 1, 199x to June 30, 199x+1

	Number of Shares at Start-Up	Additional Investors & Performance Bonus: Years 1 Through 5	Number of Shares at Year 5
ChildLife Products	2,500	0	2,500
Initial Investors	3,000	0	3,000
Future Investors		1,000	1,000
Management: Ann Mooney	150	850	1,000
Cyriac Roeding	50	250	300
Future Management	0	200	200
Total	5,700	2,300	8,000

II. Products

KidSmart™

Licensed exclusively to SmartSafety Systems by ChildLife Products, KidSmart™ is an innovative, patented audio smoke detector. The purpose of KidSmart™ life-saving product aims to prevent thousands of injuries and deaths that currently occur in households equipped with traditional smoke alarms.

KidSmart™'s distinguishing features are:

♦ **An audio recording of the parent's directive voice in the event of a fire.** This message will help to prevent the child from panicking, as proper escape instructions are provided in the familiar, reassuring voice of their parent.

♦ **A back-up battery system.** This will alert parents that the batteries need to be replaced, so homeowners no longer need to worry that their smoke detector's batteries have gone "dead" while they were away.

♦ **Three different types of alarms.** Alarms can sound in horn, buzzer or siren fashion, allowing the parent to use the alarm to which the child reacts best.

♦ **A testing system that reactivates the entire system,** allowing parents to simulate fire drills with their children.

♦ **A set of children's fire safety instructions,** educating parents on the most effective ways to prepare their children for fire emergencies.

In addition, the KidSmart™ vocal smoke detector will enable parents to leave customized messages for each child, and deluxe models will include long-life lithium batteries. The initial KidSmart™ prototype has already been developed and shown at local demonstrations. Please refer to the front cover for a picture of the prototype.

Product Awards

Inventors Club of America

KidSmart™ vocal smoke detector has won two awards given by the Inventors Club of America. These awards include the 1996 New Product Award and the 1996 Environmental Safety Product Award.

These awards recognize KidSmart™'s ability to create an outstanding impact on the fire safety market. SmartSafety Systems is very proud of these accomplishments, as many inventors each year compete for these coveted awards.

Annual Inventor's Exhibition

SmartSafety Systems premiered its KidSmart™ vocal smoke detector at the Annual Inventor's Exhibition, sponsored by the United States Patent and Trademark Office (USPTO), and the Intellectual Property Owners Association, held September 16, 1995 in Walt Disney World. The USPTO sent out approximately 44,000 applications for the expo to individual inventors. Of the 1,435 applications received, 250 were selected for exhibition, and KidSmart™ was judged to be in the top 10 inventions.

Patents and Trademarks

The KidSmart™ patent is U.S. Patent No. 5,349,338 ('338), issued September 20, 1994 (see Appendix II). The term of the patent extends to February 2, 2013. The '338 patent provides the patent owners (ChildLife Products) and their licensee (SmartSafety Systems) the right to exclude others from the unauthorized making, using or selling of any vocal smoke detector device, or method of using a vocal smoke detector device, covered by the claims of the '338 patent for the next 17 years.

The KidSmart™ trademark will be used in marketing the KidSmart™ vocal smoke detector and future SmartSafety System products. This brand name is the trademark of ChildLife Products and as such, will be included in the terms of the exclusive worldwide licensing agreement. The five-percent royalty rate and 25-percent ownership share allocated to ChildLife Products will also serve as compensation for use of the KidSmart™ trademark.

Future Products

Product Extensions

SmartSafety Systems will first expand its product lines through redesigning and offering value-added features to the original

KidSmart™ vocal smoke detector. "Designer" KidSmart™ units will be developed with household decor in mind, enabling customers to purchase the KidSmart™ unit that looks best in their house. KidSmart™ halogen units, in which a halogen bulb will automatically blink upon sensing a fire, are also being considered. This value-added feature will offer parents one more assurance that their children will react quickly in the event of a fire.

KidSmart™ Complete Home System

The KidSmart™ Complete Home System will integrate several KidSmart™ smoke detector units located throughout the household. This will offer customers the added assurance that, in the event of a fire in any part of the house, everyone will be notified clearly and immediately of the danger. Over time, SmartSafety Systems plans to further develop the KidSmart™ Complete Home System to where it will interact seamlessly with existing home security systems, such as those offered by Westinghouse. This integrated network will effectively create a comprehensive home-protection system, offering customers a total solution to their security needs.

Exhibit 1 (not shown) is a letter from Alexander T. Marinaccio, chairman of the International Hall of Fame to inventor Larry Stults complimenting him on being selected to receive their New Product Award for the invention of KidSmart™ Vocal Smoke Detector.

III. Management Team and Key Advisers

The Management Team

SmartSafety Systems' founding management team is skilled in all of the key tasks required to successfully start a company. Summaries of their pertinent experience follows:

Ann Mooney, President

Ms. Mooney will coordinate the overall operation of SmartSafety Systems. Her financial experience includes three years with Coopers & Lybrand, where she managed client engagements in the retail business assurance group and specialized in high-end retailers, such as Saks Fifth Avenue. While at Coopers & Lybrand, Ms. Mooney received recognition for outstanding service. Currently, Ms. Mooney serves as an independent consultant for AT&T. She is also certified as a CPA. *{A photograph would normally be included.}*

Cyriac Roeding, Marketing Manager

Mr. Roeding will be responsible for selling SmartSafety Systems products. His selling expertise is highlighted by his verbal communication skills, developed as a radio broadcaster in Germany and TV reporter in Lithuania. He is currently employed as a strategic management consultant in the retail sector of Roland Berger & Partner, International Management Consultants, the largest European management consulting firm. Recent projects involved Wal-Mart, Procter & Gamble and other retail industry leaders. *{A photograph would normally be included.}*

Trevor Knott, Marketing Adviser

Mr. Knott's marketing and communications background includes two years of telemarketing management with Am-Tel, Inc., a home securities system retailer. In addition, Mr. Knott has project experience in relationship marketing and direct mail with Holiday Inns Worldwide, and previously worked for three years in public service with the Social Security Administration. He will assist the team in start up, and will later rejoin SmartSafety Systems full-time as new products and markets are developed.

Indu Arora, Financial Advisor

Ms. Arora will assist SmartSafety Systems with various financial matters and will seek private investors, primarily through her contacts in the Middle East. Ms. Arora's experience includes owning and managing a real estate firm in Bahrain.

Board of Advisers

Larry W. Stults, Ph.D., Esq., Owner

Co-inventor of KidSmart™ and a part owner of ChildLife Products, Dr. Stults will serve as SmartSafety Systems' primary legal adviser. He currently practices intellectual law with the firm of Jones & Askew, Atlanta, Georgia. His practice includes domestic and foreign patent prosecution and client counseling. Dr. Stults earned his Ph.D. in cellular biology from Johns Hopkins University and his J.D., cum laude, from the University of Georgia, School of Law, where he founded the Intellectual Property Club.

Brent E. Routman, Esq., Owner

Mr. Routman, the other KidSmart™ co-inventor, received a Juris Doctor from Cleveland-Marshall College, where he graduated near the top of his class. Mr. Routman practices as a supervising attorney in the Foreign Filing Department of Merchant & Gould, Minneapolis, Minnesota. He also has extensive experience on the board of directors of several professional organizations.

John Gilsdorf, Business Consultant

Mr. Gilsdorf has served as president of Snowdent-Pencer for the past 13 years. During this period, he has increased Snowdent-Pencer's sales and profit by more than 500 percent and 1,000 percent respectively. Mr. Gilsdorf will assist SmartSafety Systems in the selection and management of the subcontractors who will produce KidSmart™, as well as with general business guidance.

James C. Thomas, Esq., Financial Advisor

Mr. Thomas is the Atlanta Branch Manager of J.C. Bradford & Company, a regional investment banking firm headquartered in the Southeast. Mr. Thomas will serve as SmartSafety Systems' primary financial advisor.

Charles W. Hofer, Ph.D., Start-up Consultant

Dr. Hofer, Regents Professor of Strategy and Entrepreneurship at the University of Georgia, will serve SmartSafety Systems as a business adviser. Dr. Hofer's vast experience with assisting start-up businesses will be critical to the success of SmartSafety Systems. His extensive personal small-business contacts will also be of great value.

Kathryn Scott Young, M.S., Behavior Consultant

Ms. Young is a Child Behavior Specialist for Family Counseling Services, Inc., in Athens, Georgia. Ms. Young's expertise will provide SmartSafety Systems with valuable insights that will help effectively market KidSmart™ and develop future safety product concepts. (See Appendix IV for testimonial from Ms. Young.)

IV. The Smoke Detector Market

Market Growth

Since the 1970s the percentage of U.S. households with at least one smoke detector has increased ninefold, from 10 percent in 1975 to 90 percent in 1995. This growth can be attributed to increased public awareness of fire safety, as well as federal, state and local government legislation mandating the installation of household smoke detectors. *While this growth has been dramatic, the smoke detector market is by no means saturated, in part because of the trend toward installing multiple units in the home, which is now gaining momentum.* In fact, the U.S. Consumer Product Safety Commission (CPSC) estimates that 28 percent of U.S. households currently have two smoke detectors in their residence, while 13 percent have three or more smoke detectors, leaving plenty of room for future growth.

Market Segmentation and Competition

The current U.S. smoke detector market has two primary segments:

1. The Consumer mass market segment, and

2. The Commercial market segment.

Each segment is dominated by a single firm: First Alert, Inc. (First Alert) and Seatt, Inc. (Seatt), respectively.

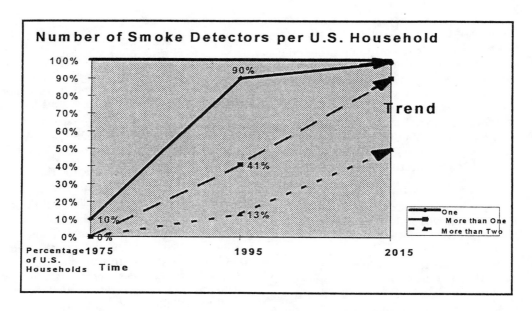

The Consumer Mass Market

U.S. sales in the consumer market is approximately $170 million. The typical products in this segment are priced between $8 and $20, and offer only limited features and a 9-volt battery. Last year, a slightly improved product offering a 10-year lithium battery was introduced to the segment for between $40 and $50. In total, this segment accounted for nearly 15 million new unit sales in the United States last year.

With an estimated 80-percent market share, First Alert clearly dominates this segment, as their nearest competitor commands less than a three-percent share. First Alert's product line includes the First Alert™ smoke detector and Family Guard™, a lower priced line offering very basic smoke detector functions. First Alert sells its products at very low prices by producing them at low coast in Mexico and then distributing its products through several mass market channels, including Wal-Mart, Home Depot, Service Merchandise and Sam's Warehouse Clubs. *At the same time, First Alert does not seem to have sought to compete with Seatt in the commercial market at any time during the last 20 years,* opting instead to diversify into fire extinguishers, flashlights and other mass market safety items.

The Commercial Market

It quickly became apparent that First Alert's low-price, residential smoke detectors would not be adequate for commercial use, leading to the development of a separate commercial detector market. Compared to the consumer segment, products in this segment typically are of a larger, bulkier, more heavy-duty design, and usually are wired into the building's electrical system.

The commercial market has about $30 million in U.S. sales, and prices begin at about $50 per unit and rise from there. One firm, Seatt, quickly emerged as the dominant firm in this segment, amassing an estimated 70-percent share, while its largest competitor has only a single-digit share. *Moreover, in the past 20 years, Seatt does not seem to have sought to compete with First Alert in the consumer mass market,* preferring instead to develop and extend its dominance in commercial smoke detectors.

A New Market Niche (the Key to SmartSafety Systems' Success!)

SmartSafety Systems does not anticipate a strong competitive reaction from either First Alert or Seatt, as neither has encroached on the other's "turf" for the past 20 years. With KidSmart™, SmartSafety Systems will develop a high-end segment to the consumer smoke detector market, offering a unique new product with several safety features—preprogrammable audio recording, multiple alarms and a backup battery system—currently not available in the marketplace.

Evidence that such a high-end segment exists includes SmartSafety Systems' market research at retail outlets, schools and craft shows. (See Appendices V and VI for surveys.) In a recent SmartSafety Systems survey conducted at a leading retail store, 100 of 130 people surveyed expressed high interest in KidSmart™ and requested follow-up information (See Exhibit 2 for customer comments and Exhibit 3 for a customer list.)

Using nontraditional distribution channels, such as specialty and upscale catalogues and stores, SmartSafety Systems will meet the unique wants and needs of this sizable target customer group.

Exhibit 2

Comments from Potential KidSmart™ Customers

"Super idea! I think this device could certainly save lives."
—Nancy Goodwin, Athens, Georgia

"Great Product. I would definitely buy one."
—Sue Terry, Athens, Georgia

"Being a firefighter, I think the need for safety is important. This product sounds great. I will recommend it."
—Tim Webb, Fire Chief, Greene County Fire Department

"I want to be on the first buyers' list."
—Kathryn Scott Young, M.S., Child Behavior Specialist, Family Counseling Service, Inc.

"This product could be instrumental in saving children's lives."
—Jan Padgett, Athens, Georgia

Exhibit 3

This exhibit, not reproduced here, listed the names and addresses of 92 people who expressed interest in buying a KidSmart™ vocal smoke detector.

V. Goals and Strategies

Goals

SmartSafety Systems will become a leading marketer of high-end, special-application protection and fire alarm systems for residential use. Its 10-year performance goals are as follows:

◆ Annual sales of 200,000 units.
◆ Sales revenue of $13 million.
◆ Net profit margins of 20 percent or better.

To meet these long-term goals, SmartSafety Systems has developed short, mid- and long-term objectives in marketing and sales, manufacturing, research & development, human resources and finance. These objectives are described in detail in Exhibit 4.

Strategies

SmartSafety Systems will initially market its KidSmart™ smoke detectors through high-end catalogues and specialty stores. The company will focus on high-end stores and catalogues in geographic markets, such as the Northeast and Southeast, which have the highest concentration of adults with young children.

Within three years of start up, Smart-Safety Systems will develop many follow-up safety products, such as Kid-Smart™ Complete Home System. By year three, Smart-Safety Systems will offer a full line of high-end, residential smoke detector products.

Finally, by year five, SmartSafety Systems plans to enter the Canadian and European markets, as well as develop and offer specialized products in the growing elderly and handicapped market segments.

(Exhibits 5 and 6 detail the scope of strategy and key competitive weapons, respectively. Exhibit 7 shows a milestone chart of achievements to date.)

Competitive Advantage

SmartSafety Systems' strategy is based on four major competitive advantages:

♦ **An Innovative Product With Unique Features.** KidSmart™ is a revolutionary product that offers safety benefits and features currently nonexistent in the marketplace.

♦ **An Exclusive License With ChildLife Products,** the holder of KidSmart™ patent ('338) and the KidSmart™ trademark.

♦ **A Unique Distribution System.** The use of high-end catalogues and specialty stores sidesteps traditional mass market channels, thereby limiting direct competition with First Alert.

♦ **High Profit Margins.** The high margins available at the high-end of the market will allow SmartSafety Systems to break even and achieve substantial profit margins at low-unit volumes.

VI. Marketing, Sales and Distribution

Target Market

The upper-middle and upper-class families of small children are SmartSafety Systems' initial target market. Although this market is only a part of the total U.S. population, it is an especially attractive segment, because it will allow SmartSafety Systems to charge higher prices for the unique product features, performance, convenience, durability and reliability offered by Kid-Smart™. A secondary target market Smart-Safety Systems will pursue after start up is adult children of elderly parents. Many elderly parents would benefit from hearing instructions from KidSmart™ smoke detectors, offering adult children a way to ensure their parents' safety without actually being there.

Sales and Distribution

SmartSafety Systems will sell and distribute its products through upscale mail order catalogues and specialty retail stores. These channels will minimize the total fixed selling costs SmartSafety Systems will incur, as well as support its premium pricing. Market entry through these channels will also enable SmartSafety Systems to avoid direct competition with First Alert, which markets primarily through mass merchandisers. SmartSafety Systems has developed four criteria for selecting the catalogues it will use for the distribution of KidSmart™. Specifically, the catalogues must:

♦ Target SmartSafety Systems high-end customers (upper-middle class young families).

♦ Regularly feature child and/or safety products.

♦ Be published regularly and delivered to a substantial and/or growing customer base.

♦ Have an image and format consistent with KidSmart™.

Exhibit 8 shows selection criteria used for catalogues. Ratings of several leading catalogues using these criteria and catalogue contact information is included in Exhibits 9 and 10, respectively.

Our First Sale: *Parenting Concepts,* a 25-page color catalogue sent to more than

70,000 parents twice a year, has already agreed to carry KidSmart™ and to make it a featured product in its Fall 1996 issue. Exhibit 11 (not shown) is a letter from Tracy Urban, president of *Parenting Concepts* magazine to Cyriac Roeding saying they will include KidSmart™ in its forthcoming catalogue.

Pricing

SmartSafety Systems will sell KidSmart™ to catalogues at $100, with a recommended retail price to consumers of $149. While conventional smoke detectors range from $10 to $25, SmartSafety Systems believes that its premium price is justified based on: 1) the multiple additional features that it offers, which will significantly decrease the chances a child will be killed or injured in a fire; 2) the responses it has received from its market surveys that suggest the price is reasonable; and 3) the fact that lithium-battery smoke detectors are selling for $40 to $100, even though they do not offer many of the KidSmart™ features. These features include the exclusive use of voice technology, a backup battery system, three types of alarms and a testing/fire drill system. These additional features support KidSmart™'s $149 premium-pricing strategy.

In order to enhance the use of smoke detectors through all elements of society, SmartSafety Systems will provide a $10 rebate to each customer who donates their existing smoke detector to local charities and fire departments for distribution to families less fortunate.

Exhibit 4

Short-term Objectives (1996-1997)

Marketing & Sales
- Introduce KidSmart$_{TM}$ in 50 to 75 catalogues and 5 specialty stores (Sharper Image etc.)
- Sell and advertise through on-line services, incl. World Wide Web
- Increase immediate demand & brand awareness through continued free publicity (magazine features, TV features etc.)

Manufacturing
- Subcontract at least one reliable manufacturer for KidSmart$_{TM}$ production
- Identify at least one potential additional manufacturer as backup resource
- Enforce manufacturer's responsibility for quality, quantity & timely delivery to catalogues through contract penalties (payment decrease, and threat of switching to potential additional manufacturer)

Research & Development
- Develop SeniorSmart$_{TM}$ smoke detector version
- Develop 2-3 new products, including KidSmart$_{TM}$ Complete Home System

Financials
- Achieve Breakeven after first FY 1996/97, with revenues of $260T
- Achieve net income of $400T and revenues of $1M in FY 1997/98

Mid-term Objectives (1998-2001)

Financials
- Increase net profits of $0.9M A.T. in FY 1998/99 to >$2.5M A.T. in FY 2000/01
- Attain revenues of $5 million or more by FY 2000/01

Marketing & Sales
- Introduce product in additional catalogues, networks & home builders
- Market new product developments (R&D 1996-1997: new versions, Home S.)

Research & Development
- Develop 3-5 new products: SeniorSmart$_{TM}$ Smoke Detector, KidSmart$_{TM}$ Direction Giver etc.
- Refine existing products (based on market demand and research)

Human Resources
- Add experienced secondary target market sales manager & representatives (for elderly & disabled people)

Manufacturing
- Decrease variable costs from $25-30/unit to $20/unit
- Manufacture basic & enhanced KidSmart$_{TM}$ versions and KidSmart$_{TM}$ Complete Home System

Exhibit 5

Business Strategy: Scope

	Short-Term: 1996-1997	Mid-Term: 1998-2001	Long-Term: 2002-2006
Products & Services Offered	• KidSmart$_{TM}$ Vocal Smoke Detector: Initial Version (with Backup Lithium Batteries, 3 Sounds etc.)	• KidSmart$_{TM}$ Vocal Smoke Detector: Initial & Enhanced • KidSmart$_{TM}$ Complete Home System	• KidSmart$_{TM}$ Systems • SeniorSmart$_{TM}$ Smoke Detector • Annual Upgrades • Other Safety Invent.
Target Markets Served	• Parents of Young Children (2-8 years)	• Parents of Young Children (2-8 years) • Grandparents: Gifts for Grandchildren	• Parents of Young Children (2-8 years) • Grandparents • Elderly & Disabled Homeowners and Nursing Home Resid.
Geographic Areas Covered	• Entire USA	• USA • Canada	• United States • Canada • Europe: Germany, Sweden, UK, France • Asia: Japan

Exhibit 6

Business Strategy: Competitive Weapons

	Short-Term: 1996-1997	Mid-Term: 1998-2001	Long-Term: 2002-2006
Customer Benefits Offered	• Improved Security for Children • "Peace of Mind" for Parents	• Additional Safety (light etc.) & Design (colors etc.) Features • Integrated Home Children Fire Safety Solution	• Enhanced Features • Safety Improvement for Senior Citizens & the Disabled • Increased Safety From New Products
Pricing Policies	High-End: • $100 Wholesale • $150 Retail Price for KidSmart$_{TM}$	Mostly High End: • Keep High Price for Enhanced Versions • Slowly Decrease Price of *Initial* Version (~$70 Ws.)	High & Middle: • Keep High Price for Enhanced Versions • Slowly Decrease Price of *Initial* Version (~$50 Ws.)
Distribution Methods	Coverage Through: • High-End Catalogues	Coverage Through: • High-End Catalogues • Selected Upscale Retail Stores	Coverage Through: • High-End Catalogues • Upscale Retail Stores • Home Shopping Networks

Exhibit 7

Milestone Chart:
Key Achievements to Date

Time

- *September 1994:*
  - Award of U.S. Patent# 5,349,338 for KidSmart™ Product Concept

- *September 1995:*
  - Formation of SmartSafety Systems New Venture Team
  - Retail Outlet Presentation: 80 Customer Requests in 1 Day
  - Selection: One of Top 10 Inventions at EPCOT Expo '95

- *October 1995:*
  - Intensive Market Research Project Completed
  - Refinement of Product Concept
  - Child Psychologist Support Letter (Kathryn Scott Young, M.S.)

- *November 1995:*
  - Identification of Potential KidSmart™ Manufacturers
  - Exclusive Worldwide KidSmart™ Licensing Agreement
  - Support from USAA Insurance (Alan Krapf, Vice President)
  - Support from Greene County Fire Chief (Tim Webb)

- *December 1995:*
  - Hall of Fame New Product Award 1995 Received for KidSmart™
  - First Large-Scale Customer Commitment: Parenting Concepts (Tracy Urban, President): 70,000 Catalogues Twice / Year

- *January 1996:*
  - Expansion & Refinement of Marketing & Promotion Concept

- *February 1996:*
  - TV Feature on KidSmart™ Vocal Smoke Detector on NBC Atlanta Evening News
  - Firm Commitment of Parenting Magazine to Publish Feature on KidSmart™ in May 1996-Edition
  - Development of Detailed Sales Agreement with Parenting Concepts, Lake Arrowhead, CA

- *March 1996:*
  - $100,000 Start-up Capital Secured by Team (20% of Total)
  - Sycamore Engineering, Cincinnati, OH, Offers to Provide Full Manufacturing Process for KidSmart™ by July 1996

Four Step Process: Selection Criteria for Catalogues

Exhibit 8

Catalogue Market Coverage
1 • High percentage of SmartSafety Systems' target market included in catalogue's market

Catalogue Product Specialization
2 • High degree of catalogue's specialization on children and/or safety items

Catalogue Distribution Intensity
3 • High frequency: No. of times catalogue sent out p.a.
• High circulation: Catalogue volume (amount & pages)
• Catalogue growth rate

Catalogue Effectiveness
4 • High customer satisfaction
• Strong catalogue image
• High unit sales
• Good positioning of KidSmart™ ad

Selection Filter

Most Successful Catalogues for Distribution of KidSmart™

Exhibit 9

Ranking of Potential Catalogues by Selection Criteria

	Catalogue Market Coverage	Catalogue Product Specialization	Catalogue Distribution Intensity	Catalogue Effective- ness	Total Catalogue Score
1. Parenting Concepts	9	10	9	10	38
2. Natural Baby Co., Inc.	8	10	9	9	36
3. F&H Safety Products	9	10	8	9	36
4. F&H Baby Products	9	10	9	9	36
5. Lilly's Kids	8	9	9	9	35
6. One Step Ahead	9	9	10	7	35
7. O'Grady Presents	7	8	10	8	33
8. Signatures	8	8	10	7	33
9. All But Grown-Ups	9	9	8	7	33
10. Fire	8	10	7	7	32
11. Delta Airl. Flightline Gifts	8	6	10	7	31
12. Direct-to-you Baby Prod.	7	10	7	7	31
13. World of Products	9	6	8	7	30
14. Salden Company	7	8	7	7	29
15. Sharper Image	7	6	9	7	29

Note: See Appendix 1 for complete list of all 50 catalogues, home shopping networks and retail stores.

Evaluation Scale: 5: Average   0: Far Below Average

                10: Excellent

Exhibit 10

Top 15-Ranked Catalogues: Contact Information

	Contact Partner	Position	Address	Telephone / Fax
1. Parenting Concepts	Tracy Urban	President	P.O Box 1437, 526 Grizzley Rd. Lake Arrowhead, CA 92352	Ph. 800-727-3683 Fax 909-337-0969
2. Natural Baby Co., Inc.	Jane Martin	President	114 West Franklin, Suite PR, Pennington, NJ 08534	Ph. 609-737-2895 Fax 609-737-7665
3. F&H Safety Products	Robert Fay	President	P.O. Box 566, Chagrin Falls, OH 44022	Ph. 800-729-7233 Fax 210-247-1680
4. F&H Baby Products	Margaret M. Fay	Marketing Manager	533 Halls Street, Sugrin Falls, OH 44022	Ph. 216-247-3937
5. Lilly's Kids	Fred P. Hochberg	President	510 South Fulton Avenue, Mt. Vernon, NY 10550	Ph. 914-699-4131 Fax 914-699-7698
6. One Step Ahead	N.A.	N.A.	P.O. Box 46, Deerfield, IL 60015	Ph. 800-274-8440
7. O'Grady Presents	Carol O'Grady	President	111 E Wacker Drive, Suite 3000, Chicago, IL 60601	Ph. 800-548-5759 Fax 312-565-4452
8. Signatures	Audrey Shaeffer	Buyer	3660 Brennan Avenue, Perris, CA 92370	Ph. 714-943-2011
9. All But Grown-Ups	N.A.	N.A.	P.O. Box 555, Berwick, ME 03901	Ph. 800-448-1550
10. Fire	Connie Gross	President	Roberts Co., 180 Franklin St., Framingham, MA 01701	Ph. 800-729-1482 Fax 508-879-3735
11. Delta Airl.Flightline Gifts	John Schreiber	President	3825 West Green Tree Road, P.O. Box, Milwaukee, WI 53209	Ph. 800-558-8990
12. Direct-to-you Baby Prod.	Sari Connolly	President	4599 Peardale Drive, Las Vegas, NV 89117	N.A.
13. World of Products	Joseph Romano	President	1737 N. 39th Avenue, Stone Park, IL 60165-1114	Ph. 708-344-0752 Fax 708-344-0768
14. Salden Company	N.A.	N.A.	P.O. Box 421, Cambridge, MA 02141	Ph. 800-800-5336
15. Sharper Image	Richard Thalheimer	President	650 Davis Street, San Francisco, CA 94111	Ph. 415-445-6148

Note: See Appendix for complete list of all 50 catalogues, home shopping networks and retail stores.

Promotion

In order to minimize the start-up costs, SmartSafety Systems will exploit cost-efficient promotional opportunities.

Free Magazine, Radio, TV and Newspaper Publicity

KidSmart™ was recently featured on the *5:00 Action News* on the Atlanta NBC-TV affiliate, as part of a week-long series on fire safety. Previously, KidSmart™ has been featured on the local Orlando, Florida, affiliate of the national radio station for kids, "Radio Ahhs."

After receiving an overwhelming response from parents visiting the Annual Inventor's Exposition, SmartSafety Systems has already been contacted by *Parenting* magazine about featuring KidSmart™ in its May 1996 issue.

Testimonials

SmartSafety Systems has received numerous testimonials from child psychologists and fire experts about the need for a product with KidSmart™'s ability to lead children to safety in the event of a fire.

(See Appendix IV for a testimonial from a child psychologist.)

Demonstrations

SmartSafety Systems is continuing to demonstrate KidSmart™ to potential customers in a variety of ways. These include retail demonstrations, a school craft show and several business plan presentations. The overwhelming support received thus far—more than 85 percent of survey respondents at demonstrations asked for an order form—indicates the importance of demonstrations in helping customers understand the benefits of KidSmart™ over those of conventional smoke detectors. (See Exhibit 3 for KidSmart™'s potential customer list, and Appendices V and VI for SmartSafety Systems' survey results.)

Insurance Agencies

While premium discounts are already given to owners of conventional smoke detectors, SmartSafety Systems believes insurance companies will give larger discounts given KidSmart™'s ability to better save lives, and thus reduce potential fire insurance claims. SmartSafety Systems has contacted several insurance companies regarding promoting KidSmart™ in newsletters sent to policy holders. To date, USAA Insurance Company has agreed to feature KidSmart™ in an upcoming newsletter, free of charge.

VII. Manufacturing and Certification

Components

Despite its unique features, KidSmart™ utilizes standard, off-the-shelf components in its construction, namely a vocal integrated circuit unit, a speaker, three types of alarms, a regular smoke detecting unit, two lithium batteries, etc.

Production

The production of KidSmart™ will be outsourced. SmartSafety Systems is currently negotiating with two manufacturers and will finalize an agreement over the next month or two. The company is confident that both manufacturers can meet SmartSafety Systems' needs for low-volume production at

start up, while still offering very large capacity for future expansion.

The first manufacturer is Sycamore Engineering, Inc. (Sycamore) of Cincinnati, Ohio, which has previous experience in smoke detector design and production. Due to its relatively small size ($500,000 average annual revenues), Sycamore is extremely interested in a partnership with SmartSafety Systems. In the first two years, Sycamore will produce KidSmart™ in-house. In future years, when larger lot sizes are required, Sycamore will meet the increased demand through existing manufacturing partnerships, maintaining control over the manufacturing process. (See Exhibits 12 and 13 and Appendix III for company profiles and price quotations.)

The second potential partner is Manufacturing, Research & Design, Inc., of Kennesaw, Georgia, which performs all types of manufacturing, ranging from specialized parts for large oil companies to the small-scale production of new inventions. Its close proximity to Athens will foster close communications between its production facility and SmartSafety Systems.

Logistics

SmartSafety Systems products will be distributed directly from its manufacturer to the premises of its mail order catalogues and specialty retail stores. Thus, manufacturing will be responsible for maintaining the required levels of inventory stipulated by its retailer agreements. The manufacturer will also be required to maintain product liability insurance.

Product Certification

While current federal and state laws require "approved" smoke detectors to be installed throughout public buildings, no regulations exist regarding their certification for private residences. Thus KidSmart™ could be sold to the public without any type of "certification." Because of the image it seeks to present, however, SmartSafety Systems will seek Underwriters Laboratories, Inc. (UL) Certification of KidSmart™. Such "certification" should take less time than usual, since KidSmart™ will be produced from standard components that have already been "certified." Put differently, the primary aspect of KidSmart™ certification will involve its packaging and its electronic circuitry, not its components. Exhibit 14 includes a description of pertinent legislation and certification.

VIII. Financials

Capital Structure and Ownership

SmartSafety Systems will have an exclusive license with ChildLife Products for use of its patented vocal smoke detector, KidSmart™. In exchange, ChildLife Products will receive a 5-percent (of net sales) royalty rate, as well as 2,500 shares of the initial 5,700 shares of SmartSafety Systems stock. The remaining shares will be assigned to management and future private investors.

SmartSafety Systems is currently completing the raising of $100,000 to fund its first prototype and initial incorporation and marketing expenses. After the prototype has been completed and passed all operating tests, an additional $400,000 will be raised from additional private investors to further the first two years of operations. In addition,

Ms. Mooney and Mr. Roeding will have the opportunity to earn stock through options as the company grows.

Contacts have already been made with other interested third parties for longer-term growth financing. Contacts include applications filed through MIT Venture Capital Network (see Appendix VII for application) and the Investors Circle, a nonprofit network of investors who invest in socially responsible start-up businesses. SmartSafety Systems is also pursuing agreements with Ham's Bank Incorporated, Women Incorporated and Women's Collateral Funding, lenders who specialize in loans to small businesses operated by women. Growth beyond five years will be funded through venture capitalists or an IPO.

	Number of Shares at Start-Up	Performance Bonus: Years 1 Through 5	Number of Shares at Year 5
ChildLife Products	2,500	0	2,500
Initial Investors	3,000	0	3,000
Future Investors		1,000	1,000
Management:			
Ann Mooney	150	850	1,000
Cyriac Roeding	50	250	300
Future Management	0	200	200
Total	5,700	2,300	8,000

Exhibit 12

Potential Manufacturer Profile (Current Negotiations): Sycamore Engineering, Cincinnati, OH

Key Company Facts

Size

- Production Capabilities: 100 Units/Month Internally >1,000: Production w/ Partners
- Annual Revenues: $500,000, Growing
- Strategic Partners: Has Existing Relationships with Multiple Mass Producers

Contact Partner

- Contact Partner: Mr. Richard Grimsley, President
- Address: 11256 Cornell Park Dr., Suite 500 Cincinnati, OH 45242
- Telephone / Fax: Tel. (513) 489-0608 Fax (513) 489-0705

Offered Services & Key Advantages

Key Services

- Engineering: Full Capabilities to Engineer Final KidSmart$_{TM}$ Prototype. One-Time Costs: $40-50,000
- Production: Full KidSmart$_{TM}$ Production & Drop Shipping Capabilities. In-house Production Capabilities of 1,200 Units/Year. Subcontracting Capabilities for up to 50,000 Units/Year at Competitive Prices.

Key Advantages for Smart Safety Systems

- Experience: Previous Smoke Detector Project for National Council Of Aging in 1995
- Full Commitment: Due to its Small Size, Sycamore has Tentatively Agreed to Place Key Emphasis on the SmartSafety Systems Contract
- High Flexibility: Fully Flexible Production Volumes Are Offered (<100-50,000 pieces per month)

Exhibit 13

Key Aspects of Manufacturing Quotation (3/18/96): Sycamore Engineering, Cincinnati, OH

Final Prototype Development

One-Time Costs
- Product Specification: $1,600
- Detailed Hardware Design: $6,500
- Software Development: $3,200
- Mechanical Engineering: $7,500
- Prototype Development: $2,800
- Enclosure Tooling: $12,500
- Total Development Costs: $34,100

Deli-verables
- 5 Engineering Prototypes
- Complete Documentation Package:
  - Drawings / Schematics
  - Software Listings / Flow Charts
  - Costed Bill of Materials

Time Frame
- Capability to Start Development Immediately:
  - Engineering Phase: 4-6 Weeks
  - System Integration & Testing: 1 Week
- Total Development Period: 5-7 Weeks

Production: Key Aspects

Variable Costs
- For 50,000 Piece Lots: $20-22 / Unit
- For Less Than 100 Piece Lots: $40 / Unit

Organi-zation
- In-house Production in Cincinnati Facilities for Order Batch Sizes of <=100
- Subcontracting to High-Volume Domestic or Off-Shore Suppliers for Larger Batch Sizes up to 50,000 Units / Month

Time Frame
- Immediate Production Capability for Both Small & Large Batches Following the Completion of the Prototype Development
- Start of Prototyping in Early May 1996 Will Secure Market Entry by July 1996

Note: See Original Quotation from Sycamore Engineering in Appendix A-3.

Exhibit 14

Pertinent Legislation & Certification

Federal Law

Title 15 of the United States Code contains federal legislation regarding fire prevention and control, and establishes the United States Fire Administration. The U.S. Fire Administration is charged with, among other things, public education regarding fire prevention and control, establishing the National Academy for Fire Prevention and Control, maintaining the National Fire Data Center, and review of fire prevention codes.

Section 2225 of Title 15 establishes Fire Prevention and Control Guidelines for Places of Public Accommodation, which includes "a requirement that hard-wired, single-station smoke detectors be installed in accordance with National Fire Protection Association Standard 74 in each guest room". The term "smoke detector" as used in the statute is defined as "an alarm that is designed to respond to the presence of visible or invisible particles of combustion". Similarly, Section 2227 of Title 15, relating to fire safety systems in Federally assisted buildings defines the term "smoke detector" as a "single or multiple station, self-contained alarm devices designed to respond to the presence of visible or invisible particles of combustion, installed in accordance with National Fire Protection Association Standard 74."

State Law

State law, such as Georgia's Title 25 of the Georgia Code relating to Fire Protection and Safety, generally requires that buildings representing a special hazard to property or life conform to certain minimum requirements. Such buildings include buildings with three or more stories, hotels, motels, schools, hospitals, theaters, churches, department stores, group day-care homes and centers. Electrically powered smoke or products of combustion detectors must be installed. Smoke or products of combustion detectors are defined as those listed by a nationally recognized testing laboratory.

Underwriters Laboratory Inc. (UL) Certification

SmartSafety Systems will bring its products to UL for safety evaluations. This will certify the quality of the Company's products, as UL is widely recognized as the most accepted, trusted and recognized safety certification Mark in the United States.

At UL, product samples will be evaluated to applicable safety requirements. Once it is shown that the SmartSafety Systems' products meet these requirements, it will be authorized to apply the appropriate UL Mark. UL will then perform periodic audits at the Company's manufacturer's location through its factory Follow-Up Services, counterchecking compliance to ascertain that products continue to meet the necessary requirements of the UL Mark.

Conclusion

Federal and state laws require approved or listed smoke detectors in certain kinds of buildings. It is important to note that private residential use does not appear to be regulated by either Federal or state law. Thus, the KidSmart vocal smoke detector can be sold to the retail public without special consideration of legal compliance. Further, the KidSmart vocal smoke detector would comply with both Federal law, because it is responsive to "visible or invisible particles", and with state laws such as those in Georgia, as it is listed by the Underwriters Laboratory Inc. (UL).

Financial Performance

SmartSafety Systems' expected financial performance for its first five years of operations is outlined below. As can be seen, SmartSafety Systems expects to break even in the first year of operations, to generate a positive cash flow for the second year of operations, and to generate sales of $5 million and profits of $2.5 million by year five.

Fiscal Year (in thousands)	1996-7	1997-8	1998-9	1991-2000	2000-1
Sales	$ 260	$ 1,000	$ 2,000	$ 3,500	$ 5,000
COGS	104	300	500	770	1,000
Gross Margin	156	700	1,500	2,730	4,000
Operating Exp.	156	150	246	348	462
Income Taxes	0	154	351	667	991
Net Income	$ 0	$396	$ 903	$1,715	$2,547
Net Cash Flows	$ 494	$ 871	$ 1,796	$ 3,520	$ 3,062

Fiscal Year (in thousands)	1996-7	1997-8	1998-9	1991-2000	2000-1
Starting Equity	$ 500	$ 500	$ 896	$ 1,799	$ 3,514
Net Income	0	396	903	1,715	2,547
Ending Equity	500	896	1,799	3,514	6,061
ROE	0 %	57 %	67 %	65 %	53 %

(See Exhibits 15 and 16 for SmartSafety Systems' monthly Pro Forma Cash Flow and Net Income statements, respectively, for Year 1. Exhibits 17, 18 and 19 include Five Year Pro Forma Cash Flow Statements, Income Statements and Balance Sheets. Appendix VII includes monthly Pro Forma Cash Flows and Income Statements for Year 2, and "worst case" and "best case" monthly income statements for Year 1 and Year 2.)

Investor Returns

SmartSafety Systems will retain all profits in order to fund its initial growth. Based on its projected sales and profits, SmartSafety Systems will not have a Return on Equity in the first year of operations, but will average 61 percent over the next four years.

Longer term, investors will recover their investment through cash dividends and/or an Initial Public Offering (IPO). Furthermore, if the high-end smoke detector market develops more slowly than SmartSafety Systems expects, its initial investors will still receive returns in excess of 20 percent annually for years two through four. On the other hand, if demand for KidSmart™ explodes, the returns to SmartSafety Systems' investors could exceed 80 percent or more annually.

IX. Key Risks and Contingencies

Slow Growth

There is a possibility that the high-end smoke detector niche could evolve more slowly than anticipated. However, SmartSafety Systems has three advantages that will see it through even an abnormally slow start up.

Exhibit 15

SmartSafety Systems -Expected Scenario
Income Statement
(July 1996- June 1997)
All numbers except Units Sold are in dollars ($)

	July	Aug	Sept	Oct	Nov	Dec	Jan	Feb	Mar	April	May	June	Fiscal Year 1
Assumption of													
Units Sold	100	100	150	150	300	300	250	250	250	250	250	250	2,600
Sales	10,000	10,000	15,000	15,000	30,000	30,000	25,000	25,000	25,000	25,000	25,000	25,000	260,000
Cost of Goods Sold	4,000	4,000	6,000	6,000	12,000	12,000	10,000	10,000	10,000	10,000	10,000	10,000	104,000
Gross Margin	6,000	6,000	9,000	9,000	18,000	18,000	15,000	15,000	15,000	15,000	15,000	15,000	156,000
Operating Expenses													
Childlife Prod. Royalties	500	500	750	750	1,500	1,500	1,250	1,250	1,250	1,250	1,250	1,250	13,000
Dev of Prototype	50,000	0	0	0	0	0	0	0	0	0	0	0	50,000
Storage	500	500	500	500	500	500	500	500	500	500	500	500	6,000
Utilities	500	500	500	500	500	500	500	500	500	500	500	500	6,000
Officer Salaries	4,000	4,000	4,000	4,000	4,000	4,000	4,000	4,000	4,000	4,000	4,000	4,000	48,000
Payroll Tax & Benefits	1,000	1,000	1,000	1,000	1,000	1,000	1,000	1,000	1,000	1,000	1,000	1,000	12,000
Insurance	200	200	200	200	200	200	200	200	200	200	200	200	2,400
Advertising & Promo	500	500	500	500	500	500	500	500	500	500	500	500	6,000
Depreciation	17	17	17	17	17	17	17	17	17	17	17	17	204
Office Exp	200	200	200	200	200	200	200	200	200	200	200	200	2,400
Legal Exp	2,000	200	200	200	200	200	200	200	200	200	200	200	4,200
Misc	500	500	500	500	500	500	500	500	500	500	500	500	6,000
Total Oper Expenses	59,917	8,117	8,367	8,367	9,117	9,117	8,867	8,867	8,867	8,867	8,867	8,867	156,204
Income Before Taxes	(53,917)	(2,117)	633	633	8,883	8,883	6,133	6,133	6,133	6,133	6,133	6,133	(204)
Income Tax	(15,097)	(593)	177	177	2,487	2,487	1,717	1,717	1,717	1,717	1,717	1,717	(60)
Net Income	(38,820)	(1,524)	456	456	6,396	6,396	4,416	4,416	4,416	4,416	4,416	4,416	(144)
Cumulative Income After Taxes	(38,820)	(40,344)	(39,888)	(39,432)	(33,036)	(26,640)	(22,224)	(17,808)	(13,392)	(8,976)	(4,560)	(144)	(144)

Key Assumptions Made:

* See line 1 of statement for assumptions of units sold per month
* Sales price of $100 per unit
* Manufacturing cost of $40 per unit. This is based on estimate received from potential manufacturer.
* Salary of $48,000 for general manager and marketing manager combined
* Benefits are 25% of salary expense
* Income Tax Rate of 28%

Exhibit 16

SmartSafety Systems -Expected Scenario
Statement of Cash Flows
(July 1996-June 1997)
All numbers in dollars ($)

	July	Aug	Sept	Oct	Nov	Dec	Jan	Feb	Mar	April	May	June	Fiscal Year 1
Cash Flow from Operating Activities													
Net Income	(38,820)	(1,524)	456	456	6,396	6,396	4,416	4,416	4,416	4,416	4,416	4,416	(144)
Adjustments to Net Income													
Change in Accts Rec	(1,667)	(1,667)	(1,667)	(1,667)	(1,667)	(1,667)	(1,667)	(1,667)	(1,667)	(1,667)	(1,667)	(1,667)	(20,004)
Change in Inventory	(100)	(100)	(100)	(100)	(100)	(100)	(100)	(100)	(100)	(100)	(100)	(100)	(1,200)
Change in Accts Pay	1,250	1,250	1,250	1,250	1,250	1,250	1,250	1,250	1,250	1,250	1,250	1,250	15,000
Depreciation	17	17	17	17	17	17	17	17	17	17	17	17	204
Net Cash Flows From Operating Activities	(39,320)	(2,024)	(44)	(44)	5,896	5,896	3,916	3,916	3,916	3,916	3,916	3,916	(6,144)
Cash Flows from Investing Activities													
Purchases of Equipment	(1,000)	0	0	0	0	0	0	0	0	0	0	0	(1,000)
Net Cash Flows Used by Investing Activities	(1,000)	0	0	0	0	0	0	0	0	0	0	0	(1,000)
Cash Flows from Financing Activities													
Cash Received from Investors	100,000	0	400,000	0	0	0	0	0	0	0	0	0	500,000
Net Cash Flow from Financing Activities	100000	0	400000	0	0	0	0	0	0	0	0	0	500,000
Net Increase (Decrease) in Cash Flows	59,680	(2,024)	399,956	(44)	5,896	5,896	3,916	3,916	3,916	3,916	3,916	3,916	492,856
Beginning Cash Balance	0	59,680	57,656	457,612	457,568	463,464	469,360	473,276	477,192	481,108	485,024	488,940	
Ending Cash Balance	59,680	57,656	457,612	457,568	463,464	469,360	473,276	477,192	481,108	485,024	488,940	492,856	492,856

Key Assumptions made
$100,000 and $400,000 of Investor Financing will be received in July and September, respectively

Exhibit 17   SmartSafety Systems -Expected Scenario
Income Statement
(June 30, 1997- June 30, 2001)
All numbers except Units Sold and
Number of Catalogues are in dollars ($)

	June 30 1997	June 30 1998	June 30 1999	June 30 2000	June 30 2001
Assumptions of Units Sold	2,600	10,000	20,000	35,000	50,000
Sales	260,000	1,000,000	2,000,000	3,500,000	5,000,000
Cost of Goods Sold	104,000	300,000	500,000	770,000	1,000,000
Gross Margin	156,000	700,000	1,500,000	2,730,000	4,000,000
Operating Expenses					
Development Prototype	50,000				
Childlife Prod Royalties	13,000	50,000	100,000	175,000	250,000
Storage	6,000	7,600	7,600	7,600	7,600
Utilities	6,000	6,000	6,000	6,000	6,000
Officers Salaries	48,000	52,800	75,000	100,000	130,000
Payroll Taxes & Benefits	12,000	13,200	18,750	25,000	32,500
Insurance	2,400	2,400	2,400	2,400	2,400
Advertising & Promotiona	6,000	6,000	11,000	11,000	11,000
Depreciation Expense	200	933	933	933	933
Office Expense	2,400	2,400	3,000	3,550	5,000
Legal Expense	4,200	2,400	15,000	11,000	11,000
Miscellaneous	6,000	6,000	6,000	6,000	6,000
Total Opeating Expenses	156,200	149,733	245,683	348,483	462,433
Income Before Taxes	(200)	550,267	1,254,317	2,381,517	3,537,567
Income Taxes	(56)	154,075	351,209	666,839	990,519
Net Income	0	396,192	903,108	1,714,678	2,547,048

Key Assumptions Made
-See line 1 of statement for assumptions of units sold per month
-Sales price of $100 per unit
-Manufacturing cost of $40, $30, $25, $22 and $20 per unit for years 1 through 5
  respectively.
        This is based on estimate received from potential manufacturer and
        consideration of economies of scale realized from increased production in
        future years.
-Salary Expenses of $48,000, $52,800, $75,000, $100,000 and $130,000 for years 1
  through 5 respectively. This assumes that a third and fourth employee will be hired
  in years 3 and 4 respectively.
-Benefits are 25% of salary expense.
-Income tax rate of 28%

-The projected unit sales were derived as follows:

	Year1	Year 2	Year 3	Year 4	Year 5
Projected number of Catalogues Carrying KidSmart	50	75	100	110	100
Projected unit sales per year through catalogues (1)	52	133	150	155	160
Total projected KidSmart unit catalogue sales	2,500	9,975	15,000	17,050	16,000
Total projected sales per year of KidSmart through retail stores	0	0	6,700	17950	34000
Total projected unit sales	2,600	10,000	20,000	35,000	50,000
Total annual unit sales of Residential smsoke detectors in the U. S.	11,500,000	11,500,000	11,500,000	11,500,000	11,500,000
Estimated market penetration	0.02%	0.09%	0.17%	0.30%	0.43%

(1) Projected unit sales per year per catalogue were determined by averaging the
yearly unit sales for all of the catalogues that SmartSafety Systems expects to carry
KidSmart (unit sales figures were found in the Annual Index of Catalogues. Amounts
increase from years 1 through 5 as catalogues with greater circulation will be carrying
KidSmart as time progresses.

SmartSafety Systems -Expected Scenario
Balance Sheet-Opening and in Five Years
(July 1996 to June 2001)
All numbers in dollars ($)

	June 30 1976	June 30 1997	June 30 1998	June 30 1999	June 30 2000	June 30 2001
ASSETS						
Current Assets						
Cash	498,800	492,856	870,651	1,795,892	3,519,535	6,061,535
Accts Receivable	0	20,000	30,000	15,000	9,000	10,000
Inventory	1,200	1,200	1,200	6,000	6,000	6,000
Totsl Current Assets	500,000	514,056	901,851	1,816,892	3,534,535	6,077,535
Property, Plant & Equip						
Office Equipment		1,000	7,300	7,300	7,330	7,330
Less: Accumulted Depreciation		200	1,133	2,066	2,999	3,932
Total PP&E Net		800	6,167	5,234	4,331	3,398
Total Assets	500,000	514,856	908,018	1,822,126	3,538,866	6,080,933
LIABILITIES						
Current Liabilities						
Accounts Payable	0	15,000	12,000	23,000	25,000	20000
Total Liabilities	0	15,000	12,000	23,000	25,000	20,000
STOCKHOLDER"S EQUITY						
Common Stock	500,000	500,000	500,000	500,000	500,000	500,000
Retained Earnings	0	(144)	396,048	1,299,156	3,013,885	5,560,933
Total Stockholder's Equity	500000	499856	896048	1799156	3513885	6060933
Total Liabilities & Equity	500,000	514,856	908,048	1,822,156	3,538,885	6,080,933

Exhibit 19 **SmartSafety Systems -Expected Scenario**
Statement of Cash Flows
(June 1997-June 2001)
All numbers in dollars ($)

	June 30 1997	June 30 1998	June 30 1999	June 30 2000	June 30 2001
Cash Flows From Operations					
Net Income	(144)	396,192	903,108	1,714,728	2,547,048
Adjustments to net income					
Change in Accounts Rec	(20,000)	(10,000)	15,000	6,000	(1,000)
Change in Inventory	(1,200)	0	(4,800)	0	0
Change in Accounts Pay	15,000	(3,000)	11,000	2,000	(5,000)
Depreciation	200	933	933	933	933
Net Cash Flow-Operations	(6,144)	384,125	925,241	1,723,661	2,541,981
Cash Flows From Investment Activities					
Purchases of Equipment	(1,000)	(6,330)	0	0	0
Investing Activity	(1,000)	(6,330)	0	0	0
Cash Flows from Financing Activities					
Proceeds from Priv Investors	500,000	0	0	0	0
Net Cash Flow Financing Activity	500,000	0	0	0	0
Net Increase (decrease) in Cash Flows	492,856	377,795	925,241	1,723,661	2,541,981
Beginning Cash Balance	0	492,856	870,651	1,795,892	3,519,554
Ending Cash balance	492,856	870,651	1,795,892	3,519,553	6,061,535

Key Assumptions Made:
----
*Financing provided by investors will be
  provided in a two step process in year 1.

First, SmartSafety Systems has very low fixed overhead, as it has outsourced most marketing and manufacturing. Second, since KidSmart™ is made from standardized parts, its variable manufacturing costs are lower than those of most premium products. Third, as a premium product, KidSmart™ can command a high price, which combined with its low fixed and variable costs, produces a low break-even point.

Strong Competitive Response

SmartSafety Systems does not expect a strong competitive response for three main reasons:

1. First Alert and Seatt are smoke detector producers with the ability to make such a response.
2. Neither has sought to enter the other's market segment during the past 20 years.
3. SmartSafety Systems' product design, pricing and distribution are all designed to avoid direct competition with either company.

Should such competition arise nevertheless, it will almost certainly be because Smart-Safety Systems' entry may affect another company's sales. Should an explosive growth occur, SmartSafety Systems will take all steps necessary to satisfy this demand before others can enter the market.

For example, SmartSafety Systems has built into its manufacturing contract a provision that allows it to use other producers if its primary producer cannot meet market demand. In addition, SmartSafety Systems has initiated discussions with J.C. Bradford and Company, a regional investment banking firm, about the possibility of a large private placement or even an IPO to finance such growth.

Also, SmartSafety Systems would consider licensing its patent to another company, both to increase the degree to which lives will be saved by better meeting market demand, and to boost cash flow through increased royalty revenues (based on a percentage of unit sales) realized from the other company's larger channels of distribution.

Finally, even if such "explosive" growth occurred and SmartSafety Systems was not able to keep others from dominating this market segment, it will still have earned enough to provide returns in excess of 500 percent to its founding investors.

X. Future Growth Opportunities

Rapid Growth in Years One to Five

It is possible that SmartSafety Systems will be able to grow more rapidly in years one to five than is projected in this plan without stimulating a strong competitive response. Should this occur, contingency plans discussed in the Competitive Response section will be implemented in order to secure additional resources. Based on financial projections in Appendix VII, this is the most attractive of all possible scenarios, as SmartSafety Systems' founding investors will earn more than 100 percent a year.

Future Growth in Years Six to 10

In years six to 10, SmartSafety Systems will extend its original product line, add products in related markets and expand geographically.

Product/Market Extensions

These include the KidSmart™ Complete Home System, which provides a separate detector for each room in the house with the entire set of detectors linked together, and the SeniorSmart™ vocal smoke detector, which will include extra loud instructions in frequencies best heard by the elderly, as well as other similar products.

Geographic Expansion

SmartSafety Systems' first international markets will be the NAFTA nations of Canada and Mexico. This will be followed by expansion into the various countries of Western Europe (in the order of: Germany, using direct contacts of Mr. Roeding, then Sweden, the U.K., France, etc.) and Australia. With its high per-capita income and safety concerns, Japan will also be a priority for international expansions, although this might be done by licensing an existing Japanese producer of smoke detectors. Japanese entry might also be built on the Senior-Smart™

vocal smoke detector, since Japan has one of the largest senior populations of all the developed countries of the world.

If necessary, SmartSafety Systems will consider an IPO during this period, both to generate the funds needed for growth and to provide an attractive exit strategy for its initial investors.

Table of Appendices

Because of space limitations, only Appendix I is included here.

Appendix I

Potential Catalogues

- QVC Express
- R&J Distributors
- The Sharper Image
- Shop the World By Mail
- Signatures
- Century Products Co.
- Direct to You Baby Products
- F&H Baby Products
- F&H Safety Products
- Lilly's Kids
- Natural Baby Co., Inc.
- Salden Company, Inc.
- Special Delivery
- J. Goodman Co.
- ABC Distributing
- All But Grown-Ups
- Attitudes
- Citiband
- Cook Bros, Inc.
- Coors & Co. Gift Catalog
- Delta Airlines Flightline Gifts
- Fingerhut Direct
- Heartland America
- Home Values & Gifts, Inc.
- Speco Gifts & Jewlery
- Spencer Gifts
- Sporty's Preferred Living Catalog
- Trifles
- United States Purchasing Exchange
- V.J.W. World of Products
- World of Products
- Seniorama, Ltd., U.S.A.
- Fire
- One Step Ahead
- Masuen First Aid & Safety Catalog
- Preparedness Resources, Inc.
- Catalogue for Home & Garden
- Vista
- Hanley-Wood
- Notions of Spring
- O'Grady Presents
- Mast General Store
- QVC
- Shoppers Advantage

Home Shopping Networks

- QVC
- The Home Shopping Network

Retail Stores

- Neiman Marcus
- Saks Fifth Avenue
- The Sharper Image
- Brookstones

⚜ Appendix II ⚜

<u>Sample Business Plan: Five Star "Personalized" Travel, Ltd.</u>

Five Star "Personalized" Travel, Ltd.
1090 Flynn Road
Rochester, NY 14612
716-225-5757
FAX 716-225-7344
E-mail address fivestar@vivanet.com

November 14, 1989

Prepared by
Marguerite Ashby-Berger

Ms. Ashby-Berger was a student of mine in an entrepreneurship course I taught at Rochester Institute of Technology in 1989. She started her business as scheduled and has now been in operation for a little more than six years. Her sales exceeded her plan for several years after she started the business, but have now leveled off at about $2 million annually. She is currently operating at a profit and has repaid the bank loan she used to start the business.

This is a well-organized and well-written plan. It is a plan for a service business and is intended to be a "road map." It is not for the purpose of raising capital.

Ms. Ashby-Berger reviewed this plan after six years in business and added comments about her actual performance compared to the plan, as well as some things she might have done differently. During the past two or three years, there have been dramatic changes in the travel industry. *Her comments, shown in italics, indicate the importance of reviewing business plans on a regular basis.*

Table of Contents

1. Executive Summary

My overall mission is to own and operate a full-service travel agency that provides quality travel services to all clients, and at the same time, focuses on being innovative in the type of services offered. Generally speaking, I prefer to give full, quality service to a few hundred repeat clients rather than having several thousand clients to whom I give less than full service.

Because of my education, work-related background and personal travel experience, I plan to write articles for local newspapers, business magazines and national publications pertaining to the travel industry. Hopefully, this will become an important asset of my agency.

I would also like Five Star "Personalized" Travel to be at the forefront of industry changes regarding things such as education of employees and qualifying criteria for owning and operating a travel business.

The flexibility to work with a client who may need only a one-night hotel reservation, as well as a client who may require a 727 airplane to transport executives on a three-day meeting in four different countries, is something I believe very few travel industry people have. This is a capability I expect to have. Serving clients' needs by offering all of the services mentioned in the Services Description section of this Business Plan should convey the message that Five Star "Personalized" Travel

will operate at the same level of professionalism and with similar fundamental philosophies as are found in most medical and law offices.

One aspect of my agency's philosophy will be my staff's understanding of how world events affect the tourism industry, so that Five Star "Personalized" Travel can capitalize on and react to such events.

Another philosophy includes the importance of the staff personally traveling extensively to gain knowledge, collect information and establish personal industry contacts in the use of the various travel-related services and destinations required by our clients.

A third philosophy, important to the overall operating standards of my company, includes the ability to actually qualify a client for the destination or service requested. Asking the right questions of the client will help determine what will satisfy their particular travel requirements and wishes. This should result in happier customers.

Owning my own business is like being the star of a Broadway show. You must give 110 percent of yourself every day to every audience; in this case the audience is my customers. In addition to expertise about the travel business, this takes a vast amount of stamina and a lot of practice. Some of the audience will cheer your efforts and come back again and again. They will tell friends, family and business associates what a good job you do for them. Others will smear your performance. Like the star of a show, I try to practice continuously to make my company the best it can be. Only the best of Broadway continue for years, and longevity is what I hope to achieve.

However, in order to achieve this longevity, it will be necessary for me to adapt to all of the recent changes in the industry. These include the imposing of a $50 commission cap by the airline industry on domestic airline tickets that

exceed $500 (which may soon extend to other travel suppliers). The overall impact of the commission cap is a reduction of revenue, in some cases by 50 percent or more. Another change is the accessibility by the general public to national information services, such as CompuServe, America Online and the Internet, through which it is now possible to make travel reservations without the personal services of a travel agent.

From this you can see that the travel industry is experiencing dramatic change.

2. Goals and Strategies

I have three short-term goals for my company:

♦ Establish credibility in the community and, eventually, worldwide.

♦ Attract customers currently using other travel agencies, and service a substantial share of the market in terms of dollars.

♦ Have sales of $750,000 my first year in operation with a 40-percent increase the next two years, and become profitable within a year or two of starting the business. I would like my company to achieve an increase in sales each year without jeopardizing the quality of service to our clients.

I have met the goals I set out in my original business plan as follows:

1. *We have established credibility in the community and worldwide by offering Five Star service in responding to inquiries and in making reservations. We also communicate constantly with hotels, cruise lines, airlines and train companies worldwide to make us better able to meet our customers' needs.*

2. *My strategy is still to hire a competent, responsible and credible employee who will assist me in growing the business and who can develop into the office manager.*

3. *While attracting customers from other agencies may sound good, it is not always a smart thing to do. Some potential customers always seem to want special "deals" and "favors," which reduce our profit and cash position. In some cases, the requests are not*

even honest. Other customers want to work with a travel agency that understands their needs and can offer travel services that meet the criteria they set forth. We are not interested in the first type of customer. The second type is usually most happy with the service we provide.

4. *The changes taking place in the industry now require my agency to develop a new strategy taking into account these new technologies. Our strategy now includes having an Internet web site, through which our present clients or others can communicate with us. This will make it possible for us to benefit from these new technologies and, hopefully, not lose the personal relationship with our customers that has in the past been one of our key strategies.*

5. *Another element of our new strategy is to employ only people with an extensive background in the travel industry. On the Internet and other information services, you see only what they want you to see and you cannot get personal advice and guidance from an experienced professional.*

6. *The ceiling on commissions recently introduced have made it necessary for us to charge a small fee for services such as reissuing tickets, changing reservations, etc., which we formerly could do at no charge. As best I can tell, the majority of our customers both understands the need for these charges and values our services to the extent that they do not object.*

3. Market Description

On Jan. 15, 1990, I plan to open and operate a full-service travel agency staffed by knowledgeable employees offering quality services to clients who demand and require such services, and to make a profit selling these travel-related services. The three markets my company will serve are corporations, individual business travelers and leisure travelers.

Corporate market

Corporate customers will help to stabilize revenue income for my company, due to the nature and type of travel services required by clients in this market. This market will also provide additional revenue generated by the travel of individuals as a result of their satisfaction with the travel services received at the corporate level. The local corporate market will also provide my company with the opportunity to offer additional services, such as meeting planning and employee incentive programs. This is a market that I understand, as a result of my three years of experience organizing and managing the internal travel department of a major area food chain.

I find that most companies are owned and operated by men. While this is not a problem for me, many men to whom I have made a sales pitch seem to prefer to do business with male-owned travel agencies. I think that most deals are made on the golf course. I now play golf.

We lost the business of three clients because they were acquired by other larger companies, and travel arrangements are now made by a central group at headquarters.

Many companies mandate that their employees travel at the most discounted tickets available, often requiring a Saturday overnight stay. While this gives them lower ticket prices, it also gives them a hotel bill and other expenses, which may not cover the savings.

The corporate market has been soft for several years, because of large staff cutbacks at many companies and expense reduction programs that limit travel. However, this situation seems to be improving. But because of the industry limitations on travel agents' commissions for travel within the U.S., this market is no longer as attractive as it was in the past.

However, I am convinced that travel to business meetings, seminars and the like will probably always be necessary and will be especially attractive to us when they require international travel, on which there are no $50 commission limits at this time.

Individual corporate traveler

This will include those individuals who usually make the final decisions in their company and who demand specialized travel services, sometimes including private aircraft chartering and limousines equipped with telephones, fax machines and personal computers. This type of client will provide my company with the challenge of serving the most demanding of people with very complex schedules and of expanding my personal expertise in private aircraft/helicopter chartering, plus other unique travel-related service requests.

This market consists mostly of smaller companies—between one and 150 employees. The individual corporate traveler is very demanding and usually highly stressed. Many changes are often necessary before the itinerary is complete. They demand a very high level of service. The word no is never mentioned.

I remember the time one of my customers wanted to rent a Porsche during a trip to San Francisco. None was to be had. I finally located one in Los Angeles, which had to be driven to San Francisco and then back to Los Angeles when my client was finished using the car. Let's just say the cost of this rental was about what most people would pay for a year's tuition for one of their children at a private school.

I have no trouble meeting the demands of these customers, no matter how unusual they may be. This type of customer has the skills necessary to utilize computer information services and communicate with us using e-mail, but they still require and value personal service. One reason for this is that many of their travel needs are unique and still require the advice and counsel of a travel professional. We pride ourselves on fulfilling customer needs, from a Porsche to a box of Godiva Chocolates.

Individual leisure traveler

These customers will range from those clients who may want a simple weekend hotel package, to those requesting a "Five Star" vacation. This market will also provide my company with the opportunity to establish contacts worldwide. Many of these travel industry contacts will be located in destinations to which corporate travelers infrequently or never travel. The individual leisure traveler will help enhance the knowledge required to organize incentive travel packages for the local corporate market and also contribute to overall revenue income.

All three markets mentioned above will give Five Star "Personalized" Travel the opportunity to provide a professional, knowledgeable solution to all travel-related requirements by a management team whose careers have been spent buying travel services and who understand and can react to the traveler's concerns. My agency's attention to detail and follow-through are expected to be key ingredients to the successful delivery of travel-related services, regardless of the nature of the request.

I find it very difficult to provide service to first-time customers over the telephone and always try to get them to come into our office for a "one-on-one" conversation. This gives me a better chance to understand their needs and gives them a better chance to understand the benefit of doing business with us.

Many travelers will call several agencies to get price quotations. I do not object to this, as long as the client understands that price is not the only thing that counts. The individual leisure traveler is often not very loyal to the agency. They do not understand it takes time to build up a relationship, as it does with a doctor, dentist or lawyer.

I have tried to determine what these customers expect from a travel agency, and this is what they say is important:

1. *Aircraft seat assignments. This is very important to many travelers. One of my clients will fly only in seat 13C. If this seat is not available, they take another flight.*

2. *Frequent flyer mileage credit verification. Some clients will fly only with an airline with which they have frequent flyer miles accumulated. The frequent flier program is one of the most successful marketing programs in the history of aviation. It helps keep the traveler loyal to an airline.*

3. *Cost. There has been a trend in the airline industry to reduce fares every four to six weeks, only to raise them again a short time later. This is as confusing for the travel agent as it is for the traveler. When an airline reduces its prices, customers already ticketed are not always entitled to the lower fare. Even new reservations do not always meet the restrictions of the new lower fares. The Clinton Administration has prevented the industry from giving advanced notice of increases or decreases in fares. Purchasing an airline ticket is like buying stock—all you can do is make an educated guess.*

4. *The Internet. Another factor, of recent importance, is that negotiating or getting special help from an information service is difficult, if even possible, for the leisure traveler, and this category of customer is less likely to have the computer skills to intelligently use these services. Also, because their knowledge of travel services is so limited, they tend to value the personal services more than the other categories of travelers.*

The travel agency is such that it cannot always meet the above list of needs. We can request a specific seat assignment, but the carrier does not always guarantee the request. We communicate the customer's frequent flyer number, but the airline tracking system is not always accurate. And thanks to deregulation, the cost of the ticket is whatever the load factor will allow. But we do try to give our customers all the help we can, so the odds are better that we can meet their needs

While we do encourage our customers to "surf" the net, we caution them of possible problems, and advise them to purchase services directly from us. The Internet does not provide security—professional agencies are bonded.

4. Description of Services

The services to be offered by Five Star "Personalized" Travel will be divided into three categories: travel services that all clients may require at any given time, travel services to meet the needs of local companies and travel services required specifically by individual leisure travelers. Although my company will be a full-service agency and any client may request and receive any of the services offered, I have divided the services into these three categories so that we can refine our marketing strategy to continuously add, change or eliminate services as the needs of each market change. All travel services will be provided to both domestic and international destinations.

The following legend applies to the list of services shown below:

* All local travel agencies offer these services.

** A majority of local travel agencies do not offer these services.

*** No local travel agency offers these services. Five Star "Personalized" Travel hopes to be the first.

Category 1: General travel services

* Airline reservations and tickets.

* Boarding passes and seat assignments.

* Complete and confidential traveler information.

* Railroad reservations and ticketing.

* Hotel and condominium reservations.

* Car rental reservations.

** Maintain complete traveler profile records so that pertinent information will not have to be repeated by clients each time they make a reservation.

** Delivery of all travel documents when requested.

** All services necessary to utilize frequent flyer awards.

** Travelers checks.

** Passport and visa applications.

*** Frequent Flyer reports and individual mileage tracking system with quarterly reports and updates.

*** 24-hour personalized service to all clients.

*** Multilingual interpreter service.

*** Personalized calls to client's home or office.

*** Quality, personalized luggage for sale.

Category 2: Corporate travel services and individual business traveler services

** Complete understanding of the company's culture in terms of travel-related services.

** Management travel reports, either weekly or monthly.

** Incentive travel programs for valued employees, including special promotion marketing and meetings.

** Complete meeting planning services.

** Trip giveaways for company's customers.

*** Consultation for writing and enforcing a company's travel policy.

*** Corporate travel budgeting analysis, including cost-saving criteria, travel pattern assessment and cost savings to the company.

*** Domestic and international destination guidelines and consulting, including culture barriers and world travel security and safety.

*** Delivery of sensitive business documents and/or products point to point.

*** Private aircraft/helicopter chartering services, including individual audits of each chartering company utilized, as well as flight plans and custom services.

Category 3: Individual leisure travel services

* Travel insurance.

* Cruise and steamship reservations.

* Honeymoon packages.

* Specialized group travel (e.g., trips for the handicapped, etc.).

* Escorted group tours.

* Adventure package tours.

* Gift certificates.

** Theater tickets.

** Complete spa vacations.

** Anniversary packages.

*** Imported suntan products (as giveaways).

Based upon our experience, we no longer offer the following services:

1. *Quality personalized luggage. People just do not buy luggage from a travel agent.*

2. *24-hour personalized service. To provide this, I contracted out the work to a company in California. I had complaints from customers, because the people in California did not understand the problem the call referred to and did not give personalized service. I decided that waiting until morning or leaving a message on an answering machine was less of a problem than trying to educate the people at the California company.*

3. *Travelers checks. My clients preferred to deal with their own banks rather than with us.*

However, a new service that we do offer is a willingness to go to the customer's home to discuss specific travel needs with him or her personally. E-mail and the Internet cannot do this, nor, in most cases, can they answer even the simplest question. All other services listed are still being offered.

5. General Industry Description

The economic changes of Western Europe, advances in technology, continuing world globalization, deregulated domestic air traffic and increasing level of sophistication of air travelers will all contribute to a variety of challenges and changes in the travel industry. As these changes occur, people providing travel services will have to become more proficient in their operations in order to survive. Prior to deregulation, travel agency owners and operators did not require substantial knowledge of the industry. For example, there were only three air fare levels: First class, coach class and economy class. Today there are more than 30,000 air fares published, with a majority of them updated on a daily basis.

Five Star "Personalized" Travel will use the latest in computer technology, so that the services we provide will be efficient and profitable. One of the major resources of Five Star "Personalized" Travel, that will contribute to its overall success, is the fact that my manager and I both hold college degrees in Travel Management and have been in the travel field for more than seven years. This college background and work experience will help us determine what future trends will be and how to capitalize on these trends.

A major percentage of travel agencies today are operating their businesses on pre-deregulation standards and procedures. Five Star "Personalized" Travel will operate on a professional business level in terms of the current local and world climate.

It is my assumption that a small travel agency can play an important role in serving corporate travel needs. While some experts advise that consolidation and large travel agencies are the wave of the future, others defend the role of the smaller agency that can provide a standardization of services, plus other intrinsic benefits. As competition in the business community intensifies and all employees are required to maximize their work performance, travel-related practices and policies will be a more important factor in the operating strategies of many companies.

6. Competition

In Rochester there are approximately 100 travel agencies. Most of these agencies started as "mom and pop" entities and still operate that way today. Travel agency sales volume in Rochester ranges from $250,000 to well over $100 million per year. The overall selling strategy of most local travel agencies is in the form of price, either by offering a "rebate" or by promoting low-priced tours. The use of a price-only approach reduces the agency's profits and perhaps credibility, and also attracts customers who are price-conscious and will not necessarily be loyal.

I consider all local travel agencies to be my competition, with my direct competition being "XYZ" Travel, one of the large agencies in the area. The strengths of "XYZ" Travel include the fact that they have serviced the community for more than 20 years, their computer technology includes information from two separate computer systems (Apollo and Sabre), they offer travelers checks, they have two offices (one on the west side and one on the east side of the city), they have established the Kodak leisure market, including retirees, and they have a large advertising budget.

Their weaknesses include the location of one of their offices (which is difficult to reach, because it is located on a one-way street), their hours of operation (8 a.m. to 5 p.m., Monday through Friday) and the lack of 24-hour service to all of its clients. Those select clients who can use the 24-hour service communicate their questions and problems to a person who they may never have been in contact with before and who has limited decision-making authority.

In addition, "XYZ" has high employee turnover, which is typical for this industry (in the past three years, five different agents have been assigned to one large local corporate account), and they assign defined tasks to individual employees, which means that a problem or question can be resolved only by that particular employee.

Another weakness is that travel documents are not presented to the customer in a standardized format.

Some local companies, individual business travelers and individual leisure travelers change travel agencies frequently, because of some of the weaknesses noted above, as well as other factors. The travel community has not been successful in providing added value to services in order to gain and retain loyal customers.

Since January 1990, two travel agencies opened in my community and two closed. In March 1990, an agency opened on the other side of the city with a name similar to mine. When I discovered this, I contacted my lawyer and was told the only thing I could do was file a lawsuit against New York. State. The state is not supposed to permit another company to incorporate with the same name as a company already incorporated.

Apparently, this did not work in my case. I decided not to bring action, because of the cost involved and the time that would be required. This other agency is no longer in business, so the problem is gone.

Some travel agencies outside of Rochester have begun advertising for clients in our local newspaper. My counter to this was to always try to explain to my clients what "Personalized Travel Services" means. Most of my customers apparently still prefer doing business with a local agency.

The information services (CompuServe, America Online and the Internet) have changed this to a certain extent, and as a practical matter, we now do business in a national, and even global, market.

7. Marketing and Selling Strategy

My selling strategy to the local corporation will be different than that followed by many other agencies. Before approaching a local organization, I will analyze the targeted company's culture, history and top management personnel and identify the travel agency currently serving them.

After doing this preliminary research, I will send a letter of introduction, including a listing of innovative services my company offers, and request a meeting, either at their office or mine. I will prepare a three-ring binder with actual examples of the services I have provided to other companies, as well as examples of other specific services, plus a list of my present clients. My general marketing and selling strategy will not include cold calls.

Fortunately, I have several comprehensive lists of local companies and the names of their senior executives. Many of these executives currently charter and/or own private aircraft. Other top-level business people who are not on this mailing list but who could be considered potential clients will have to be identified in other ways.

In addition, I will also put a major effort into contacting the secretaries of these senior executives, who often have the authority to decide which travel agency is used.

My selling strategy to the individual leisure market will include hand-delivering new brochures to homes within a three-mile radius, advertising in local publications, becoming active in the community (sponsoring local little league baseball teams), setting up a booth at bridal shows and guest-speaking for various organizations and schools.

My overall general selling strategy to all my markets will include having a grand opening (with trip giveaways) and inviting business associates, friends, local residents and reporters. I'll write travel articles for local publications, as well as for travel magazines. I will join local business organizations and hire outside sales staff already knowledgeable on the travel industry. After a client of Five Star "Personalized" Travel completes a trip, I will personally send that client a thank-you note with my business card enclosed.

Part of my selling strategy will also include being a guest on local radio talk shows and speaking to as many local professional and social organizations as I can arrange. This will enhance my company's overall credibility in the community.

I have generally followed the marketing and selling strategy outlined in my original business plan. However, I try very hard to recognize the changing needs of my customers and adapt my strategy to their needs.

One thing that helps sell travel services is the agent's knowledge about the place the traveler plans to go. I try to keep my knowledge and my employees knowledge as up-to-date as possible. We travel a lot.

Did I do any "dumb" things? Yes, a few.

1. *Advertising in local newspapers was not productive.*

2. *Donating money to various worthy local causes does not bring in business.*

3. *Participating in local bridal shows did not bring in business either—only one of the decision makers is usually in attendance.*

All-in-all, I think my original strategy has been successful.

One factor that I did not fully appreciate when I first wrote this business plan was the importance of referrals as a source of new customers. A large percentage of my new customers is a result of referrals from loyal customers who have been satisfied with the service I provide them. I now have people calling me from all over the country as a result of referrals, even though they all could have used travel agents located a mile or so from where they live.

I am now wondering what things I can do to show my appreciation to the people who make these referrals, so that this source of new business will continue.

8. Quality Control

Assuring quality travel services will be accomplished by having the latest in technology and by implementing controls to determine which staff members will be responsible for which aspect of the overall travel service sold to the customer. It will be my company's philosophy to provide the same level of service to every corporate and individual client. It takes less energy to give 100 percent service all the time than to give less than 100 percent service some of the time.

Assuring quality service to clients will also be accomplished by identifying vendors and suppliers (hotels, resorts, airlines, cruise lines, etc.) who can consistently deliver top-quality services.

Doing it right the first time is the best way to provide quality service to our customers. Doing anything a second time just costs too much time, money and aggravation. I have a "quality check list" for every employee and make them personally responsible for providing quality service. I try to reward them for a continuous commitment to quality. Every reservation is checked three times before it is ready for the customer.

9. Management

Initially there will be two individuals employed full-time for the Five Star "Personalized" Travel: Mr. John Doe (fictional name) as manager and myself as president. I will be the sole owner of the company. My biography is included as an appendix to this plan.

Mr. Doe has worked for an airline, a retail travel agency and two wholesale tour operators. He has contacts established with all the international airline representatives, and has personally traveled to countries in the orient and many destinations in the United States. Mr. Doe will be responsible for servicing leisure clients, as well as overall office management.

I will be responsible for attracting and servicing local corporate businesses and the individual business traveler. Mr. Doe and I will alternate attending industry seminars and courses. The hours of operation (when the office will be readily accessible to clients) will include: Monday through Friday, 8 a.m. to 8 p.m.; Saturday, 9 a.m. to 1 p.m.

People have been by far my biggest problem. John Doe, mentioned above, and I did not get along. I had hoped he would become a key employee, but it just did not work out and he left the agency. I also had problems with other employees and I decided that I did not do a good enough job interviewing, nor did I adequately communicate to new employees what I expected of them. I was naive in that I assumed people I hired were hard workers, took pride in their work and were honest. These turned out to be false assumptions.

I started to lower my standards, which was clearly the wrong thing to do. Instead, I now use a selection criteria check list, and each candidate must meet every criteria. I also read a number of books on interviewing techniques and hiring practices that helped me a lot.

Now I follow my "gut," rather than my "heart." My hiring decision is based upon whether I think the potential employee can do the job, not whether he or she needs the job. This approach has worked and we now have a quality staff of top-notch professionals—three full-time and three part-time. And they do an excellent job serving our customers.

Another thing I did recently, which I should have done on my first day in business, was to prepare an employee manual. To educate myself, I borrowed manuals used by others to serve as a guide. I have each employee read and sign the manual, which I keep in their file. Also, I had the Department of Labor review the manual to give me a bit of protection.

10. Board of Advisers

My board of advisers will include Dr. Richard Marecki, Ms. Gilda Gimple and Mr. Bruce Ashby. Dr. Marecki is a full-time professor at Rochester Institute of Technology. He was one of my professors in the travel management program, as well as my adviser. Ms. Gimple is the marketing and sales director of an area service business. Mr. Ashby is my father and an experienced business executive.

The board will meet quarterly. Members do not have a financial interest in the company.

I suggest that every new business form a board of advisers or board of directors, whichever is appropriate. I continually consult with my board, either through face-to-face meetings or telephone conversations. They have been most willing to advise me and suggest new directions. They share their experience and contacts and never charge for this counsel.

11. Financial Plan

I have a commitment from Norstar Bank for a $50,000 loan at two percent above prime, with interest only the first year and interest plus principal the last five years. This loan is secured by a lien on my home and is guaranteed by my father and will be used to purchase capital equipment and for working capital.

Projected Capital Expenditures

Item	Estimated Cost
Telephone system	$3,000
Conference table and chairs	1,000
Personal computer	3,000
Computer table	200
Computer	1,000
Alarm System	1,000
FAX Machine	1,000
Three desks	1,500
Three computer tables	750
Three desk chairs	800
Six client chairs	1,200
Office supplies and printing	3,500
Outdoor sign	1,000
Window blinds	1,000
Copier	2,000
Carpeting	1,250
Typewriter	200
Typewriter table	100
Coat rack	200
Office refrigerator	100
Coffee service and stand	100
Two file cabinets	600
Total	$25,000

Sales forecast

Sales for the first year in business are projected to be about $750,000. For the second and third years, sales are projected to be $900,000 and $1.25 million.

The $50,000 I borrowed to start the business turned out to be enough. Originally I had a six-year note, but was able to pay it off entirely by the start of my fourth year. My company is now debt-free and the lien on my home has been released. My revenues the first year, 1990, were $750,000, in 1991 they were $1,050,000 and in 1992 they were $1,470,000. In 1993 sales exceeded $2,000,000. These were well ahead of my initial projections. Since then, however, sales have stabilized in this range. I am now trying to decide what my future goals should be. My agency now employs six people. I make a comfortable living, I thoroughly enjoy having my own business and I enjoy the relationship I have with my customers. Whether or not I want to grow further is uncertain.

One method of growing would be to open a second office on the other side of the city. However, since my major thrust is providing personal service to my customers, having a second office will make it more difficult to continue this personal service strategy, which has been so important. This is a subject that will require a great deal of thought and some very tough decisions in the coming months.

My relationship with the bank with which I had the loan and with which I still do business has been somewhat of a problem. In four years I have had to work with three different people responsible for my account. One left the bank and two were transferred to other jobs.

My conclusion is that it is good to routinely do business with and establish a relationship with more than one bank. This can hardly be wrong and may become important. Finally, I found that the existence of a good business plan helped a lot in establishing a good banking relationship.

Cash flow projections for the first two years are on the following 2 pages.

Sample Business Plan: Five Star "Personalized" Travel, Ltd.

Five Star Travel Cash Flow Year One

	Jan	Feb	Mar	Apr	May	June	July	Aug	Sept	Oct	Nov	Dec	Total
Starting Cash	0	18746	17092	15500	14484	15080	15226	14882	14478	15674	17920	21666	
Cash In													
Cash/CC/Fees	3000	4000	4000	5000	6000	6000	5000	5000	7000	8000	9000	9000	71000
Bank Loan	25000	0	0	0	0	0	0	0	0	0	0	0	25000
Total Cash In	28000	22746	21092	20500	20484	21080	20226	19882	21478	23674	26920	30666	
Cash Out													
Rent	900	900	900	900	900	900	900	900	900	900	900	900	10800
Office Supplies	1000	100	100	100	0	100	0	0	100	0	0	100	1600
Printing	1000	0	0	100	0	100	0	100	0	0	0	100	1400
Maintenance	0	0	0	0	100	0	100	0	0	100	0	100	400
Postage	250	100	100	200	200	200	200	200	200	250	250	250	2400
Telephone	300	300	300	300	300	300	300	300	300	300	300	300	3600
Legal	500	0	0	0	0	0	200	0	0	0	0	200	900
Accounting	300	0	0	200	200	0	0	200	0	0	0	0	900
Education	0	0	0	200	0	200	0	0	200	200	200	200	1200
Contributions	0	0	0	0	0	250	0	0	0	0	0	0	250
Insurance	150	150	150	150	150	150	150	150	150	150	150	150	1800
Payroll Exp	64	64	64	64	64	64	64	64	64	64	64	64	768
Utilities	150	150	150	150	150	150	150	150	150	150	150	150	1800
Computer Lease	500	500	500	500	500	500	500	500	500	500	500	500	6000
Letter of Credit	400	0	0	0	0	0	0	0	0	0	0	0	400
Misc	300	300	300	300	300	300	300	300	300	300	300	300	3600
Loan Interest/Ex	500	500	500	500	500	500	500	500	500	500	500	500	6000
Dues & Subscript	600	250	100	100	0	100	0	0	100	0	0	0	1250
NAB	700	700	700	700	700	700	700	700	700	700	700	700	8400
FTE	770	770	770	770	770	770	770	770	770	770	770	770	9240
PTE	0	0	0	0	0	0	0	0	0	0	0	0	0
Employment Taxes	200	200	200	200	200	200	200	200	200	200	200	200	2400
Auto Milage	70	70	70	70	70	70	70	70	70	70	70	70	840
Travel (FANS)	0	0	0	0	0	0	0	0	0	0	0	0	0
Entertainment	100	100	100	100	100	100	100	100	100	100	0	300	1300
Advertisement	500	500	500	500	200	200	200	200	500	500	200	500	4500
Total Cash Out	9254	5654	5504	6104	5404	5854	5404	5404	5804	5754	5254	6354	71748
Ending Balance	18746	17092	15588	14396	15080	15226	14822	14478	15674	17920	21666	24312	

Five Star Travel Cash Flow Year Two

	Jan	Feb	Mar	Apr	May	June	July	Aug	Sept	Oct	Nov	Dec	Total
Starting Cash	24312	23472	25592	26512	27432	28052	26322	24982	23902	24222	26282	29042	
Cash In													
Cash/CC/Fees	8000	9000	8000	8000	7000	6000	5000	7000	8000	9000	10000	10000	95000
Bank Loan	0	0	0	0	0	0	0	0	0	0	0	0	0
Total Cash In	32312	32472	33592	34512	34432	34052	31322	31982	31902	33222	36282	39042	
Cash Out													
Rent	1000	1000	1000	1000	1000	1000	1000	1000	1000	1000	1000	1000	12000
Office Supplies	100	100	200	100	100	50	50	50	100	100	100	200	1250
Printing	1000	0	500	0	0	500	0	0	500	100	500	0	3000
Maintenance	100	40	40	40	40	40	100	40	40	100	100	100	780
Postage	200	200	200	200	200	200	200	200	200	200	200	200	2400
Telephone	350	350	350	350	350	300	300	300	350	350	350	350	4050
Legal	300	0	0	0	0	300	0	0	0	0	0	0	900
Accounting	300	0	0	300	0	0	0	300	0	0	0	300	1200
Education	0	200	0	0	0	200	200	200	200	0	0	0	1000
Comtributions	0	0	0	0	0	250	0	0	0	0	0	0	250
Insurance	175	175	175	175	175	175	175	175	175	175	175	175	2100
Payroll Exp	75	75	75	75	75	75	75	75	75	75	75	75	900
Utilities	165	165	165	165	165	165	165	165	165	165	165	165	1980
Computer Lease	500	500	500	500	500	500	500	500	500	500	500	500	6000
Letter of Credit	400	0	0	0	0	0	0	0	0	0	0	0	400
Misc	300	300	300	300	300	300	300	300	300	300	300	300	3600
Loan Interest/Ex	1000	1000	1000	1000	1000	1000	1000	1000	1000	1000	1000	1000	12000
Dues & Subscript	200	200	200	500	200	0	0	800	200	200	200	0	2500
NAB/FTE	900	900	900	900	900	900	900	900	900	900	900	900	10800
PTE	800	800	800	800	800	800	800	800	800	800	800	800	9600
Employment Taxes	0	0	0	0	0	0	0	0	0	0	0	0	0
Auto Milage	300	300	300	300	300	300	300	300	300	300	300	300	3600
Travel (FANS)	75	75	75	75	75	75	75	75	75	75	75	75	900
Entertainment	0	0	0	0	0	400	0	400	200	0	0	0	1000
Advertisement	100	100	100	100	100	100	100	100	100	100	100	100	1200
Other	500	400	200	200	100	100	100	400	500	500	400	400	3800
Total Cash Out	8840	6880	7080	7080	6380	7730	6340	8080	7680	6940	7240	6940	87210
Ending Balance	23472	25592	26512	27432	28052	26322	24982	23902	24222	26282	29042	32102	

✣ About the author ✤

In 1961, Bill Stolze was the founder of RF Communications, Inc., in Rochester, N.Y. In eight years, RF became a worldwide leading producer of single sideband radio communications equipment. With three colleagues, he raised $150,000 of start-up capital in a public offering without the services of an underwriter. After a first quarter loss, RF was profitable for its entire history as an independent company.

When it merged with Harris Corporation in 1969, RF was a firm with about 800 employees and 4,000 shareholders, selling equipment in more than 100 countries and enjoying remarkable success on the American Stock Exchange. RF now has about 2,000 employees and annual sales in the $200-million range. It remains a consistently profitable growth business unit of Harris and a world leader in long-range communications.

After 15 years with Harris, where he served as vice president and group executive and as a consultant, Stolze launched a private consulting business. He is now an adviser to numerous new and growing companies, a venture investor, author and the founder of the Rochester Venture Capital Group.

A recognized authority on entrepreneurship and new venture management, he taught both subjects for many years in the graduate business programs at the University of Rochester and Rochester Institute of Technology.

In 1989, Stolze wrote and self-published the first edition of this book. Subsequent editions were published by Career Press. As this fourth edition goes to press, total sales are approaching 50,000.

Stolze is an electrical engineering graduate of the Polytechnic University of New York, which named him Fellow of the Institute and Distinguished Alumnus. In 1960 he was a Sloan Fellow at MIT.

He began his career at RCA Laboratories, where he received an award for outstanding work in research. At the time he started RF Communications, he was general product manager of the Electronics Division of General Dynamics.

In 1989, Stolze was named Engineer of the Year by the Rochester Engineering Society and in 1995, he was designated Entrepreneur of the Year for Upstate New York in the category of Supporter of Entrepreneurs, in a program sponsored by *Inc.* magazine, Ernst & Young and Merrill Lynch. A business editor of a Gannett Rochester newspaper described him as "mentor-at-large" for small businesses in this region.

Stolze is a frequent speaker at seminars and professional meetings and has been published extensively on various aspects of starting and managing a new business.

Index